Feminist Politics

Feminist Politics

Identity, Difference, and Agency

Edited by
Deborah Orr, Dianna Taylor, Eileen Kahl,
Kathleen Earle, Christa Rainwater,
and Linda López McAlister

ROWMAN & LITTLEFIELD PUBLISHERS, INC.
Lanham • Boulder • New York • Toronto • Plymouth, UK

ROWMAN & LITTLEFIELD PUBLISHERS, INC.

Published in the United States of America
by Rowman & Littlefield Publishers, Inc.
A wholly owned subsidiary of The Rowman & Littlefield Publishing Group, Inc.
4501 Forbes Boulevard, Suite 200, Lanham, Maryland 20706
www.rowmanlittlefield.com

Estover Road
Plymouth PL6 7PY
United Kingdom

British Library Cataloguing in Publication Information Available

Library of Congress Cataloging-in-Publication Data

Feminist politics : identity, difference, and agency / edited By Deborah Orr . . . [et al.]
    p. cm.
  Includes index.
  ISBN-13: 978-0-7425-4777-3 (cloth : alk. paper)
  ISBN-10: 0-7425-4777-9 (cloth : alk. paper)
  ISBN-13: 978-0-7425-4778-0 (pbk. : alk. paper)
  ISBN-10: 0-7425-4778-7 (pbk. : alk. paper)
  1. Feminist theory. 2. Women in politics. 3. Identity (Philosophical concept) 4. Sex
role. I. Orr, Deborah, 1946–
  HQ1190.F46311 2007
  305.42—dc22   200610142

Printed in the United States of America

⊗™ The paper used in this publication meets the minimum requirements of
American National Standard for Information Sciences—Permanence of Paper
for Printed Library Materials, ANSI/NISO Z39.48-1992.

Contents

~

Preface

This book is, in part, a testimony to, and an example of, the importance of the International Association of Women Philosophers/*Internationale Assoziation von Philosophinnen (IAPh)*. In the preface to its companion volume, *Beliefs, Bodies, and Being* (Rowman and Littlefield, 2006), I wrote in some detail about the founding of that organization, in which I was privileged to play a small part. It was founded in the 1970s in order to give German-speaking women philosophers, and later women philosophers from other countries and cultures, a place to share their work and ideas on philosophical topics that, at the beginning of the second wave of feminism, were hardly in the mainstream.

It was clear from the start that among the purposes of the organization was to foster the work of women and feminist philosophers in mostly European countries where their numbers were few and where the opportunities to present their work on still unfamiliar topics were extremely limited. To the IAPh's great credit, it has succeeded in sponsoring eleven major symposia since 1980 in Germany, Switzerland, Austria, the Netherlands, the United States, Spain, Sweden, with the twelfth coming up this year in Rome, Italy. It has published the proceedings of nearly all of these symposia, making the work available to an even wider audience.

For a number of years, U.S. feminist philosophers were, for the most part, on the periphery of the IAPh. While a couple of us were there at the first meeting of German women philosophers in Würzburg in 1974, hoping that the meeting would be the start of an organization in Germany similar to

SWIP (Society for Women in Philosophy), which had recently been started in the United States, our continuing involvement with IAPh tended to be somewhat sporadic. We would occasionally participate in IAPh symposia, but mostly when we were in Europe on sabbaticals or for other reasons. Only with the eighth Symposium (held in Boston in 1998 just prior to the World Congress of Philosophy), the one at which the articles in this volume were originally presented, did the importance of IAPh to American women philosophers become clearer. Due to the way the publishing industry in the United States functions, translations of the work of European women philosophers were seldom available to us, except for the work of a few famous, mainly French, feminist philosophers. And, sad to say, not many of us are fluent enough in other languages to read the work of European scholars in their native languages. Hence, U.S. feminist philosophers remained fairly isolated from the work of their European counterparts, not to mention the work of women philosophers from elsewhere in the world, unless the work was written in English and could be located in sometimes difficult-to-access publications. What the IAPh Symposium in Boston did was to expose U.S. feminist philosophers in large numbers to their counterparts from throughout the world, and give them a chance to hear, in some cases for the first time, new and different approaches to some of the same issues and themes that they themselves had been working on. This volume is a good illustration of that. At the time, the main themes of this volume, "political divisions" and "identity politics," might be said to have come to something of an impasse within U.S. feminist philosophy in the wake of the critiques of "identities" by social constructionists. Many of the papers presented at the symposium, however, seemed to present new ways of examining traditional political dichotomies, on the one hand, or to deal with more sophistication and in more detail with the concept of identity and the need to reexamine its importance to politics.

That 1998 IAPh symposium brought together literally hundreds of feminist philosophers from eighteen countries throughout the world. Since then, more U.S. women philosophers have participated in these international forums, there has been a special issue of *Hypatia: A Journal of Feminist Philosophy* on feminist philosophy in German, and, wonder of wonders, an American publisher has even published a work of German feminist philosophy translated into English, namely Herta Nagl-Docekal's *Feminist Philosophy* (Boulder, CO: Westview, 2004). These may seem small advances, but anything that can expand our thinking about important feminist philosophical issues, encourage international cooperation, and reduce the potential parochiality of our discourse, is, I submit, a step in the right direction.

I feel I need to address the question of why this collection has taken so long to appear in print. Immediately after the eighth Symposium—which I organized with the help of a group of graduate students in the departments of Philosophy and Women's Studies at the University of South Florida—the question of publishing the papers arose. The proceedings of almost all of the previous IAPh symposia had been published in short order in the countries in which the symposia were held. But since the publishing industry in the United States operates rather differently than publishers in European countries, it was clear that it would be impossible to publish the complete proceedings of this huge conference. Instead, we invited the presenters to submit their papers for possible publication in thematic volumes instead. Since I had just completed eight years as editor of *Hypatia: A Journal of Feminist Philosophy*, I still had an excellent group of experienced assistant editors at hand who were willing to work on the project: Eileen Kahl, Kathleen Earle, and Christa Elrod Rainwater. We reviewed the submissions and developed four potential volumes on the themes of the body, identity, ethics, and history of women philosophers. Rowman & Littlefield offered to contract with us to publish the first two of these collections.

When I retired in 1999, I expected to have time to finish preparing these volumes for publication. Unfortunately, a series of health and family problems prevented me from carrying out this plan, and it looked as if nothing would be published. Then, Dr. Deborah Orr of York University in Toronto volunteered to take over the final editorial work for the first volume, *Beliefs, Bodies, and Being* and, subsequently, Dr. Diana Taylor of John Carroll University, pitched in and offered her editorial assistance on this volume. It is thanks to them that this volume is finally about to appear in print. The authors have kindly revised and updated their papers, so this collection remains timely and relevant despite the long delay in publication. Finally, I want to express my deeply felt gratitude to all the editors and authors of this volume and my hope that it will prove of value to its readers.

Linda López McAlister
Albuquerque, NM
February, 2006

~

Acknowledgments

Deborah Orr and Dianna Taylor would like to thank our coeditors Kathleen Earle, Eileen Kahl, Linda López McAlister, and Christa Rainwater for their work in selecting the essays included in this volume from among those presented at the 1998 IAPh conference in Boston. Additional thanks go to Eileen Kahl for her work on the volume's index. Special thanks are extended to Linda López McAlister for her work in the early days of IAPh, in organizing the 1998 conference, and in initiating the volume. Linda has made an important contribution to feminist philosophy throughout her career. We also wish to thank Ross Miller, Ruth Gilbert, and Molly Ahearn of Rowman & Littlefield for all of their help and patience in bringing this project to press. Finally, we wish to thank the *Journal of Political Philosophy* for granting permission to reprint Amy R. Baehr's essay, "Feminist Politics and Feminist Pluralism: Can We Do Feminist Political Theory without Theories of Gender?," *Hypatia* for granting permission to reprint Alison Bailey's essay, "Locating Traitorous Identities: Toward a View of Privilege Cognizant White Character," Princeton University Press for granting permission to reprint Sigal Ben-Porath's essay, "Feminism Under Fire," and Rowman & Littlefield for granting permission to reprint Marla Brettschneider's essay, "To Race, To Class, To Queer: Jewish Contributions to Feminist Theory."

PART I

RECONCEPTUALIZING CHALLENGES TO ENTRENCHED POLITICAL DIVIDES

CHAPTER ONE

~

Introduction to *Feminist Politics: Identity, Difference, and Agency*

Deborah Orr

Philosophical efforts to ontologically differentiate female and male and to make this identity difference grounds not only for their social separation, but also for their assignment to positions of relative subordination and domination date from the founding moment of the Western patriarchal tradition. In the fragments of his metaphysical poem that have come down to us, Parmenides (c. 515–399 BCE) schematized the logic of a patriarchal culture of domination by dividing "reality" and our talk about it into mutually exclusive and oppositional pairs—what "is" and what "is not," which are arranged in a value hierarchy. What is, is one, eternal, indivisible, imperishable, unchanging, and grounds Truth; what is not is multiple, temporal, changing, mixed, ultimately nonexistent, and grounds error and "mortal belief." While the context of fragment 17 of Parmenides' poem is unclear, with "On the right boys, on the left girls" (Kirk, Raven, and Schofield 1991, 260), he is clearly marking out sex as one of his binaristic pairs. This logic has been written and rewritten by millennia of male philosophers but rarely challenged or changed. Even apparently dissenting voices, such as Plato's in his *Republic*, resulted in little, it anything, by way of real social alternatives for girls and women. Thus the social organization this logic validates remained little changed in its organization of sex until the work of first-wave feminists bore fruit. Theoretically the dominant strain of that early feminist work was grounded in the newly emerging liberal ideology, and this orientation remained into the early days of the second wave. However, powerful new voices from the margins—women of color, lesbian feminists, Marxist and

Socialist feminists, feminists from the full range of the world's spiritual traditions, and others—soon began to challenge the central tenant of liberal feminism, that rationality is the *sine qua non* of the human and the key to the feminist endeavor. A vigorous debate developed not only around the issue of the difference, or lack thereof, between women and men, but around the differential identities of women occupying a range of sociopolitical sites. These debates in turn informed both theory construction and the strategies and tactics developed to bring about change.

In her preface to this volume, Linda López McAlister states, "At the time [of the Eighth International Association of Women Philosophers Symposium held in Boston in 1998], the main themes of this volume, 'political divisions' and 'identity politics,' might be said to have come to something of an impasse within U.S. feminist philosophy in the wake of the critiques of 'identities' by social constructionists. Many of the papers presented at the symposium, however, seemed to present new ways of examining traditional political dichotomies, on the one hand, or to deal with more sophistication and in more detail with the concept of identity and the need to reexamine its importance to politics." The chapters in this volume contest some of the prevailing conceptualizations of identity and difference as well as the functions of these concepts in feminist political discourse and praxis. Since the time of that conference there has been a renewal of interest in these topics, and so it is of particular importance to note that the original papers have been updated by their authors for publication in this volume. Further, these chapters bring an international perspective to the issues they raise because they are drawn from the work of women who were educated and/or work in locations as diverse as the United States, Canada, Germany, and Israel, among others. Thus these chapters represent cutting-edge thinking from an international perspective in these important and pressing areas for feminist research and praxis.

When work began on this volume, the chapters were organized by the previous editors into two parts, and that organization has been retained. These parts are "Reconceptualizing Challenges to Entrenched Political Divides" and "Putting Identity Back into Politics." While this division is in some ways useful, it is also somewhat misleading. As I worked on these chapters I could not help repeating to myself, almost as a mantra, the old feminist slogan, "The personal is political, the political is personal." Most of the chapters in this volume could easily be shifted from one part to the other because, whether they do so explicitly or implicitly, they deal with both sides of that binarism. Whether addressing such issues as identity politics, the need to connect with feminist women who occupy other identity sites, education, the role of third-wave feminists, or even questioning the importance of identity for an effective feminist praxis, these chapters display a deep concern to foreground the mutual implication of the personal and the political. Another pervasive theme of many of these works is the desire to correct some of the excesses of postmodern feminism, in particular the erasure of the subject and/or of the body. Thus the questions of authenticity, the lived and living body, and nature are raised here in fresh ways in order not simply to explore abstract issues, but also to make the point that these are real issues that matter in the lives of feminists and that their resolution has implications for social and political praxis. But what is perhaps most striking and heartening about these chapters is their spirit. Without exception these chapters display the deeply held conviction that building bridges among differently identified feminists is not only important but a necessary and achievable goal.

The first part of this volume, "Reconceptualizing Challenges to Entrenched Political Divides," opens with my chapter "The Mind/Body Paradigm Crisis and a New Paradigm for Feminism." Mind/body dualism is a paradigm in the Kuhnian sense(s) that has circulated in all of the three forms of feminist theory that Christine Di Stefano has schematically identified: rationalism, antirationalism, and postrationalism. Although each of these forms of feminism has attempted to address the negative effects of modernist preoccupations with rationality, their often trenchant critiques and successful praxes have been vitiated to some degree by the workings of this paradigm. Thus I argue, along Kuhnian lines, that this paradigm has outlived its usefulness. I look first to the mature work of Wittgenstein to begin to limn out an alternative picture of the human that avoids not only reified and ontologized dualisms, but also essentialism, behaviorism, and radical constructionism. Then consonant with Wittgenstein's utilization of the notion of a "human form of life" in which language-games and constructed subjectivity are rooted, Gad Horowitz appeals to a nonessentialized "erotic dimension of human experience" in order to ground resistant political theory and praxis. Horowitz maintains that the Western philosophical tradition cannot provide the resources needed to elucidate the political contribution made possible by a position that is nonessentialist but at the same time nondualist and nonmonist. Thus to fill in that deficit in the development of his own work, Horowitz accesses aspects of Buddhist philosophy with which Wittgenstein's work has also been found to have affinities. In particular, the concept of *sunyata* (emptiness, suchness, or nonessentialism) provides the conceptual tools Horowitz seeks in order to develop a "groundless democracy," one that draws on the givens of human life while refusing to essentialize identity. I then continue with the development of a further application of Buddhist thought by exploring its concept of compassionate action (*Karuna*), and arguing that Buddhist meditation practices, and especially *Vipassana*, or mindfulness meditation, can provide a means of fostering the personal change that must compliment and ground any real social and political transformation.

Jutta Weber's chapter, "Who's Afraid of Nature? The Rise and Fall of 'Denaturalization' in Contemporary Feminist Thought," continues the exploration of the theoretical tension between nature and constructionism. She reflects on the results of postmodern feminist theory's strategy of denaturalization as a way to overcome the problems engendered by modernist naturalism, positivism, and essentialism. She draws on the work of Donna Haraway, Katherine Hayles, and Karen Barad in order to interrogate the "distinction between denaturalization as a critical and negative strategy on one hand and dematerialization as a kind of naturalized denaturalization with hidden ontological statements on the other." In asking the question, "Why do we have to deny anything outside of human discourse to acknowledge the responsibility for our undertakings?" she points to the "blind spots and problematic effects" of dogmatic denaturalization and to dematerialization's radical negation of "everything beyond cultural discourse" as a form of silencing. Her position is that the postmodernist theoretical stance vis-à-vis nature has been an overreaction that has not served its political purpose of undermining sexism or racism, but has cost us access to the very category necessary to rein in some of the more extreme "anything goes" tendencies of postmodernism and the undesirable political positions they can be used to support. Thus she calls for "situated ontologies" that enable us to speak of nature while not denying our relationship to it.

Writing from the context of Canadian Québécois culture, law professor Marie-Claire Belleau uses the concept of "strategic intersectionality" to interrogate the interactions between feminism and the national and/or cultural identity politics of Québec and the rest of Canada. In her chapter "'L'intersectionnalité': Feminisms in a Divided World," she deploys her concept of intersectionality to challenge both essentialism (which eternalizes differences) and universalism (which erases them). The aim of her work is to preserve and celebrate the real cultural, institutional, and political differences between these two identity feminisms while working toward the development of new forms of coalitions rooted in these differences. This balance of preserving difference while seeking new coalitions may, she believes, open a space for dialogue between feminists in Québec and in the rest of Canada that could issue in the imaginative creation of new strategies for the feminist struggle. Clearly, Marie-Claire Belleau's work has applications well beyond the Canadian context from which she writes, applications for all those feminists seeking to build coalitions while retaining a distinct identity.

In "Feminism Under Fire," Sigal Ben-Porath brings her interests in political philosophy and education to bear on an issue that is of particularly pressing contemporary significance, the theoretical and practical relationship between militarism and patriarchalism. She takes a comparative approach, moving between the Israeli and American contexts, to explore the ways in which protracted conflict, such as the American "war on terror," tends to move a society toward conservative and undemocratic attitudes and institutions and especially toward conservative conceptions of gender roles. She holds that "Societies enduring a protracted conflict, such as the war on terror, tend to reconceptualize citizenship as a narrow notion, which I call 'belligerent citizenship,'" and it is this notion that serves to ground the problematic social attitudes and the restricted civic standing of women, which seems to inevitably accompany such situations. This discussion occupies the first part of her chapter; she then turns to an examination of the role the educational system can play in strengthening democracy, even during wartime. While, as she shows, the educational system is often used to strengthen militarism and gendered divisions, she brings to bear work such as that of Sara Ruddick and Virginia Woolf to argue that women's lives and experiences render them uniquely placed to introduce a "philosophy of peace" into education. Their pedagogical praxis is not grounded in an essentialized female nature, she argues, but rather in the social roles they have traditionally played and continue to play as mothers, caregivers, and teachers. Further, she maintains that feminist theory provides the tools necessary for a feminist pedagogical praxis of peace that includes well-developed theories of nonviolence, recognition and respect for the Other, resistance to social prejudice and oppressive practices, and the positive self concept necessary for the creation of a better future. Thus she concludes, "The mere infusion of the public discourse—or its miniature educational equivalent—with the silenced voices of women, can serve the aim of expansive education to diversify the public sphere and thus to offer further option, further visions, and further voices beyond the oppressive unity of belligerent citizenship."

In "When Girls Just Wanna Have Fun: Third-wave Cultural Engagement as Political Activism," Cathryn Bailey argues for the political meaningfulness of third-wave feminist activism. Perhaps the cultural production of this new wave of young women has been overlooked because these young feminists work in cultural sites not always accessed by older feminists, and so the influence of their work, even its very existence, may not always be recognized. Among these areas of cultural production are music, zines, and Internet websites. Cathryn Bailey surveys a wide range of work in these areas, as well as in more mainstream venues such as TV and movies, to make the case that third-wave feminists are not only active, but are also engaged in vigorous, informed cultural critiques that, while different in form, continue to address many of the areas of concern that have exercised first- and second-wave feminists—sexism, heterosexism, racism, injustice, and, especially, freedom. At the same time, this third-wave work embraces the themes and strategies of the postmodern movement, and this is especially evident, she argues, in the deployment of cultural rather than political strategies in much of their work. While this shift may have developed, in part, from their disenchantment with politics, it can also be read as a form of "politics by other means." Thus Cathryn Bailey, speaking for third-wave feminists, maintains, "We contest a politics of purity that would separate political activism from cultural production. We acknowledge the tension between criticism and the pleasures of consumption, and we work the border between a critical, even cynical, questioning of things-as-they-are and a motivation to do something anyway, without the 'support' of a utopian vision."

In the last chapter in this part, "My Once and Future Self," Marlene Benjamin offers an excerpt from her larger project that aims to examine the conception of the self in the face of catastrophic illness. In this portion of her work she argues, "In important, gender-specific ways, the body's violated promises irrevocably alter—practically *and* metaphysically—how one lives in the world. Much of this has to do with experience and the language available for its expression." Thus, from the perspective of her own experiences with tuberculosis, cancer, and then surgery to prevent the possible occurrence of the ovarian cancer that runs in her family, she engages the Cartesian distinction between the objective and subjective selves to explore their deployment in the context of "prophylactic" surgery. Her foci in this are gender-specific "body alterations" and the language associated with them, as well as the moral implications and consequences of the gendering of this language. Although she does not wish to entirely reject her philosophical tradition, she finds that the language of analytic philosophy is not adequate to her attempts "to speak *from* the lived body—from the body that is both *Korper* [the physical body in the Cartesian sense] and *Leib* [the living/lived body], rather than *about* the lived body"—and, importantly, to speak from *her* lived body.

Part II, "Putting Identity Back into Politics," opens with Morwenna Griffiths' "Keeping Authenticity in Play—Or Being Naughty to Be Good." In her chapter she argues that playfulness has an important role in the achievement of what is usually taken to be a most serious goal, personal authenticity. Women's struggles for justice frequently involve individual and/or collective changes in identity, and so Griffiths undertakes to explore "how a nonunitary self may come to authenticity." Her strategy is to explore the notion of authenticity in some important feminist ontologies of the self to arrive at a "patchwork model of the self." In this patchwork model, the self is neither fixed nor fragmented. She then explores the insights provided by this model, using her methodology of "critical autobiography," in autobiographical narratives of change. In this study she argues that "playfulness, especially naughty playfulness, is helpful in coming to authenticity."

Alison Bailey's work in this volume explores a different strand in the complex issue of identity. She develops a pressing area for feminist-standpoint epistemology by foregrounding in an original way the epistemological dimension of the social and political factors that grant or withhold privilege. With a focus on white identity, in her chapter, "Locating Traitorous Identities: Toward a View of Privilege-Cognizant White Character," she reconsiders the notion of traitorous identities, or "those who belong to dominant groups yet resist the usual assumptions and practices of those groups." As she notes, the methodologies, concepts, and theoretical frameworks of traditional philosophy and feminist theory have been problematized by a range of counterdiscourses situated in global, postcolonial, and multicultural positions. She develops her contribution to this reworking, the distinction between "privilege-cognizant" and "privilege-evasive" white identity scripts, through a critical analysis of Sandra Harding's description of the traitor as insider who becomes marginalized. Harding's work, in turn, draws on Patricia Hill Collins' important analysis of the "double-consciousness" of black domestic workers whose employment position gives them unique access to the realities of white women's privilege and thus produces a "more complete view," which can be used to open the eyes of both self and others. Alison Bailey argues that, while she believes Harding's work is headed in the right direction and makes an important contribution, her concept of the marginalized white race traitor is misleading. The problem she identified here is the conflation of epistemology and positionality, what Bailey calls the "cartography of margin and center," in standpoint theory. Bailey works to clarify this issue by the introduction of the distinction between privilege-evasive scripts, which may articulate an awareness of privilege but do not challenge, and so reproduce privilege; and privilege-cognizant scripts that are traitorous in that they develop out of a critical reflective consciousness of privilege and then take responsibility for its deployment. Because of this, privilege-cognizant scripts are capable of destabilizing the center. She ends with a discussion of the cultivation of a traitorous character and the strategic deployment of Lugones' "world"-traveling to enable the traitor to "see oneself in the Other."

Central to Birge Korndorfer's project in "Mobility–Unlimitation–Acceleration: General Insights and Feminist Intentions" is the rethinking of postmodern identity. In keeping with many of the chapters in this anthology, she wishes to develop a position that takes into account the lived experiences of women. Thus, in her chapter she seeks to address the disconnect between feminist academic theorizing and the level of concrete experience and knowledge. Her chapter does not purport to be conventionally academic, nor does she claim to be pursuing specific research goals. However, she wishes to discuss a kind of knowledge that foregrounds connections and reconceives "the spilt between knowledge and action." She maintains, "This kind of knowledge would be a philosophy of practice and (the production of) theory considered from a feminist point of view, but also with feminist intentions, intentions that enormously complicate the point of view in every respect."

Marjorie C. Miller engages questions from both metaphysics and politics to explore the relationships between empowerment, identity, place, and movement. In "Place, Movement, and Identity: Rethinking Empowerment," she seeks to clarify the concept of empowerment in order to foreground a distinctly feminist notion of empowerment that does not involve "power over," and that is fluid and multidimensional. Her stated purpose in this is to "help to answer questions about who we are and where we want movement [both in the sense of political action and in the sense of change of place] to take us." As are other authors in this collection, Marjorie Miller is especially concerned with the postmodernist tendency, represented by a feature of the work of Judith Butler, to depoliticize identity by denying "the legitimacy of the identities that locate common oppression" and thus diminish the ability of women to work together for change, in particular to exert the power solidarity provides to effect civil change. Instead Miller proposes a movement to decenter that changes the conception of identity rather than erases it. Again in company with other authors in this collection, her conception of identity recognizes the multiplicity and complexity of an individual's sites of identity: "It is situational, overlapping, and 'thick.'" At the same time, no aspect of identity is accorded primacy or centrality.

Marla Brettschneider begins her chapter by recognizing the necessity of contextualizing her topic within the evolving historical context of feminism. That broader feminist context provides the realization that identities are not simply multiple, nor do they simply intersect; rather, they are mutually constitutive. Thus from that perspective, in "Theorizing Identities as Mutually

Constitutive: A Critical Reading of Spelman, Aristotle, and Jewish Law," she raises issues from queer studies and the queering of race studies within a Jewish context: "The personal and social constructions of one's life as a Jewish lesbian feminist is a Jewishly and gendered sexing, a sexed and gendered Jewing, and simultaneously a sexed and Jewed gendering." In the body of her chapter she first discusses an early work by Elizabeth V. Spelman for the insights it provides for her concerns, but also criticizes its tendency to privilege race as an identity category. This, she argues, is owing to Spelman's reliance on Aristotle. She then seeks an alternative to Spelman's work by providing a critical reading of a Talmudic text that she uses as a countertext to provide an example of particularism that is used to destabilize the myth of the dominant culture's universalism as represented by Aristotelianism in Spelman. Finally, she turns to works by Rebecca Alpert and Melanie Kaye/Kantrowitz to explore how insights drawn from her first two areas can be found in Jewish feminist queer discussions of identity politics.

Amy R. Baehr's chapter, "Feminist Politics and Pluralism: Can We Do Feminist Political Theory without Theories of Gender?" takes the perspective of liberal political theory to argue that a feminist political theory can best be developed by laying aside a theory of the person (gender). She begins with an extended examination of the theoretical work of two prominent theorists, Luce Irigaray and Judith Butler, to show that both make claims about the fundamental nature of gender, claims that are incompatible, from which they draw conclusions about "the appropriate goals and practices of the women's movement." She continues, "Even if both theorists are read as proposing accounts of the limits of our knowledge about gender, and not accounts of what gender is, their theories still have serious implications for feminist thinking about gender ontology." The incompatibility of Irigaray's and Butler's accounts sets her problematic question, how can we develop a feminist political theory that is compatible with diverse theories of gender? She turns to the work of John Rawls to provide a model for this undertaking. Stressing that the dependency conception of the person and its associated conception of justice that inform her argument are only a part of a feminist conception of justice, she develops a model that is "rightly flexible" along important dimensions. This development is grounded not in any particular conception of gender—which necessarily, in the context of feminist pluralism, will be unacceptable to many—but rather in the specific, contemporary experiences of domination and subordination, particularly as these arise out of the reality of the differential work experience of women (in both the domestic and public spheres concurrently) and men (almost exclusively in the public sphere). She ends her chapter by reaffirming the importance of gender theory for contesting forms of discrimination and ac-knowledges that, while some may worry that the theory she develops waters down feminist critiques, in fact "the feminist contractualism sketched here is quite hostile to traditional gender roles, if those depend on a significantly unequal distribution of social power."

The concluding chapter in this part continues the discussion of the de-velopment of an inclusive feminist politics. In the process of revising an ear-lier version of her chapter in light of ensuing sociopolitical events, particu-larly those associated with September 11, 2001, Dianna Taylor was concerned for the relevance of her earlier work on Arendt and Foucault. However, she argues in "Arendt, Foucault, and Feminist Politics: A Critical Reappraisal" that these two important theorists are still relevant to her proj-ect of articulating a feminist politics committed to promoting freedom and resisting domination. Like Amy Baehr, Dianna Taylor addresses the problem of how to develop an inclusive political process, in this case, how feminists can be included in the conversation of the progressive movement in the United States. She proceeds by examining and providing feminist critiques of a number of ways in which "the orthodox left," as represented by the "First Principles" series run by *The Nation* in 1997, marginalizes feminist concerns. Two major issues she identifies and analyzes are the privileging of economic over cultural concerns and the conflation of feminism with identity politics. She maintains, "The orthodox left was imposing its views about progressive politics, in the form of an objective universal, on the whole of the left in the name of promoting unity. Alternatively, feminist views about what consti-tutes unity and how to achieve it, as well as feminist critiques of the domi-nant perspective, were routinely dismissed, criticized, or subordinated in ways that were oppressive to persons relegated to the margins and which, in-sofar as they inhibited the development of a truly progressive politics, were harmful to the whole of the left as well." She ties this to the current scene by asserting, "Looking back on them now, I believe the orthodox left's actions can be seen as . . . promoting both conformity with a preexisting standard or norm and obedience to a single, dominant vision of and for progressive pol-itics. And it is these specific aspects of the situation within the left during the late 1990s that resonate within the post-September 11, 2001, U.S. polit-ical context," in particular with the agenda of the Bush administration. It is because the issues of conformity and obedience remain definitive of the po-litical culture of the Bush administration era that the central features of fem-inist politics that she had earlier identified remain relevant. Again in com-pany with Amy Baehr, Dianna Taylor seeks a "pragmatic" politics that is concerned with "specific practical and political problems" and so she utilizes the work of Arendt and Foucault on agonism, creativity, identity, their differently theorized notions of "thinking differently," and antinormalization to articulate such a political stance.

The chapters in this collection amply demonstrate that issues of identity and difference have a central place in contemporary feminist research. Throughout their range, the authors of these essays have worked to develop new ways of understanding and living out our differences that will both preserve and celebrate them while at the same time fostering the necessary conditions for opening dialogue and forming new coalitions. The intent of these efforts has been to thereby engender imaginative new strategies for the personal, spiritual, and sociopolitical changes that will enable human growth, wellbeing, and flourishing. While the focus of the work represented here is understandably on women, the issues that are raised are given additional urgency, explicitly in some of the chapters and implicitly in others, by the situation of their concerns in the context of the world created by the Bush administration. Because that administration has foregrounded issues of identity and difference in ways that are not only inhumane and often inaccurate, but also dangerous for all of us, the new ways of thinking and acting that are proposed here have a much broader application. Thus these chapters truly invite not only feminists but all people to move in new directions.

Bibliography

Kirk, G. S., J. E. Raven, and M. Schofield. *The Presocratic Philosophers: A Critical History with a Selection of Texts.* Cambridge: Cambridge University Press, 1991.

CHAPTER TWO

~

The Mind/Body Paradigm Crisis and a New Paradigm for Feminism

Deborah Orr

Modernist preoccupations with rationality have been deeply inscribed in feminist theories and consequently, since the time of their first-wave inceptions, have structured feminist critiques of the projects of modernity, their theoretical and practical attempts to rectify injustices, and also intrafeminist debates. Questions regarding the nature of reason, of mind and its relationship—or lack of relationship—to body, and of the role of language/discourse and social convention/construction remain pivotal to ongoing interrogations and contestations of the concepts of sex, gender, and woman. They are, of course, at the crux of debates over the multitude of current issues surrounding questions of identity and difference (Plumwood 1993, 31–36, passim). Implicated in these questions are parallel issues concerning the body and, conjoined with these, issues concerning other dualistic pairs—for example, masculine/feminine, active/passive, culture/nature—which have served to organize Western social and political discourse. For our concerns in this chapter, the most important of these pairs is mind/body dualism. In what follows, I will argue that mind/body dualism in all of its formulations is incoherent. When applied to living human beings, neither member of this pair can be radically separated from its opposite while retaining conceptual sense or coherence, let alone deployed independent of its opposite, as is suggested by the slash between them. This is not simply because the construction of one term of the pair relies on the existence of the other, as many have argued, but because their very creation as an absolute disjunct[1] is entirely artificial, resting not on ontological difference but, as Wittgenstein (1968, sec. 371, 773, 104, 664, passim) points out, on the projection of the grammar of natural language onto the world. I will draw on the philosophical investigations of Wittgenstein's mature period to argue that this dualistic pair has been created not only by "subliming the logic of our language" but also by narrowing and restricting the natural language concepts of "mind" and "body" to a degree that makes them virtually inapplicable to living human beings. The sorts of conceptual problems that Wittgenstein has uncovered in the dominant theoretical deployments of this binaristic pair, taken together with the issues raised by feminist deployments of it, strongly suggest that the time has come for a Kuhnian paradigm shift. Most certainly a simple return to a naïve employment of natural language, which is the direction in which Wittgenstein's work might appear to lead us, can hardy be counted upon to resolve the multiplicity of social and political ills that feminism and other antioppressive discourses and praxis wish to address; however, I will suggest that a reconsideration of natural language does open up some new possibilities for dealing with these issues. In order to expand the possibilities opened up by Wittgenstein's work, I will turn to an exploration of some elements of Buddhist philosophy that are both consonant with his work and suggestive of a more satisfactory theory and praxis of identity and difference than is offered by those positions that draw, explicitly or implicitly, on mind/body dualism.

The argument I am making is a purely conceptual one and so may seem, on the face of it, to have little direct importance for feminist social, political, or spiritual praxis. Further, it does not directly address the multiple axes of social discrimination other than gender that many women and men find even more significant for understanding their experience. That may seem to limit its usefulness even further. However, what I am proposing, in a fairly straightforward application of Wittgenstein's work, is a shift in focus from the demonstrably incoherent models of human being that have been developed out of mind/body dualism and toward a model that is not only coherent but is, in fact, already widely utilized by natural language speakers. More specifically, I am arguing that the natural language "picture" of human beings that Wittgenstein developed in his later work undercuts the dualisms that Western culture has taken, either explicitly or implicitly, as ontologically grounded. Since these dualistic structures are, in fact, derived from the natural language picture by means of the reification of its grammar and so cannot be given ontological validation, we will see that shifting focus to the natural language picture of human being will make two vitally important contributions to feminist and other antioppressive projects: It will remove the (false) rational for the construction of alterity in terms of ontologically gender-linked hierarchies of mind/corporality as opposed to reason/emotion, and it will provide an understanding of human being that foregrounds embodiment and relationship. In doing this it will strike at the root of the cultural assumption identified by Simone de Beauvoir (1970), that woman as Other is defined by deficiency and lack. It will do this through showing not only that "immanence"/corporeality is the *human* condition, but that it is the *necessary* condition of "transcendence"/reason/spirit. In Wittgenstein's terms, the use of language, and thus the functioning of mind, is interwoven with embodied, lived experience. What this argument will not do, of course, is address the multiplicity of forms that social difference and disadvantage take, nor will it, by itself, ameliorate those problems. While these many and complex issues demand a range of strategies, I will suggest that Buddhist *Vipassana*, or mindfulness, meditation techniques hold out the promise of affecting on the personal level the deep attitudinal changes that must ground any satisfactory and lasting social change.

The Mind/Body Paradigm in Feminist Theory

Thomas Kuhn's groundbreaking *The Structure of Scientific Revolutions* (1970) provides an apt approach for the argument of this chapter. There he argued that the proceedings of "normal science"—in our case "normal philosophy"—are grounded in past achievements that are acknowledged as foundational by the scientific community, that provide that community with the problems with which they occupy themselves, and that thus provide shared "paradigms" for that community. In explaining his use of "paradigm," Kuhn said, "By choosing it, I mean to suggest that some accepted examples of actual scientific practice—examples which include law, theory, application, and instrumentation together—provide models from which spring particular coherent traditions of scientific research." (p. 10) In his 1969 postscript to *The Structure of Scientific Revolutions*, Kuhn distinguishes two senses of paradigm: the sociological sense in which it "stands for the entire constellation of beliefs, values, techniques, and so on shared by the members of a given community; and a second sense that denotes "one sort of element in that constellation." (p. 175) My contention is that in a similar manner philosophy has provided impressive and fruitful achievements that have circulated as paradigms, in both of Kuhn's senses of the word, within the philosophical community, and further that the products of these achievements have then informed the discourse of the broader, nonphilosophical community, just as scientific discourse production has done. Following on with this analogy, the philosophical paradigm at issue, in Kuhn's second sense of the word *paradigm*, has been the production of mind/body dualism with its valorization of mind and the concomitant pitting of reason against "mere nature," "subjectivity," emotion, and the body. On the sociological level, this paradigm has structured a multitude of social formations. Among these we must include not only gender relations, but also other social structures, such as race, class, sexuality, ethnicities, and so forth that are grounded in the mind/body distinction. I will not belabor the point, demonstrated by critics ranging from Mary Wollstonecraft (1986/1792) to Edward Said (1978), that a, if not *the*, chief mechanism of inferiorization has been to consign the target group to the more corporeal, and thus necessarily less rational, side of the divide. More broadly, we can see that the full range of cultural production is rooted in this distinction, most fundamentally in culture's root definition of itself as a grounded in and a product of reason, as distinct from nonrational "nature," that is, from the material and the bodily.

Importantly, while scientists, and likewise philosophers, may agree on a paradigm, they may not agree on, "or even attempt . . . to produce, a full *interpretation* or *rationalization* of it." (Kuhn 1970, 44; italics in original) Paradigms may be differently interpreted or applied in accord with varying rules by scientists or by philosophers; "Indeed, the existence of a paradigm need not even imply that any full set of rules exists." (p. 44) Kuhn appeals to Wittgenstein's concept of family resemblance to explain how this is possible. Just as words in natural language, for instance, *game, number,* or *leaf,* can be used without appeal to a shared essence, so too can the paradigms of science or philosophy. What ties these uses of a word together under a common concept, Wittgenstein argues, is sharing in a set of features in a way that is analogous to the way that traits are shared among family members—some may share a similar nose, others lack the nose but share a build, and so forth. The similarities in uses of a word or paradigm "overlap and criss-cross" just as the resemblances between the members of human families do (Wittgenstein 1968, sec. 67). Thus we can identify a family of uses of the mind/body dualism that runs through the history of Western culture without having to identify any one trait, set of rules, or "essence" common to them all. Awareness of the family resemblance character of this paradigm allows us to see that this dualism grounds both radical materialism (which begins by suppressing mind and then must account for it) and radical idealism (which suppresses matter/body and then must reconstruct it), as well as those theories that overtly or covertly deploy both terms of the binarism while valorizing one of them (e.g., Cartesianism). Postmodern theorizing often moves in both directions, problematizing the body and also constructed "subjectivity," the latter frequently a loose stand-in for "mind."[2]

Christine Di Stefano has provided a useful schematization of the major positions taken by current feminist theories in response to the Enlightenment project's valorization of mind and reason, its linkage of these to maleness and masculinity, and its denigration of feminized corporeality and emotion. A review of the three positions she identifies—rationalism, antirationalism, and postrationalism—reveals the uses to which each position puts the mind/body dualism and shows the sorts of problems that arise for feminist theory when the theorization of mind and body are framed by a dualistic paradigm.

The *rationalist* position is grounded in Enlightenment ideals of rationalism and humanism. Here the ideal of reason is that utilized initially and primarily by science, although it has now been extended to virtually every sphere of human endeavor, from literary criticism to ethics, from sociology to political theory. Here reason is instrumental-technological, and its proper employment calls for the erasure of all purportedly extraneous aspects of personal experience (e.g., emotion, inclination, affiliation, intuition, and so forth) in order to produce results that are "objective," "neutral," and "replicable." Proponents of feminist rationalism hold that the body as well as gendered psychology and other dimensions of socially differentiated experience can be set aside to enable the unencumbered operation of reason. Clearly, for this position the radical separation of mind and body is foundational; indeed, Descartes is most often cited as its chief architect.

This position undergirds much first-wave feminism as well as second-wave liberal feminism. It is foundational to classical liberalism and early on was applied to "the woman question" by John Stuart Mill. Although Mill acknowledged that he lacked empirical proof to support his belief, it was his conviction, and the thrust of his argument in *The Subjection of Women* (1986/1869), that, given a chance, women could prove themselves the equals of men in the realm of reason and thus fit subjects of that "principle of perfect equality," (p. 219) the applicability of which he argued for in all social and political matters. Liberal feminism maintained that with access to education, the vote, and equal social—especially employment—opportunities, women would take their place beside men in the public sphere.

The problems in principle and in practice for white, educated, and middle-class women who attempted to follow the creed of liberal feminism have been well analyzed (Jaggar 1983, 173–206), but it fell to analysts such as bell hooks to begin to expose the deeper and differential layers of consciousness and experience in the lives of women socially marginalized by race and class. Quoting Rita Mae Brown on class, for instance, hooks writes, "Class involves your behavior, your basic assumptions about life. Your experience (determined by your class) validates those assumptions, how you are taught to behave, what you expect from yourself and from others, your concept of a future, how you understand problems and solve them, how you think, feel, act." (1984, 3) What is here true of class, we now realize, is equally true of gender, race, sexual orientation, and so forth. In this deeply divided society one form of reason, instrumental reason, has been hived off and claimed by an elite not only as their own but as the only valid form, while all other forms are dismissed as inferior and inadequate. It is a form of reason that serves their interests and that can best, if not only, be deployed by them or by those to whom they have granted honorary status as "one of us."

The position of the rationalist camp is turned on its head by *antirationalism*. That which makes woman Other—immanence, or the body, procreation, irrationality, emotion—is now valorized, and a distinctly female form of reason, if not always directly determined by her body, is grounded in her experience as a woman. Most often the theoretical core of that experience is maternity. From the work of such early feminists as Nelly McClung (1972) and Charlotte Perkins Gillman (1998), to Luce Irigaray (2004) and Carol McMillan, whose *Woman, Reason and Nature: Some Philosophical Problems with Feminism* (1982) Di Stefano reviews, these feminists have celebrated not only the differences between women's way(s) of thinking and men's way, but its superiority, most especially in the realm of morality. Here again, clearly, mind/body dualism is at work; although women's antirationalism is sometimes merely *linked* to their corporeal experience of being a woman, it is frequently determined by it in keeping with a theoretical position articulated early on by Aristotle (1947, bk. 1, ch. 12–13), which received one of its best-known statements in Rousseau's *Emile* (1958/1763).

Rousseau's book was, in fact, an attempt to theoretically ground women's *subordinate* position by reference to physical sexual difference. His work received its importance and social impact from the Enlightenment's rejection of theologically embedded sexual hierarchy and its concomitant embrace of material science's emphasis on the importance of physical, in this case sexual, difference (see Laqueur 1990). Proponents of this position, as Di Stefano points out in her critique of McMillan, tend to assume a heterosexist (not to mention white, middle class, etc.) perspective and fail to problematize femininity or the sexual division of labor or to understand the role of a purported special female form of reason in constituting sexual difference (1990, pp. 68–73). We must also note that this position bodes ill for relations between the sexes since women and men will inevitably be forever talking past each other owing to their differential logics and values. On the positive side, work such as that of the authors just cited as well as such influential research as that of Mary Belenky and her colleagues (1986), Carol Gilligan (1982) and all those who have followed up her original work, and others (Orr 1989, 1995) have begun to make the case first, that the ideal of reason favored by the post-Enlightenment West[3] does not exhaust the possibilities and, second, to point us in the direction of exploring more fully the relationship between reason and embodied, lived experience.

Postrationalism is presented as a position that purportedly eludes the dilemma inherent in the rationalism-antirationalism debate, that of a forced choice between "a politics and epistemology of identity (sameness) or difference." (Di Stefano 1990, 72) But, it does so at the price of promoting a "postfeminist tendency, an inclination which is fostered by a refusal to systematically document or privilege any particular form of difference or identity against the hegemonic mainstream." (p. 73) Postrationalism rejects not only the master narratives of the Enlightenment and "overly coherent theory" (p. 74), but also anything that is construed to be an attempt to naturalize or essentialize "the human." On both the epistemological and political levels, contestation, violation, refusal, partiality, and fragmentation are the hallmarks of acceptable positions and responses.

As with rationalism and antirationalism, this position is embraced at a price; in fact it has several drawbacks. Chief among these are that the major postmodern theorists have been white, middle-class, and almost exclusively male academics who not only represent their social position in their work, but who have also been obsessed with the work of similarly placed males and, further, who have been blind to issues not only of gender but, once again, of race, class, and so on. Of special import for the development of a feminist politics is the rejection of any semblance of shared, nondiscursive identity or commonality in subjectivity among women. Not only does that preclude any but a negative solidarity grounded in resistance, as Di Stefano correctly points out, but it gives us no basis for even conceiving of substantive and enduring alternatives to the status quo. Generally, political opposition in the past has not merely involved a shared sense of grievance and oppression; these have been grounded in some deeper conception of the human good for which protesters sought recognition and protection. Across their range[4] the positions comprehended by postrationalism leave us with little more to look forward to than a ceaseless process of resistance for resistance's sake, for if we are nothing more than the effects of "discourse," then there can be nothing to work for that might give us satisfaction, fulfillment, or peace. As well, with its prioritizing of issues of epistemology and discourse, this theoretical group once again grounds itself in the mind/body distinction. That this is so is clear when we consider both the degree to which the humanist notion of "subjectivity," which is the target of these theories and which is to be replaced by discourse or performance, is in turn a reconfigured notion of mind, as well as the dependence of the constructed body on the constitutive activity of discourse. This line of thought, it has been argued, crosses over into idealism, for instance in Butler's critical rejection of Foucault's assertion that the body exists prediscursively to be inscribed by regimes of power and discourse (1997, 1999) and in her appropriation of "the Kantian tradition" by way of Derrida in her more recent work (see Costera Meijer and Prins 1998, 279; Butler 1999).

Each of these three positions has undeniably made major contributions to feminist theory and to the social and political advancement of women and other socially marginalized groups. Rationalism made the historically necessary case that women can function equally as well as men in the public sphere and as rational agents; antirationalism foregrounded the differential experiences of women as embodied beings; and, in the hands of feminist postmodernists, postrationalism has gone far to expose the degree to which women's subjectivities and lives are constructed.

At the same time, each of these positions contains theoretical and practical problems that limit their usefulness. I have suggested that in each case these positions are grounded in the influence on their construction of a particular paradigm, mind/body dualism, or some variation of it. It seems to me that this paradigm is in a state of crisis owing to its inability to coherently deal with the research field to which it is applied, or to provide a methodology for satisfactorily resolving issues that are of current and pressing interest on both the theoretical and practical levels. Kuhn (1970) has argued that it is such a state of crisis that leads to paradigm change. To foster that shift I will now turn to the work of Wittgenstein's mature period to explore the emergence of a new paradigm or, more accurately, the uncovering of a paradigm of an integrated and relational human being that already exists in natural language. That paradigm is utilized in the political work of Gad Horowitz (1987, 1992) where he employs it in ways that are highly promising for a new political theory and praxis. Following a discussion of Horowitz's work I will draw some parallels between Wittgenstein's work and that of Nagarjuna, the philosophical voice of Mahayana Buddhism, and then suggest some of the implications of these affinities for a more adequate theory and praxis of identity and difference.

Wittgenstein, Horowitz, and a Holistic Paradigm

Wittgenstein's work is useful in responding to the mind/body paradigm because he both tested its logic as it was employed in its major Western philosophical forms—classical mind/body dualism, behaviorism, and idealism—and explored an alternative to it in natural language and the "picture" of human being embedded in that language. In his work he argued strenuously both against essentialism and against the production of any final ontological truth, both key targets of postrationalism. As a corrective and an alternative to these he explored natural language, which provides the words with which philosophical paradigms and theories are constructed. One point of this examination of natural language, and a point that tells as much against his own earlier work (Wittgenstein 1961) as against the other philosophical models he critiqued, is that it is in these natural language-games that the words employed to construct philosophical theories have their sense. What has been overlooked by many Western philosophers, including the young Wittgenstein, is that these words are deprived of that sense when philosophers put them to specialized uses (e.g., ontological, metaphysical) while futilely attempting to draw on their original, but now lost, sense (Wittgenstein 1968, sec. 116–124, passim).

Wittgenstein held that natural language is pragmatic in that its primary purpose is to facilitate human relationships and projects. It is like a box of tools (Wittgenstein 1968, sec. 11) and, like tools, can be best understood by examining how people used each to perform various tasks. Thus his examination of natural language revealed the conceptual grammar of language-games, that is, the relationships not only between words but also between words and the human purposes and experiences into which they were woven (sec. 7). For our purposes it is important to bear this in mind, that the conceptual grammar of language-games that gives words their sense *necessarily* involves not only valid relationships between words but also between words and human lived experience, for it is this human element that provides the medium that gives words their life, their sense. Without it, like fish out of water, words shrivel up and die.

Wittgenstein's work is not easily summarized because he did not approach the conceptual issues he investigated in a linear fashion, by presenting a thesis and defending it. Instead he moved in on his targets from many different directions and rarely drew conclusions, instead letting the force of what he did accumulate until his reader began to "see things differently." This methodology relates to his understanding of what his philosophizing could accomplish. It was a kind of "therapy of the understanding," which worked by lessening the hold of ideas that, he believed, are confused and misguided and that, consequently, functioned as a sort of malignancy in people's lives. Thus the point of his work was to enable his readers to effect a change not only in the way they thought, but concomitant with this, in the way they lived (see especially Wittgenstein 1980). In this respect his philosophical methodology is similar to psychoanalysis in that the analyst may quickly apprehend what the analysand's problems are, but it does no good to tell them this; for a cure to be effected analysands must come upon the cause of their dis-ease themselves. "Working in philosophy . . . is really more a working on oneself." (Wittgenstein 1980, 16) The promise here is that in gaining a clearer understanding of how language works—for example, words such as *mind* and *body*—we can begin to ameliorate some of the problems engendered by misunderstanding them. I will return to this point below.

Thus, much against Wittgenstein's desire for how he should be read, I will schematically outline some of the problems he uncovered that are associated with mind/body dualism. Chief among these in the post-Enlightenment period are the problem of other minds and the private language problem. Both of these develop out of the projection of the grammar of two types of language-games into a visual metaphor. These two grammars, the grammar of human bodies and the grammar of subjective states, are projected to become an opaque container that houses subjective experiences to which only their possessor (the container) has access. The resulting myth, which Gilbert Ryle called "the Myth of the Ghost in the Machine," permeates not only modernist Western philosophy but also most of its intellectual production, from medicine to psychology to religion to politics.

In its philosophical usages, this picture is conjoined with the referential theory of meaning in which words mean the things to which they refer or for which they stand (Wittgenstein 1968, sec. 1, passim). But if subjective experience—reasoning, feeling, emoting, and so on—is sequestered in the body, knowledge of the subjective experience of others becomes problematic to the point that we can doubt that "others" even have such experience, and, pushing this logic to its end point, we can doubt that those entities that we have been taking to be "others" are, in fact, humans; perhaps they are simply complex automata (cf. Descartes' worry, Wittgenstein 1968, sec. 420).

Analogical reasoning has been proposed as a solution to this problem; I know that *pain* means pain in my own case—my experience of pain is my criterion of correct application of *pain*. However, this move establishes a logically private language since only I can know what I mean by *pain*. I also know, so the argument goes, that I act in particular ways when I am in pain, and so I can deduce that another person has pain when they act in those ways. On the basis of this reasoning, it is argued, I can correctly apply *pain* to them. But this fails on the initial assumption that one can know in one's own case that *pain* means pain, for on this criteriological model *correct* connections must be set up between pain and *pain*. However, there is no way of ascertaining from case to case that the word is being used consistently in one's own case and so there is no way of applying it correctly either to oneself or to others. Calling on memory is no help here for memory, as with the original use of the word *pain*, requires a criterion of correctness. Thus, on this model language is reduced first to solipsism and then to nonsense; on the grounds of its own logic it can mean nothing. Wittgenstein denied that this leads him into behaviorism; rather than denying human subjective experience he is simply rejecting "a *grammatical* fiction" (sec. 307), or "the Myth of the Ghost in the Machine," along with the referential theory of meaning that produced it.

In the case of the private language problem and the problem of other minds, philosophical confusions arise when language is removed from the context of human life in which it functions, from its home in natural language-games (sec. 116), and is given entirely new uses, and likewise, Wittgenstein argued, other major philosophical positions rest on mistakes about conceptual grammar and the overuse of the referential model of meaning: "For *this* is what disputes between Idealists, Solipsists and Realists look like, The one party attack [sic] the normal form of expression as if they were attacking a statement; the others defend it, as if they were stating facts recognized by every reasonable human being." (sec. 402)

As a general piece of advice Wittgenstein recommends that, when in difficulty, "Always ask yourself: How did we *learn* the meaning of this word . . . ? From what sort of examples? In what language-games?" (sec. 77; italics in original) Doing so undermines the referential theory of meaning and dispenses with the need for criteria in many first- and second-person uses of words. It does so by turning the philosopher's attention to the "prelinguistic" actions and interactions with others that "a language game is based on," that are "the prototype of a way of thinking and not the result of thought." (Wittgenstein 1970, sec. 540–541) For instance, a child hurts herself, or she laughs, or is hungry and so reaches for the breast, and the people around her teach her to use words in the context of these behaviors. She thus learns new, linguistic behaviors that replace, rather than refer to or stand for, the primitive, prelinguistic ones (Wittgenstein 1968, sec. 244). Her use of the word *hungry* replaces crying; it does not refer to her inner sensation of hunger. As Wittgenstein pointed out in sec. 402, her use of language in these cases is not a "statement" but a mode of expression and relationship.

In order to foreground human lived experience as the context of linguistic sense, Wittgenstein returns again and again to what he calls human "natural history" (sec. 25), the behaviors and reactions that are common to human beings and that provide the context for language acquisition and use. His notion of a human natural history comprehends not only the expressive behaviors of a person but also their reactions to and interactions with others, and with the rest of their world. For instance, he reminds us, "It is a primitive reaction to tend, to treat, the part that hurts when someone else is in pain . . . and so to pay attention to other people's pain-behaviour" (Wittgenstein 1970, sec. 540). A thought experiment can help demonstrate the importance of the behavior of others; try to imagine a stone in pain. This seems absurd, impossible to do. What could possibly give us the idea that a stone had pain? What behaviors would we react to? But, "Now look at a wiggling fly and at once these difficulties vanish and pain seems able to get a foothold here, where before everything was, so to speak, too smooth for it." (Wittgenstein 1968, sec. 284) We react to the behaviors of other sentient beings, flies as well as people, in ways that are inconceivable for us with rocks or trees. In the case of other people, we react to them as *people*, and not either as bodies or as minds, "One looks into his face" (sec. 286) when another is in pain and one seeks to comfort them. One does not look at a mere physical body, much less reason by analogy to ascertain what its "inner sensations" might be.

In sum, in his study of natural language Wittgenstein developed the picture of human beings that is found in that language. The picture he found embedded there helps to illuminate our way of understanding others and ourselves. This picture of the human being is holistic, integrated, and relational. In many of its aspects it is continuous with the natural world. Mind and body are not separate entities conjoined to form a person, nor does a person create/construct the Other on the basis of the behaviors of their bodies or by some other process of reasoning. It is on the basis of the behaviors, experiences, and interactions of human *persons*, not mere bodies, that the language of mind and body are developed. Thus our concepts of mind and body are rooted in our experiences as integrated and relational beings; we cannot logically reverse this to "build up" the concept of a person from the concepts of mind and of body. Further, human persons respond to and interact with others in ways that, at a primitive level, are typical of human beings in general. But to say this is not to deny that a great deal of shaping and developing of these primitive behaviors goes into forming a member of any given social or cultural group. Thus Wittgenstein's philosophy allows us to acknowledge and explore that "social construction of the subjectivity of the person" without denying its rootedness in presocial and prelinguistic behavior and experience.

Wittgenstein worked at length to uncover the role of mind/body dualism in behaviorism, idealism, and Cartesian positions. The problem of language acquisition and use and the covert working of mind/body dualism are endemic to postmodernist and poststructuralist theory as we can clearly see when we bring Wittgenstein's considerations to bear. They are, for example, shown in a particularly vivid form when we consider Judith Butler's work in the context of Wittgenstein's advice. While she concedes in *Bodies That Matter* that "surely bodies live and die; eat and sleep; feel pain, pleasure; endure illness and violence; and these 'facts,' one might skeptically proclaim, cannot be dismissed as mere construction. Surely there must be some kind of necessity that accompanies these primary and irrefutable experiences. And surely there is." (1993, xi) However, she argues, this is no argument against their "constructedness" but rather a reason for rethinking what is meant by construction, a project she undertakes in *Bodies That Matter*. Thus the intent of her work is to "offer an account of how it is that bodies materialize," (p. 69) "a developmental account of how the *idea* of one's own body comes into being," (p. 71; my italics) that is, to explain how the body is "known" (passim) by the subject. In one specific example, in taking issue with Kristeva's account of the role of an infant's relationship with "the maternal body" (not, tellingly, "with its mother") in inaugurating its "relation to speech," Butler states, "The maternal body prior to the formation of the subject is always and only *known* by a subject who by definition postdates that hypothetical scene." (p. 71; my italics)

This language, typical of the book as a whole, betrays two important problems: First it reveals the workings of her recasting of mind/body in terms of discourse/materiality. On this account human subjectivity becomes entirely discursive—what is constructed through discourse and known through discourse exhausts it without remainder. Second, it reveals the misunderstanding, which is entailed by the first problem and which Wittgenstein attributed to the misreading of conceptual grammar, that human bodies, experiences, and relationships are objects of *knowledge* rather than the lived experiences of human beings. On Butler's account a child cannot even be said to be in a relationship with its mother—another living being—until *after* it acquires language. Consequently, in theories such as Butler's, to the extent that both the *human* body itself as well as *all* subjective experience is a function of performative discourse, these cannot serve as a part of the natural, prelinguistic "human form of life" (see Wittgenstein 1968, sec. 23) into which language is woven to form language-games. To say that they can is to undercut *radical* constructionism. The problem here is much the same as that with private language; because of the theorized nature of human beings, language acquisition and use becomes logically impossible, for how—if that upon which form is imposed is, *per impossible*, mute and unresponsive—can a prediscursive Kantian noumenon (see Costera Meijer and Prins 1998, 279) ever learn to use such words as pain, pleasure, or hunger? How ever become the phenomenon we call a human being? But, as we have said, if it is not so theorized, then *radical* constructionism fails. While Wittgenstein is able to adduce the

natural behavior and reactions of children to provide a context for their acquisition of language, what theories such as Butler's leave us with is, at best,
something closer to a stone than a baby—in Gad Horowitz's word "primal
matter" (Horowitz 1987, 71)—and how can we conceive of that learning language? Further, "primal matter" would have no way of ever coming to distinguish between the mother's breast and a baby bottle for the natural experiences on which that *linguistic* distinction will later rest—a differential
reaction to another living being and to an inanimate object—are lacking and
cannot be supplied. Either human *babies* come equipped to experience pain
and pleasure, to desire and avoid, to eat and sleep, or they cannot learn to
speak, to think, or to know. Thus, to admit that they do come so equipped
with this rudimentary subjectivity would undermine *radical* constructionism
but not constructionism *per se*; in fact, as I have indicated and will argue further, it leaves it much room in which to perform.

In a paper addressing Foucault's constructionism—a position that Butler
generally endorses except when he slips up with such statements as that it is
"the body" that is "inscribed" or "imprinted" by history (see Butler 1999)—
Gad Horowitz (1987) puts his finger on one aspect of the problem for theorists such as Foucault—as well as Butler and others—that results from their refusal to admit any nonconstructed aspects of human being. Horowitz's
concern is with political resistance and he finds Foucault's ceaseless dance of
power and resistance unsatisfactory either as an explanation of dominated
subjectivity or as providing a ground for opposition to power. He brings Freud
and Marcuse into his discussion in order to introduce an "erotic dimension of
human experience" (p. 61) that will provide Foucault with the needed ground
for opposition, an "inherent positive direction that underlies and serves as a
source of resistance and orients that resistance toward a positive goal." (p. 65)

The problem that stands in the way of Foucault's incorporation of the
Freudian-Marcusian position is, Horowitz says, "the taboo of essentialism."
(p. 70) Horowitz rejects this taboo as ungrounded in this case since Freud's
central concepts, most especially Eros, do not cohere with the key meanings
of essentialism, a term which, it has been persuasively argued, actually has no
essence of its own (Fuss 1989) and which, in consequence, is used ambigu-
ously in much "antiessentialist" discourse. The point Horowitz makes, one
which applies as much to Wittgenstein's use of such terms as "the human
form of life" and "human natural history" as it does to Freud's Eros, is that not
every general observation about human beings commits us to essentialism in
the sense of a commitment to the existence of "a true essence—that which
is most irreducible, unchanging, and therefore constitutive of a given person
or thing." (Fuss 1989, 2) While Eros is often conflated with sex, Horowitz

points out that in Freud's usage it comprehends much more, "the striving of the living to bond, to attach, to be united with the living. . . . It is the child's need for love." (1987, 71) It is out of the child's need that Eros is played out in the development of the adult but, Horowitz charges, "Foucault's male antiessentialism represses knowledge of the child." (p. 71) What he says is worth quoting at length:

> Without being the all-inclusive or self-subsisting "essence" of the human, infancy is transhistorical. Any human infant has much more in common with all other human infants in all other times and places than with the older humans of its own time and place. The infant is not a subject—her subjectivity will be constructed—but she is not merely resistant primal matter. She needs. It is not merely a need for physical sustenance and bodily pleasure. Those who do not throw out the baby can be radical [as Foucault cannot], for the infant's need for love is the root of the self. Even deeper than the need for love is the terror that Freud found in the infant deprived of love. It is the terror of annihilation. We are not superficial beings. Liberation is not simply the liberation of pleasure. It is liberation from the terror, and from the numbness that wards off terror, that pervades our existence in the patriarchal hate cultures. (p. 71)

If we can resist the urge to jump to the conclusion that every substantive noun refers to an essence, then we can begin to develop a picture of the human that reflects our actual human condition, including those elements of it to which Horowitz points, while enabling an analysis of the formation of identity through the acquisition of language-games. Indeed, it will enable the formation of a picture that allows for the very acquisition of language for, as I have indicated above, on postrationalist accounts it is no easier to account for language acquisition by "primal matter" than it would be to account for language acquisition by a stone or a tree. Those aspects of the human form of life that Wittgenstein and Horowitz point to (e.g., the need for love and fear of abandonment and consequent annihilation, natural expressions of primitive experiences, instinctive reactions to others, and so forth) are shaped and molded virtually from the moment of birth—to a large extent but certainly not entirely by the acquisition of language-games—to construct an individual who will fit the requirements of her or his social position. Here neither term of mind/body dualism is prioritized or valorized; rather language-games are a synthesis of words and human behaviors (Wittgenstein 1968, sec. 7), in the broadest sense of the word *behaviors*. Thus we can avoid the problems attendant on the valorization of one or the other term of the dualism by rationalism and antirationalism, while at the same time providing just the ground we need for opposition to power and domination, a ground

unavailable to the postrationalist. That ground lies in the common humanity that we all begin with and in the needs, desires, abilities, and inclinations
that we thus have. Crucially, this account allows us to use with impunity, and
without fear of essentialism, that "forbidden vocabulary" that Christine Di
Stefano says some postmodern feminists have "smuggled in" in order to provide a plausible feminist politics (1990, 76). Those words include *health,
flourishing, identity, unity, solidarity,* and others.

Nagarjuna and Mindfulness

In "Groundless Democracy" (1992) Horowitz elucidates the political contribution that a position that is nonessentialist, and at the same time nondualist and nonmonist, can make. He maintains that the philosophical traditions
of the West cannot provide the resources needed for this and so he turns to
the philosophical traditions of the East, especially to Buddhism (p. 158) and
its concept of emptiness, groundlessness, or suchness (*sunyata*). This is an interesting move in itself and is made even more so by the facts that, on the
one hand, Wittgenstein's work has been found to have many affinities with
this Buddhist philosophical tradition (Gudmunsen 1977; Katz 1981; Streng
1967), and on the other hand that feminists (Gross 1993; Klein, 1994, 1995,
1997) and other antioppressive theorists (Forbes 2003, 2004, 2005; Orr 2004,
2005) are now beginning to draw on this tradition—or more accurately, this
body of traditions—to provide both theory and praxis for their projects. At
this point I will not attempt either to formulate a feminist political stance(s),
nor will I be able to fully discuss the uses to which a feminist praxis might put
the resources offered by Buddhist philosophy and the yogic practices it has
developed to foster human liberation from suffering. What I will do is look
briefly at the work of the primary voice of Mahayana, or Middle Way, Buddhism, (Nagarjuna 1995; see also Streng 1967) in order to point to some of
the implications of a nonessentialized concept of human being such as is also
to be found in the works of both Wittgenstein and Horowitz, and then to indicate how this nonessentialized concept leads to a praxis useful for feminists.
In doing this I believe we can avoid what Joan Scott has called the "difference dilemma" that arises from normatively constructed views of difference,
such as are found in rationalism and antirationalism, while making the two
moves she calls for in a critical feminism: first, to expose and reject the hierarchies of normative discourse, and second, to formulate a concept of equality that rests on a notion of differences that disrupts the normative discourse
(1990, 145–146); however, we can do so without either falling prey either to

the postrationalist "postfeminist tendency" that Di Stefano identified (1990, 73), or the concomitant undermining of radicalism discussed by Horowitz.

There are many affinities to be found between the works of Wittgenstein and Nagarjuna. Importantly for our concerns, they both argue strenuously against all metaphysical views, and most especially essentialism; they both ground language and human understanding in conventional, everyday experience (Nagarjuna 1995, ch. 24, v. 8–10; ch. 14); and they both uncover the deep relationality at the heart of human existence. The concept of emptiness (*sunyata*) in Buddhist thought is precisely the denial of an essence or self-subsistent nature of things (ch. 24, passim). As in the work of Wittgenstein, this denial does not lead Nagarjuna into idealism, materialism, or the radical constructionism of postrationalism; rather, and again in company with Wittgenstein, it leads to the everyday world of human life, the matrix in which words have their meaning. Nagarjuna called this flip side of emptiness *pratityasamutpada*, or dependent arising. By this he rejected all forms of atomism—logical or social—and referred us instead to the interconnectedness of all things.

> If dependent arising [*pratityasamutpada*] is denied,
> Emptiness [*sunyata*] itself is rejected.
> This would contradict
> All of the worldly conventions. (ch. 24, v. 36)

In construing this verse Garfield has said, "Common sense holds the world to be a network of dependently arisen phenomena [i.e., things are interconnected and interrelated]. So common sense only makes sense if the world is asserted to be empty [i.e., *sunyata*, without essences]." (1995, 313) In this Nagarjuna was rejecting all metaphysical theories, "emptiness is the relinquishing of all views," (1995, ch. 13, v. 8) and turning attention to the everyday world of "worldly conventions" to assert its irreducible importance for establishing a healthy, nondeluded understanding. Wittgenstein made a similar point when he complained that trying to apply philosophical theories to real life is like trying to walk on slippery ice; to walk we must return to the "rough ground" (Wittgenstein 1968, sec. 107) of human life: "One might say: the axis of reference of our examination must be rotated, but about the fixed point of our real need." (sec. 108) That "real need," for Wittgenstein, as for Nagarjuna, is to develop a less confused and distorted view of the human form of life and of our own individual lives. This, they both held, is the key to overcoming suffering and thus to human health and flourishing.

As I have indicated above, in exploring the "rough ground" of human life Wittgenstein foregrounded the importance for language acquisition of natural human reactions, not only to other humans but also to other things in the world. Relationships and spontaneous reactions and behaviors are natural and fundamental to the human form of life. However, in his philosophical work, although not in his personal life (Monk 1990), Wittgenstein was blind to issues of gender, race, class, sexuality, and so forth. Nevertheless, it is safe to say that the implication of his work is that there is a commonality and a sharing of experiences among those beings who share in the human form of life and thus a sense of identity that at the same time opens space for the recognition of difference. For instance, difference is interwoven into a shared human experience through the construction of gender that is affected by the acquisition of sex-linked language-games. This difference is further nuanced through the introduction of the language-games of race, class, sexuality, historical and cultural positioning, and much more. However, whether we construe any particular difference as natural or as socially constructed, it is experientially and conceptually subsumed under the more primitive identity of all members of the human form of life that does not admit of inequality or hierarchy, that is, under *sunyata*.

Through its concept of *pratityasamutpada*, dependent arising, which is the obverse of emptiness (*sunyata*) (see Nagarjuna 1995, 24), Buddhist thought has developed the ethical implications of emptiness. Nagarjuna's move here parallels Wittgenstein's rejection of the atomism of the *Tractatus* and the development of the picture of a relational human form of life in the *Investigations*; because of the rejection of essentialism and atomism in Buddhist thought, all beings are understood as interrelated and interdependent. Consequently actions done to others are, in a real sense, done to oneself. In this respect the Sanskrit term *pratityasamutpada* effectively undercuts the radical dualism of the dominant Western philosophical tradition's thinking about self and Other. This nondualistic, relational orientation is at the core of the Buddhist concept of *karuna* or compassion. The etymology of the English word "compassion" is instructive. It conjoins the Latin roots *cum* meaning "with" or "together" and *patior* meaning "to bear, suffer, undergo, or experience."[5] Thus the primary sense of compassion for Buddhist thought is not something along the lines of having a positive emotional reaction such as pity for another being. Emotion need not play a part in this, nor is a self-Other dualism implied. Rather it is "to experience *with* the other," *as* the other, in the nondualistic sense I have just indicated. At the same time that *karuna* avoids egoistic self-regard, it also avoids the extremes of altruistic self-sacrifice since its practice derives from an experiential and nonhierarchical connectedness with others. Thus *ahimsa*, nonviolence to others and oneself, emerges as the central ethical principle of Buddhist thought. It is by drawing on this understanding of groundlessness (i.e., emptiness, suchness, or *sunyata*) that Horowitz is able to argue, "When the evanescence and suchness of the constructed identity is *feelingly experienced*, there is compassion, the listening and feeling together of self and other. Groundlessness as compassion is the no-ground of democracy." (1992, 163; italics in original)

Wittgenstein expressed some confidence that philosophy could dissolve its own problems; that the "bewitchment of our intelligence" brought about by misunderstanding language (Wittgenstein 1968, sec. 109) and the resultant "diseases" (sec. 594) that infect our lives, could thus be cured. Put another way, he held that "a change in the way people live" (Wittgenstein 1980, 61) would make philosophical questions superfluous since this would entail a more clear-sighted relationship with our language-games as well as the development of some different, more healthy language-games. But the form of cure he developed, an extended, intense course of philosophical study that demands both leisure and privilege for its pursuit, hardly seems a cure available to most people.

Nagarjuna also believed that people are deeply deluded about their own nature and their relationships with others; that this delusion is supported by mistaken notions about the meanings of words, in particular the tendency to essentialism and, most especially, the reification of one's own ego; and that this delusion causes suffering in their own lives and, perforce, in the lives of others. While it is not the only form that delusion takes, its most problematic manifestation is the human tendency to reify the self or ego. This self-reification and its many ramifications then becomes the basis of egotism, hierarchical difference, and discriminatory practices—the belief that "I" am essentially different than, separate from, and better than the Other.

In Buddhist traditions, and also in the Hindu traditions in which they are rooted (see Iyengar 1993),[6] philosophical study is only one way in which this tendency to delusion can be overcome. Yogic practices, which include not only the asanas (postures) (Boccio 2004; Iyengar 1976) now familiar to the West but also a vast range of meditation and ritual practices (Boucher 1997; Goldstein 2003; Kornfield 1993; Palmo n.d., 2002; Salzberg 1999), have been developed in a variety of forms appropriate for people in all walks of life. The purpose of these is to address and "dissolve" the delusions that lie at the root of our suffering, be that suffering grounded in the reified ego, internalized oppressive discourses regarding ourselves and others, the emotional reactions we have to our beliefs and attitudes, or the bodily experiences and behaviors that are a part of them. In this respect, then, yogic practices are much more comprehensive in their ability to reach and treat the full range of human experience that is affected by a given language-game than is Wittgenstein's more limited, strictly conceptual, philosophical approach. This is especially significant when we consider that both a holistic picture of the person and the notion of language-games entail that our relationship with our ideas does not exist solely "in the mind." Rather it affects all aspects of human experience—social behaviors, somatic responses, emotional reactions, spiritual responsiveness, attitudes, interpersonal relationships, and so forth. Thus the importance for feminist praxis of techniques that can treat the multiple levels on which a diseased understanding functions in the person cannot be overestimated. The potential of the rich resources developed by these traditions is now being recognized by Western researchers in areas ranging from medicine to psychotherapy, from sports to mediation. They are especially promising for application in antioppressive pedagogies, and exciting work is being done in that area as well (Forbes 2003, 2004, 2005; Miller et al. 2005; Orr 2004, 2005). I am suggesting here that, just as Horowitz (1992) has begun to make the theoretical case for a "groundless" political praxis, these researchers are beginning to show how we can use yogic practices to overcome Joan Scott's "difference dilemma" (1990) while sacrificing neither identity and solidarity nor (nonhierarchical) difference.

In this chapter I have argued that mind/body dualism lies at the root of the troubles feminists have experienced in their attempts to critique the projects of modernity and to rectify the injustices suffered by women and other socially marginalized groups. Rationalism, antirationalism, and postrationalism have each drawn on this dualistic construction, although often unwittingly. While each of these approaches has produced valuable theory and has contributed to social change, each remains hampered, both in their theorization of identity and difference and in their political theory and praxis, by the operation at its root of that dualistic structure. Thus I have accessed the work of Wittgenstein, Horowitz, and Nagarjuna to begin to sketch out a way to conceptualize a de-essentialized "woman" that avoids the mind/body binarism and thus the problems it generates for rationalist, antirationalist, and postrationalist feminist approaches. Further, I have argued that we can begin to effect change on both the individual and social/cultural levels through engagement with yogic techniques. I have not attempted to explore specific social issues generated by dilemmas of identity and difference, nor to theorize the tactics and strategies that could most effectively be employed to combat them; that task has been taken up by the many other contributors to this volume. Space will allow me to do nothing more at this point than to indicate that mindful yogic practices and the understanding of human community that ground them can be usefully synthesized with, in fact often demands, the application of a broader range of treatments designed to address specific problems, some of which are indicated by those other chapters.

Notes

1. Val Plumwood (2002) distinguishes a dualism from a simple dichotomy as "a special kind of distinction or dichotomy, one involving particular features which result from domination." (p. 22) Karen Warren (1988) also analyzes the domination/subordination relationship of the two terms, in particular as these apply to issues in science, ethics, and critical thinking.

2. See Judith Bulter's opus for a strong articulation of postmodernist problematizing of the body and subjectivity and Nancy Hartsock (1990) for a critique of this type of project. The operation of one manifestation of mind/body dualism is made abundantly clear, for instance, in Bulter's *Bodies That Matter* (1993) where she attempts to offer an account of the role of "regulatory regimes" or "regulatory schemas" in the production of "intelligibility," as in, for example, "normative heterosexuality is clearly not the only regulatory regime operative in the production of bodily contours or setting the limits to bodily intelligibility." (p. 17) What Butler overlooks is that it is constitutive of the concept of a human being that bodies are what we *are*, not what we *have*, and in consequence it is only in a derivative sense that we *know*, as opposed to *experience*, them.

3. There is a growing body of work demonstrating relationships between social embeddedness and patterns of thinking that challenges the simple alignment of rational style and sex/gender. For instance, Johnson's research (1988) has shown that, when given an opportunity, both boys and girls can use both of the "moral voices" that Gilligan (1982) identified. She suggests that there is a gender-linked socialization to a *preference* to one voice or the other. Further, Stack's research with African Americans "suggest[s] that under conditions of economic deprivation there is a convergence between women and men in their construction of themselves in relationship to others, and that these conditions produce a convergence also in women's and men's vocabulary of rights, morality, and the social good." (1993, 109) Looking beyond the West, Hall and Ames (1998), Kasulis (2002), Berling (1992), and Nisbett (2003) are a few of the current researchers who explore relationships between culture and modes of reasoning that cannot be fit comfortably into the Western model.

4. See Sarup (1993) for a useful survey of major postmodern voices and critiques of their positions.

5. I would like to thank Professor James Rives, York University, Division of Humanities, for help in sorting out my Latin on this point.

6. Patanjali codified the Classical Yoga school, which has become prominent in the West through the work of B. K. S. Iyengar and other students of Krishnamacharia.

Bibliography

Aristotle. "Politics." In *Introduction to Aristotle*, edited by Richard McKeon, 545–617. New York: The Modern Library, 1947.

Beauvoir, Simone de. *The Second Sex*. Translated and edited by H. M. Parshley. Toronto, New York, London: Bantam Books, 1970.

Belenky, Mary Field, Blythe McVicker Clinchy, Nancy Rule Goldberger, and Jill Mattuck Tarule. *Women's Ways of Knowing: The Development of Self, Voice, and Mind*. New York: Basic Books, Inc., Publishers, 1986.

Berling, Judith. "Embodying Philosophy: Some Preliminary Reflections from a Chinese Perspective." In *Discourse and Practice*, edited by Frank Reynolds and David Tracy, 233–260. New York: State University of New York Press, 1992.

Boccio, Frank Jude. *Mindfulness Yoga*. Boston: Wisdom Publications, 2004.

Boucher, Sandy. *Opening the Lotus: A Woman's Guide to Buddhism*. Boston: Beacon Press, 1997.

Butler, Judith. *Bodies That Matter: On the Discursive Limits of "Sex."* New York and London: Routledge, 1993.

———. *The Psychic Life of Power: Theories in Subjection*. Stanford, CA: Stanford University Press, 1997.

———. "Foucault and the Paradox of Bodily Inscriptions." In *The Body: Classic and Contemporary Readings*, edited and introduced by Donn Welton, 301–313. Malden, MA and Oxford: Blackwell, 1999.

Costera Meijer, Irene, and Baukje Prins. "How Bodies Come to Matter: An Interview with Judith Butler." *Signs* 23, no. 2 (Winter 1998): 275–286.

Di Stefano, Christine. "Dilemmas of Difference: Feminism, Modernity, and Postmodernism." In *Feminism/Postmodernism*, edited and with an introduction by Linda J. Nicholson, 63–82. New York and London: Routledge, 1990.

Forbes, David. "Turn the Wheel: Integral School Counseling for Male Adolescents." *Journal of Counseling and Development* 81 (Spring 2003): 142–149.

———. *Boyz 2 Buddhas: Counseling Urban High School Male Athletes in the Zone*. New York, Washington, D.C./Baltimore, Bern, Frankfurt am Main, Berlin, Brussels, Vienna, Oxford: Peter Lang, 2004.

———. "In Da Zone: Meditation, Masculinity, and a Meaningful Life." In *Holistic Learning and Spirituality in Education*, edited by John P. Miller, Selia Karsten, Diana Denton, Deborah Orr, and Isabella Colalillo Kates, 153–160. Albany: State University of New York Press, 2005.

Fuss, Diana. *Essentially Speaking: Feminism, Nature & Difference*. New York and London: Routledge, 1989.

Garfield, Jay L. *The Fundamental Wisdom of the Middle Way: Nagarjuna's Mulamadhyamakakarika*, translated and commentary by Jay L. Garfield. New York and Oxford: Oxford University Press, 1995.

Gilligan, Carol. *In A Different Voice: Psychological Theory and Women's Development*. Cambridge, MA, and London, England: Harvard University Press, 1982.

Gillman, Charlotte Perkins. *Herland*. Mineola, NY: Dover Publications, 1998.

Goldstein, Joseph. *Insight Meditation: The Practice of Freedom*. Boston and London: Shambhala, 2003.

Gross, Rita M. *Buddhism after Patriarchy: A Feminist History, Analysis, and Reconstruction of Buddhism*. Albany: State University of New York Press, 1993.

Gudmunsen, Chris. *Wittgenstein and Buddhism*. London and Basingstoke: The Macmillan Press Ltd, 1977.

Hall, David L., and Roger T. Ames. *Thinking from the Han: Self, Truth, and Transcendence in Chinese and Western Culture*. Albany: State University of New York Press, 1998.

Hartsock, Nancy. "Foucault on Power: A Theory for Women?" In *Feminism/Postmodernism*, edited and with an introduction by Linda J. Nicholson, 157–175. New York and London: Routledge, 1990.

hooks, bell. *Feminist Theory: From Margin to Center*. Boston: South End Press, 1984.

Horowitz, Gad. "The Foucaultian Impasse: No Sex, No Self, No Revolution." *Political Theory* 15, no. 1 (February 1987): 61–80.

———. "Groundless Democracy." In *Shadow of Spirit: Postmodernism and Religion*, edited by Phillipa Berry and Andrew Wernick, 156–164. London and New York: Routledge, 1992.

Irigaray, Luce. *Key Writings*. Edited by Luce Irigaray. London and New York: Continuum, 2004.

Iyengar, B. K. S. *Light on Yoga*. Hammersmith, London: Thorsons, An Imprint of HarperCollins Publishers, 1976.

———. *Light on the Yoga Sutras of Patanjali*. Hammersmith and London: Thorsons, An Imprint of HarperCollins Publishers, 1993.

Jaggar, Alison M. *Feminist Politics and Human Nature*. Totowa, NJ: Rowman & Allanheld, 1983.

Johnson, D. Kay. "Adolescents' Solutions to Dilemmas in Fables: Two Moral Orientations—Two Problem Solving Strategies." In *Mapping the Moral Domain: A Contribution of Women's Thinking to Psychological Theory and Education*, edited by Carol Gilligan, Janie Victoria Ward, and Jill McLean Taylor with Betty Bardige, 73–86. Center for the Study of Gender, Education and Human Development, Harvard University Graduate School of Education, Cambridge, Massachusetts: Distributed by Harvard University Press, 1988.

Kasulis, Thomas P. *Intimacy or Integrity: Philosophy and Cultural Difference*. Honolulu: University of Hawaii Press, 2002.

Katz, Nathan. "Nagarjuna and Wittgenstein on Error." In *Buddhist and Western Philosophy*, edited by Nathan Katz, 306–327. Atlantic Highlands, NJ: Humanities Press, 1981.

Klein, Anne Carolyn. "Presence with a Difference: Buddhists and Feminists on Subjectivity." *Hypatia: A Journal of Feminist Philosophy* 9, no. 1 (1994): 112–130.

———. *Meeting the Great Bliss Queen: Buddhists, Feminists, and the Art of the Self*. Boston: Beacon Press, 1995.

————. "Finding a Self: Buddhist and Feminist Perspectives." In *Shaping New Visions: Gender and Values in American Culture*, edited by Clarrissa W. Atkinson, Constance H. Buchanan, and Margaret R. Miles, 191–218. Ann Arbor: U.M.I. Research Press, 1997.

Kornfield, Jack. *A Path with Heart: A Guide Through the Perils and Promises of Spiritual Life*. New York, Toronto, London, Sydney, Auckland: Bantam Books, 1993.

Kuhn, Thomas S. *The Structure of Scientific Revolutions*, 2nd ed. Vol. 2 of *International Encyclopedia of Unified Science*. Chicago: University of Chicago Press, 1970.

Laqueur, Thomas. *Making Sex, Body and Gender from the Greeks to Freud*. Cambridge, MA, and London, England: Harvard University Press, 1990.

McClung, Nelly. *In Times Like These*, introduction by Veronica Strong-Boag. Toronto: University of Toronto Press, 1972.

McMillan, Carol. *Women, Reason and Nature: Some Philosophical Problems with Feminism*. Oxford: Basil Blackwell, 1982.

Mill, John Stuart. *The Subjection of Women*. In *Mary Wollstonecraft, A Vindication of the Rights of Woman, John Stuart Mill, The Subjection of Women*, introduction by Mary Warnock. London and Melbourne: Dent, 1986/1869.

Miller, Jack, Selia Karsten, Diane Denton, Deborah Orr, and Isabella Kates, eds. *Holistic Learning and Spirituality in Education: Breaking New Ground*. New York: State University of New York Press, 2005.

Monk, Ray. *Ludwig Wittgenstein: The Duty of Genius*. London: Jonathan Cape, 1990.

Nagarjuna. *Mulamadhyamakakarika*. In *The Fundamental Wisdom of the Middle Way: Nagarjuna's Mulamadhyamakakarika*, translated and commentary by Jay L. Garfield. New York and Oxford: Oxford University Press, 1995.

Nisbett, Richard W. *The Geography of Thought: How Asians and Westerners Think Differently . . . and Why*. New York, London, Toronto, Sydney, Singapore: The Free Press, 2003.

Orr, Deborah. "Just the Facts Ma'am." *Informal Logic* 11, no. 1 (1989): 1–10.

————. "On Logic and Moral Voice." *Informal Logic* 17, no. 3 (1995): 347–359.

————. "The Uses of Mindfulness in Feminist Anti-Oppressive Pedagogies: Philosophy and Praxis." *Canadian Journal of Education* 27, no. 4 (2004): 477–498.

————. "Minding the Soul in Education: Conceptualizing and Teaching to the Whole Person." In *Holistic Learning and Spirituality in Education: Breaking New Ground*, edited by Jack Miller, Selia Karsten, Diana Denton, Deborah Orr, and Isabella Kates, 87–100. New York: State University of New York Press, 2005.

Palmo, Tenzin. *Three Teachings*. Dongyu Gatsal Ling Nunnery. www.tenzinpalmo.com.

————. *Reflections on a Mountain Lake: Teachings on Practical Buddhism*. Ithaca, NY, and Boulder, CO: Snow Lion Publications, 2002.

Plumwood, Val. *Feminism and the Mastery of Nature*. London and New York: Routledge, 1993.

————. "The Politics of Reason: Toward a Feminist Logic." In *Representing Reason: Feminist Theory and Formal Logic*, edited by Rachel Joffe Falmagne and Marjorie

Hass, 11–44. Latham, Boulder, New York, Oxford: Rowman & Littlefield Publishers, Inc., 2002.

Rousseau, Jean Jacques. *Emile*, translated and edited by William Boyd. New York: Teachers College Press, 1958/1763.

Said, Edward. *Orientalism*. London: Routledge & Kegan Paul, 1978.

Salzberg, Sharon, ed. *Voices of Insight*. Boston and London: Shambhalal, 1999.

Sarup, Madan. *An Introductory Guide to Post-Structuralism and Postmodernism*, 2nd ed. Athens: University of Georgia Press, 1993.

Scott, Joan W. "Deconstructing Equality-Versus-Difference: Or, the Uses of Post-structuralist Theory for Feminism." In *Conflicts in Feminism*, edited by Marianne Hirsch and Evelyn Fox Keller, 134–148. New York and London: Routledge, 1990.

Stack, Carol B. "The Culture of Gender: Women and Men of Color." In *An Ethic of Care: Feminist and Interdisciplinary Perspectives*, edited by Mary Jeanne Larrabee, 108–111. New York and London: Routledge, 1993.

Streng, Frederick J. *Emptiness: A Study in Religious Meaning*. Nashville and New York: Abingdon Press, 1967.

Warren, Karen. "Critical Thinking and Feminism." *Informal Logic* 10, no. 1 (Winter 1988): 31–44.

Wittgenstein, Ludwig. *Tractatus Logico-Philosophicus*, translated by D. F. Pears and B. F. McGuinness, introduction by Bertrand Russell. London: Routledge & Kegan Paul, 1961.

———. *Philosophical Investigations*, translated by G. E. M. Anscombe. Oxford: Basil Blackwell, 1968.

———. *Zettel*, edited by G. E. M. Anscombe and G. H. von Wright, translated by G. E. M. Anscombe. Berkeley and Los Angeles: University of California Press, 1970.

———. *Culture and Value*, translated by Peter Winch. Chicago: University of Chicago Press, 1980.

Wollstonecraft, Mary. *A Vindication of the Rights of Woman*. In *Mary Wollstonecraft, A Vindication of the Rights of Woman, John Stuart Mill, The Subjection of Women*, introduction by Mary Warnock. London and Melbourne: Dent, 1986/1792.

~

CHAPTER THREE

Who's Afraid of Nature? The Rise and Fall of "Denaturalization" in Contemporary Feminist Thought

Jutta Weber[1]

"Feminism loves another science: the sciences and politics of interpretation, translation, stuttering, and the partly understood." (Haraway 1991a, 195)

This statement of Donna Haraway about feminist epistemology encouraged me in my somehow clumsy attempt to come to terms with writing in a foreign language and finding the courage to present my "thinking fragments" (Flax 1990) about "denaturalization" in contemporary feminist thought.

The theoretical strategy of denaturalization, reinvented by postmodern[2] thought, has been known at least since Immanuel Kant, who wrote in his *Critique of Pure Reason* "that we cognize a priori of things only what we have put into them ourselves." (1982a, 3)[3] This strategy follows the insight that—as Katherine Hayles puts it today: "We are always already within the theater of representation." (1993, 1) We cannot have any direct and unmediated access to reality, and every claim to mirror or speak *for* nature is part of a more than dubious politics of representation. Postmodern theory worked out this strategy of denaturalization in an attempt to get rid of naturalism, positivism, as well as essentialism with its more than problematic political effects.

In analyzing this strategy, however, I have become more and more convinced that many contemporary critics confuse the ideological purposes and effects of naturalizing strategies with the problem of reflecting on human or nonhuman nature in general. Speaking *of* nature does not automatically imply preexisting entities that we can grasp and that we have to speak *for*. Reflecting on nature can also mean remembering that there is something that is not totally *produced* by human beings and that we therefore do not have totally at our disposal.[4] Indeed, we cannot have positive knowledge of that which is outside of cultural discourse; nevertheless it seems that there is a boundary to our different undertakings. If there is not, then science is nothing more than an arbitrary enterprise, and our knowledge of the world is only the result of solipsism and radical subjectivism.[5]

Bearing this in mind, my intention is to differentiate between certain effects of denaturalization. Therefore I will draw a distinction between denaturalization as a critical and negative strategy on one hand and dematerialization as a kind of naturalized denaturalization with hidden ontological statements on the other. With a little help from Donna Haraway, Katherine Hayles, and Karen Barad I will look for ways to reflect on nature beyond renaturalization or cultural overdetermination, and in search of more reflexive politics of representation I will argue in favor of "situated ontologies."

"Denaturalization" in the Last Two Decades

During the last two decades feminist epistemology has become more and more involved with the theoretical strategy of denaturalization. The reinvention of this strategy was part of a theoretical shift evoked by postmodern thought in general, a shift that seemed very promising for the purposes of feminism because it criticizes the hierarchical dichotomies of Western thought and deconstructs reified categories such as "nature," "Woman," "sex," and so on.

These categories, which were often naturalized by Humanist thought, which constructed them as self-evident and everlasting, had been shown to be an effect of discourse, of language as well as dubious politics of representation masqueraded as objectivity and universality.

The politics of denaturalization asserts the social and cultural construction of categories by analyzing their linguistic mediation as well as locating their social, historical, and political offspring and context. It was supposed to overcome the dangerous and seductive strategies of essentialism as well as of biologism, which had—even in its feminist versions—only reinforced traditional Western dichotomies and the double bind of "Woman" as "Other" or as the minor version of "Man."[6]

These postmodern U.S.-American approaches to denaturalize Humanist thought I find quite enlightening and inspiring, but from a European continental perspective, I wonder about this kind of inquisitive suspicion of even the most highly differentiated theories that dare to refer to or reflect on nature.

One reason for this radical suspicion may be that biologist or sociobiologist positions have hitherto had much more influence in U.S.-American than German feminist discourse—mostly, I think, for historical reasons. In addition, the disputed sex-gender-distinction—which doesn't exist in the German language—may have supplied this kind of either/or discussion about culture and nature, of cultural monism versus essentialism, of antirealism versus realism.[7]

But today, in Continental as well as in Anglo-Saxon feminist discourse, denaturalization itself—having been "naturalized" in its turn—is at stake. There are a growing number of feminist theorists who are informed by the linguistic turn but who are nevertheless focused on the blind spots and problematic effects of the strategy of denaturalization—at least in its dogmatic form. To explicate the problems of dogmatic denaturalization I want to follow the conceptual distinction between the strategies of denaturalization and dematerialization, which was drawn by Donna Haraway.[8]

In my opinion, denaturalization is kind of a "negative" strategy: It criticizes the reifying and naturalizing use of categories and insists on the social and cultural construction and linguistic mediation of "entities" such as nature, materiality, or the body. These entities are by themselves not preexisting ones, but come into being via historical, societal, and technoscientific processes. Consequent denaturalization insists that there is no positive, unmediated access to reality defined as an independent ontological realm and tries to avoid what Michel Callon describes very well as the effect of the politics of representation pursued by biologism or scientific realism: "To speak for others is to first silence those in whose name we speak." (1986, 216; cited by Star 1991, 40)[9]

In contrast to denaturalization, dematerialization is the radical negation not only of the prediscursive, but of everything beyond cultural discourse. Insisting on the more or less literal *production* of nature by culture, discourse, and language, dematerialization makes itself an ontological statement. The result is a shift to a more monistic way of thinking, leaving out *that* part of the dualism one feels uncomfortable with and thereby covering certain theoretical contradictions and ambiguities.[10]

Feminism like other critical discourses has been trying to get rid of ideologically contaminated categories such as "nature" or "materiality,"' which had often been understood as static, unchangeable, and prediscursive not only by the natural but also by the human sciences. Transforming them in discursive and constructed entities carried not only the promise of overcoming biologism or essentialism, but also of dissolving this very old problem of Western discourse: the dualistic structure of thought.

But the obliteration of one part of classical dualisms—for example nature—produces an effect that is already well known from the history of Enlightenment and that Haraway calls "hyperproductionism." It is a claim that is typical for cultural monism: that there is nothing beyond the order of man, of society, or discourse, that "There's nothing beyond the text." (Derrida 1974) Even if deconstruction had shown that textual displacements of meaning, language-games, and rules of discourse are not driven by our intentions, many postmodern theorists are seduced into thinking of everything not as the result of the mutual interaction of nature and culture, but as being the result of human *production* and insisting that there is nothing beyond the realm of culture.

Listen to postmodern hero Richard Rorty, who wants "to free mankind from . . . the notion that outside the haphazard and perilous experiments we perform there lies something (God, Science, Knowledge, Rationality or Truth) which will, if only we perform the correct rituals, step in to save us." (1982, 208)

But why do we have to deny anything outside of human discourse to acknowledge the responsibility for our undertakings?

In my opinion, theoretical approaches of dematerialization often unintentionally confuse and conflate their critique of naive realist epistemologies with their own ontological statements—for example the claim of the nonexistence of an outside of culture. Considering "nature" as nothing more than an invention of the naive scientific worldview, a trick of biologist and essentialist ideologies, is obviously a kind of overreaction—and a quite interesting stance at a historical moment when: "Our developed powers over nature have brought about a situation in which we are today far more at the mercy of what culture enforces than we are subject to biological dictate." (Soper 1995, 326)

Devaluing, idealizing, or obliterating central categories of theoretical discourse has always been linked to certain politics of representation and a certain "logic of identity." (Adorno 1966) Time does not permit me to analyze and compare different versions of these politics here.[11] All I want to do now is to remind you that the devaluing or obliteration of nature is not new; both idealist and rationalist theories have been practicing it for centuries.

On the other hand, to be able to conceptualize the relationship of nature and culture not as a one-way street but as a mutual interaction, reflecting the asymmetric relation of these categories grounded in its linguistic mediation while keeping in mind that nature and culture are themselves historical and made categories, is an old philosophical desire which has not yet been fulfilled.

Confusion of Borders: Culture and Nature

Nevertheless, it is necessary to see the obliteration of "nature" not only in its contemporary theoretical context, but also in the newer social and technoscientific developments. As Donna Haraway has argued, technoscientific processes in the field of communication and biotechnologies have led to the profound "implosion" of central organic dualisms. In my opinion there is not a total implosion but rather a series of displacements of categories in Western theoretical discourse.[12]

I share Donna Haraway's diagnosis that these developments are linked to new ways of semiotically and materially processing and cultivating nature— performed by technoscience with its accelerated production of hybrids, cyborgs, and chimeras. For example, "Communications sciences and modern biologies are constructed by a common move—*the translation of the world into a problem of coding*, a search for a common language in which . . . all heterogeneity can be submitted to disassembly, reassembly, investment, and exchange." (1991b, 164)

Obviously, science itself confuses the traditional borders of culture and nature, undermining what was once regarded as natural architectures. With the new tools of cybernetics and genetics, it is possible to rewrite what counts as an object by dissolving it to contingent parts, reassembling it, and building completely new entities.

While contemporary critical theory is occupied with denaturalizing and even dematerializing humanist categories to get rid of naturalist and biologist ideologies in the context of scientific realism and positivism, technoscience itself is already through with "nature" in its Humanist sense.

At the same time the more and more common habit of theorizing sexist or racist ideas without referring to so-called natural categories, but to cultural differences, rang the alarm of feminist and other oppositional intellectuals.[13] The hope of getting rid of racism or sexism by deconstructing certain categories obviously failed: "At the level of ideology, we see translations of racism and colonialism into languages of development and under-development, rates and constraints of modernization." (Haraway, 1991b, 162)

"Reinventing Nature?"[14]

Aware of these problematic developments in critical theory as well as in technoscientific practices, some theorists are looking for new ways "to understand the technologies by which nature and culture interact." (Barad 1996, 163)

Especially in the field of science studies, there are U.S.-American feminist scholars who seek to avoid the polarization between scientific realism and postmodern antirealism, between the traditional positivist approaches in the philosophy of science and the extreme social constructivist ones in science studies.

Many of these scholars have been scientists themselves like Karen Barad, Katherine Hayles, and Donna Haraway. It is not my intention to get involved very deeply with their theories here, but to use some of their ideas for my own purposes. With these three I share the desire for a theory beyond naive realism as well as cultural overdetermination, and they support me in my attempts to reflect on the problem of the ontology of our world. Together with physicist Karen Barad I wonder: "Is it possible to take . . . these questions seriously within the academy, in the U.S., in the late twentieth century? Won't this still sound too much like metaphysics to those trained during the various states of decay of positivist culture? And if we don't ask these questions what will be the consequences? For as Donna Haraway reminds us, 'what counts as an object is precisely what world history turns out to be about' (1988, 588), I seek some way of trying to understand the nature of the material and the cultural in the crafting of an ontology." (cited in Barad 1996, 164)

At the end of our century the definition of nature, objects, the material, as well as others are at stake, not the least because of the radical material-semiotic changes linked to sociotechnical processes.

I am impressed by the engagement of these science studies scholars in taking this challenge seriously by analyzing technoscientific processes and the production of knowledge as well as developing new concepts of nature beyond a "transcendental naturalism" (Haraway 1992b, 297) or radical social constructivism.

Unlike most German feminist approaches to science, U.S.-American feminism started quite early to look for possibilities of participating in the semiotic-material technoscientific processes, recognizing that they are among the most powerful discourses in contemporary knowledge societies. Fifteen years ago Donna Haraway's cyborg-manifesto called for feminists to get involved with technoscience. She urged them to go beyond criticizing the consequences of new technologies (as others had done before); she encouraged them to intervene as well in the technoscientific production of knowledge, to assert their own power of definition and to establish new ways of doing science.

The politics of knowledge that result from this approach are at least twofold and contradictory. On the one hand I am in search of semiotic and narrative technologies, which are self-conscious of their epistemological as well as their ontological claims. Meanwhile, having followed the discussion about denaturalization versus essentialism for some time, I am convinced that it is not possible to avoid ontological claims altogether but only to limit them by being conscious of them and situating them. We have to find ways to speak *of* nature, not to deny our relationship to it—without ever being able to know its character. As Donna Haraway puts it: "Nature is for me, . . . one of those impossible things characterized by Gayatri Spivak as that which we cannot not desire. Excruciatingly conscious of nature's discursive consti-tution as 'other' in the histories of colonialism, racism, sexism, and class domination of many kinds, we nonetheless find in this problematic, ethno-specific, long-lived, and mobile concept something we cannot do without, but can never 'have.'" (1992b, 296)

Trying to avoid dematerialization, I think it is far more reflexive and help-ful to claim the existence of nature or reality to which we do not have any unmediated access. Therefore we do not obliterate nature, but must reflect on it and leave it at the same time in its "elusive negativity." Listen to Katherine Hayles: "In negation, possibilities for articulation exist that can elude the reflexive mirroring that would encapsulate us within textuality and nothing but textuality. This elusive negativity authorizes a position that grants the full weight of the constructivist argument but draws back from say-ing anything goes." (1993, 2)

The end of Katherine Hayles' statement points to the other side of these twofold politics of knowledge: Nevertheless being aware of our situated on-tological as well as our epistemological claims, we must insist that some the-ories are more consistent with reality than others. And there are at least po-litical reasons not to give up objectivity: "Objectivity of any kind has gotten a bad name. I think this is a mistake, for the possibility of distinguishing a theory consistent with reality from one that is not can also be liberating. If there is no way to tell whether the claim that blacks and women have infe-rior brains is a less accurate account of reality than the claim that they do, we have lost a valuable asset in the fight for liberation." (1993, 8)

People who are not at the center but on the margins of power must find ways to tell their stories about nature, to intervene in semiotic-material fights to bring their own definitions of reality, objects, and entities into power, modifying the influential practices of technoscience as well as others, important discourses of meaning production. Fighting for "more livable worlds" will only be successful if we are able to insist and to explain why some scientific enterprises perceive and describe the world in a more convincing way than others.

I think we must develop situated ontologies with a theoretical framework that enables us to give up positive statements concerning nature but to recognize our active participation within reality. We don't need to make claims—as Karen Barad puts it—"about representations of an independent reality, but about the real consequences, interventions, creative possibilities, and responsibilities of intra-acting within the world. Finally, materiality matters: there are social and material reasons for knowledge claims . . . and socially constructed knowledges have real material consequences." (1996, 188) Karen Barads reminds us once again that theories or scientific concepts are constructs that describe neither an independent reality or a pure effect of cultural discourse but the in between of nature and culture.

Having this in mind, I think, we should not be afraid of nature as so many feminists have been in the last decades.

Notes

1. I am heavily in debt to Angelika Saupe and Sylvia Pritsch for their critical and inspiring remarks on this chapter and being the midwifes for my term "situated ontologies." I also want to thank Janet Sutherland for her helpful suggestions and careful reading of my German attempt to write (American) English.

2. "It is the word 'postmodern' as commonly used in the United States, that perhaps most accurately applies to the specific set of writers important here: those writing, self-consciously, from within the (intellectual, scientific, philosophical, literary) *epistemological* crisis specific to the postwar period." Jardine 1985, 23

3. "daß wir nämlich von den Dingen nur das a priori erkennen, was wir selbst in sie legen." Kant, Kritik der reinen Vernunf (Stuttgart: Reclam, 1982b), B XVIII.

4. See also Weber 1997.

5. See Hayles 1995, 8.

6. See Alcoff 1988.

7. See Knapp 1994; for Norwegian language see Berg and Lie: "Essentialism is also related to the traditional distinction between biological sex and social gender. . . . In Norwegian, the one word, *kjónn*, is used for both sex and gender." (1995, 342)

8. See Haraway 1992a.

9. See also Said 1978.

10. See also Weber 1998.
11. For an analysis of the devaluing of nature by Judith Butler, see Weber 1997.
12. See Weber 1998.
13. About "cultural essentialism," see Narayan 1998.
14. See Soulé and Lease (1995).

Bibliography

Adorno, Theodor W. *Negative Dialektik*, 1st ed. Frankfurt am Main: Suhrkamp, 1966.
Alcoff, Linda. "Cultural Feminism versus Poststructuralism: The Identity Crisis in Feminist Theory." *Signs* 13, no. 3 (1988): 405–438.
Barad, Karen. "Meeting the Universe Halfway: Realism and Social Constructivism without Contradiction." In *Feminism, Science, and the Philosophy of Science*, edited by Hankinson Lynn Nelson and Jack Nelson, 161–194. Dordrecht, Boston, London: Kluwer, 1996.
Berg, Anne-Jorunn, and Merete Lie. "Feminism and Constructivism: Do Artifacts Have Gender?" In *Science, Technology & Human Values* 20, no. 3 (Summer 1995): 332–351.
Derrida, Jacques. *Of Grammatology*. Baltimore: The Johns Hopkins University Press, 1974.
Flax, Jane. "Thinking Fragments." In *Psychoanalysis, Feminism, and Postmodernism in the Contemporary West*. Berkeley, Los Angeles, Oxford: University of California Press, 1990.
Haraway, Donna. "Situated Knowledges: The Science Question in Feminism and the Privilege of Partial Perspective." In *Simians, Cyborgs and Women: The Reinvention of Nature*, 183–202. New York: Routledge, 1991a.
———. "A Cyborg Manifesto: Science, Technology, and Socialist-Feminism in the Late Twentieth Century." In *Simians, Cyborgs and Women: The Reinvention of Nature*, 149–182. New York: Routledge, 1991b.
———. "Otherworldly Conversations, Terran Topics, Local Terms." In *Science as Culture* 3, no. 1 (1992a): 59–92.
———. "The Promises of Monsters: A Regenerative Politics for Inappropriate/d Others." In *Cultural Studies*, edited by Lawrence Grossberg, Cary Nelson, and Paula Treichler, 295–337. New York and London: Routledge, 1992b.
———. *Modest_Witness@Second_Millenium. FemaleMan_Meets_OncoMouse™: Feminism and Technoscience*. New York and London: Routledge, 1997.
Hayles, N. Katherine. "Constrained Constructivism: Locating Scientific Inquiry in the Theater of Representation." In *New Orleans Review* 18 (Spring 1993): 76–85. englishwww.humnet.ucla.edu/ Individuals/Hayles/Cusp.html.
———. "Searching for Common Ground." In Soulé, Michael, and Gary Lease, ed. *Reinventing Nature? Responses to Postmodern Deconstruction*, 47–63. Washington, D.C. and Covelo, CA: Island Press, 1995.

Jardine, Alice. *Gynesis: Configurations of Woman and Modernity*. Ithaca and London: Cornell University Press, 1985.

Kant, Immanuel. *Critique of Pure Reason*, translated by Wolfgang Schwarz. Aalen: Scientia, 1982a.

———. *Kritik der reinen Vernunft*. Stuttgart: Reclam, 1982b.

Knapp, Gudrun-Axeli. "Politik der Unterscheidung." In *Institut für Sozialforschung (Hg.): Geschlechterverhältnisse und Politik*, 262–287. Frankfurt am Main: Suhrkamp, 1994.

Narayan, Uma. "Essence of Culture and a Sense of History." Paper presented at the Eighth Conference of the International Association of Women Philosophers (IAPh), Boston, MA, August 1998.

Rorty, Richard. "Method, Social Science, and Social Hope." In *Consequences of Pragmatism*. Minneapolis: University of Minnesota Press, 1982.

Said, Edward. *Orientalism*. New York: Pantheon Books, 1978.

Soper, Kate. *What Is Nature? Culture, Politics and the non-Human*. Oxford and Cambridge, MA: Blackwell, 1995.

Soulé, Michael, and Gary Lease, eds. *Reinventing Nature? Responses to Postmodern Deconstruction*. Washington, D.C. and Covelo, CA: Island Press, 1995.

Star, Susan Leigh. "Power, Technology and the Phenomenology of Conventions: On Being Allergic to Onions." In John Law, ed., *A Sociology of Monsters: Essays on Power, Technology and Domination*, 26–56. London and New York: Routledge, 1991.

Weber, Jutta. "Sprechen wovon sich nicht sprechen läßt? Zum Naturbegriff in der aktuellen feministischen Debatte." In *Feministische Studien* 2, (1997): 109–120.

———. "Feminismus & Konstruktivimus. Oder: Die Verlockungen unendlicher Rekombination. Zur Netzwerktheorie bei Donna Haraway." In *Das Argument. Zeitschrift für Philosophie und Sozialwissenschaften* 227, Heft 5, S.699–712.

CHAPTER FOUR

~

"L'intersectionnalité": Feminisms in a Divided World; Québec-Canada

Marie-Claire Belleau[1]

Emancipatory struggles, such as feminism and national or cultural identity politics, produce exhilaration and anxiety. If national or cultural identity politics (hereinafter "nat-cult"[2]) and feminism form complex struggles when viewed separately, their intersection in the cultural, political, and socioeconomic settings of Québec and the "rest of Canada" (hereinafter ROC) creates seemingly infinite complexities. In this chapter, I advance the notion of "strategic intersectionality" as a way of describing some of the consequences of the intricate interactions between feminism and nat-cult in Québec and the ROC. Playing the intricate, if dangerous, game of strategic intersectionality can empower us to imagine innovative tactics and create new coalitions both within and between the communities of Québec and ROC feminists.

This chapter constitutes an attempt to reconceptualize the relationship between the feminisms of Québec and the ROC. I focus on a rejection of differences that portrays one feminism as more or less developed than the other. I seek to replace common clichés about "distinct feminisms" with strategic intersectionality to explain differences as emerging out of separate political contexts and struggles. I thus hope to promote dialogue based on better understanding of the Québec and ROC situations.

My thesis works against the common understanding of the differences between feminism in Québec and in the ROC. Indeed, at times, we French Canadian women argue that feminism in Québec essentially differs from the feminism prevalent in the ROC. Proponents of Québec culture often position themselves at the intersection of two worlds: Québec people are too North American to be European and too European to be North American. Québec feminists at times point to this cultural difference to explain the distinct manifestations of feminism in law in the two main Canadian legal systems.

I, too, take for granted differences between feminisms in Québec and in the ROC. I argue that differences among the two groups are unavoidable because of the divergent political positions that feminists occupy in their respective settings. Québec women thus engage in nat-cult struggles in ways distinct from the ways feminists are implicated in such struggles in the ROC. However, I advocate neither eternalizing such differences (essentialism) nor erasing them (universalism) but rather seeing these differences as inscribed in specific cultural practices, political settings, and institutional frameworks. From this perspective, I celebrate differences between feminists in Québec and in the ROC as expressing the strategic deployment of differences in differently situated feminist struggles; yet I also call for new kinds of coalitions based on these differences.

If both feminism and nat-cult are sensitive subjects, the combination of the two generates even more delicate issues requiring, at the outset, two cautionary comments that will be the subject of Part I. The first relates to the use of the term "nat-cult," while the second concerns issues about Québec and ROC identities. In Part II, I describe what I mean by strategic intersectionality. In Part III, I describe some of the processes of dissociation and projection that lead to a "distinct feminism" thesis in Québec. I also briefly illustrate the potential of strategic thinking for Québec and ROC feminists around the theme of "distinct feminisms."

The Meanings of Expression: "Nat-Cult" and "Québec" and "ROC"

"Nat-cult": The Coining of an Expression

First, I will use the term "nat-cult" throughout this chapter to refer to the necessary critique of Québec's position in Canada for feminist purposes. I will abstain from taking a position in the nationalist/federalist political debate because my critique should concern all feminists, Québec nationalists and federalists alike. At this moment, both structures of federalism and of Québec nationalism engender detrimental consequences for women. The harmful effects of Québec's position in Canada for women will not necessarily be eradicated either by sovereignty or by remaining in Canada. Neither political outcome, for example, will eliminate the problematic private/public dichotomy reinforced by the civil law/common law split in Québec's legal system. For these reasons, when I describe an intersectional move made by a Québec feminist, I do not mean that she is or is not a Québec nationalist but rather that she displays a maneuver that emerges, in part, out of a critique of Québec's position in Canada. Finally, I use the term nat-cult because not all those concerned by Québec's cultural issues identify with nationalist politics. Similarly, I do not make any assessment about the political positions of ROC feminists about Québec or Canada.

Québec and the ROC as Complex Mosaics
Second, the way I seem to have generalized Québec and ROC identities may cast doubt on my simultaneous antiessentialist and antiuniversalistic appeal. Yet, I aspire to address issues relating to Québec and ROC identity without denying their historical and contemporary complexities. Québec people rarely admit, let alone confront, their difficult and contradictory position as both colonizers and colonized. Indeed, Québec people occupy a site of complex relations as both conquerors of the first nations and as a people conquered by the royalist English. Québec people also seldom face their problematic relations to the many French Canadian communities outside of Québec which form important and diverse, but always endangered, culturally specific Francophone populations. In addition, Québec participates in an intricate web of metropole/provincial relationships to France, related to the history of colonization, and to a continued set of shared origins, history, language, and legal system linking them across the Atlantic for centuries. The place of Québec people both as a minority within a majority—that of the ROC—yet a majority in its territory complicates its predicament even further. This singular Québec positionality carries important gender implications as well as repercussions relating to relations with its "own" minority groups.

Similarly, some readers may justly object to any generalizations about the "rest of Canada." The ROC forms a mosaic of wide regional and cultural differences that also give rise to their own sets of complex webs of identities and nat-cult encounters. Like Québec, the ROC combines intricate sets of relations between minorities and majorities over numerous identity struggles as well as issues related to its own colonial encounters. Feminist issues in one English Canadian province may resemble those in another region, yet have little in common with the experience of women from other parts of Canada, because of strong differences and similarities concerning linguistic, socioeconomic, religious, and nat-cult questions. Indeed, some of these regions and provinces share more striking commonalities with Québec than with other parts of English Canada. In addition, some ROC feminists neglect acknowledging the way their own ethnic and linguistic position inflects their feminism, making their practices more or less adapted to their own needs or those of others.

As I will argue in the next part of my chapter, strategic intersectionality attempts to substitute analysis of differences based on essences to those based on political and cultural contexts—thereby creating the possibility for deeper comprehension and political alliances between feminists. Strategic intersectionality opens up an infinite number of partnerships between sites of cultural practices, both dominant and marginal.

To summarize, I use the terms "Québec" and "ROC" throughout this chapter as shorthand to designate the complex set of identities that each of these sites encompass. I thus propose reconceptualizing Québec and ROC identities in order to imagine new stratagems and build new coalitions.

Strategic Intersectionality

The concept of intersectionality implies an understanding of the simultaneous engagement in more than one distinct, but intertwined, emancipatory battle. Moreover, one of these emancipatory fights must not be perceived as subordinated to the other. Therefore, in this particular case, the feminist struggle is not subject to nat-cult aspirations and vice versa.

In advocating the concept of intersectionality, I argue against both essentialism and universalism. I reject claims that attempt to make Québec's feminism, Québec's nat-cult, or Québec's civil law as necessarily, objectively, and abstractly distinct from ROC's feminism, nat-cult, federalism, or common law. Yet, I also reject assimilationist attempts that silence cultural distinctions and aim at an undifferentiated sense of "universal" belonging. For example, merely adding the experiences of Québec women to a ROC research project may constitute an essentialist move when conducted abstractly and without examining Québec's political and cultural context. Similarly, generalizing French Canadian experiences to all Canadian women without an effort to comprehend English Canadian identities in their complex settings would be unduly universalistic. I do not mean to suggest that the Québec or ROC contexts by themselves provide determinateness to otherwise indeterminate concepts; rather, they enrich our understanding of the various possible meanings of those concepts in particular struggles.

Strategic intersectionality demands a contextual examination of how nat-cult and feminism interact with one another. Imagining new strategies requires consideration of dimensions of experiences invisible to those who view feminism and nat-cult in isolation from each other, thus failing to capture intersecting patterns of gender and national subordination in both Québec and the ROC. Imagining such new strategies presupposes stating hidden differences or similarities, deconstructing myths, revealing processes of projection and dissociation, and building new kinds of coalitions. These measures may apply inside one site of struggle or between sites to support innovative practices, to foster original strategies and to create shifting and productive alliances.

My particular interest consists in highlighting the specific context of Québec feminists who participate simultaneously in both nat-cult and feminist emancipatory struggles. By restarting a dialogue between Québec and the ROC feminists based on tactical thinking rather than on essentialist or universalistic desires of recognition and demands, conversations will ultimately be fostered.

Distinct Feminisms

In this part of my chapter I describe the "distinct feminisms" theme in an effort to uncover its hidden premises and assumptions. Each component of the theme brings to the fore the intersection between feminism and nat-cult. Often, feminists situated at the crossroad of these emancipatory struggles maneuver to avoid subsuming one to the other. Indeed, their nat-cult endeavors may remain hidden by the boundaries of gender struggles and vice versa. Thus, their emancipatory strategies can only be fully envisioned by looking at the crossing of these roads.

In this part of my chapter I will discuss first identity politics and second the processes of subordination and of dissociation in the creation of a Québec feminist identity in the legal world. However, I believe that some of the generalizations I am about to make could be extended to other domains and fields of knowledge.

Feminism and Identity Politics

At times, we Québec feminists attempt to explain and to justify the marginality of feminism in Québec law schools through a "cultural" argument based on a purported essential division between two Canadian cultures—a division often generalized to differences between "Latin" and "Anglo" historical origins and contemporary cultures. Such attempts to explain the indifference, antagonism, and even patent rejection of outspoken feminism in Québec law schools often involve the deployment of at least three claims, which should be put aside for the following reasons.

First, we reject the dubious assumption that all Québec feminist jurists suffer from a severe case of "false consciousness." Indeed, the fact that feminism in Québec's legal community may have a different expression than that of Anglo-feminism should not lead to the conclusion that Québec feminism does not exist. The supposition that all Québec women are the helpless victims of patriarchy and gender oppression verges on the absurd.

Second, we refuse to explain the split between Québec and ROC feminisms as merely an excuse invoked by Québec feminists and nonfeminists to avoid facing the "real" issues raised by Anglo-feminism out of fear or incapacity to do so.

Third, we would be projecting a "combative," "aggressive," and even "belligerent" Anglo-feminist tradition that serves as a "straw woman" in relation to the distinct Québec feminism. This last argument hinges on a highly problematic—even if strategic—projection of "Anglo-feminism." Indeed, we Québec feminists often project an image of a well-recognized and accepted ROC feminism in English Canadian law schools. These projections have been beneficial to Québec feminists. They provide us with hope and encouragement. These projections are also deployed, in part, to convince colleagues of the fundamental importance and interest of feminism as an unavoidable movement of legal thought—to provoke a sense of urgency among Québec jurists, a sense that if they do not recognize feminism, they will lag behind in cutting-edge legal thought. However, the deployment of such projections also carries risks. Indeed, these Québec projections minimize the severe backlashes that have assailed women professors in English Canada. Threats of violence and acts of discrimination as well as the resulting "silencing" have deeply affected women students and professors in ROC law schools in recent years.

Invoking these controversial and ambivalent projections, some Québec feminists argue that the "aggressive" and "confrontational" approach of Anglo-feminism does not suit Québec society. Such authors contend that since the 1970s, Québec women have exercised a "power of influence" as opposed to a "power of confrontation." The nat-cult struggle thus intersects with feminist demands, in part, by specifically asserting the existence of a "distinct feminism": Québec feminism has, and should have, a different face. Québec women succeed in achieving the same advances in the battles against patriarchal oppression by more subtle but as effective moves as their English Canadian counterparts. Indeed, these contentions have a strong measure of truth in Québec. For example, there are as many women law professors and judges proportionately in Québec as in the ROC legal communities. Indeed, for the past twenty years, twenty percent more women law students enrolled in Québec law schools than in the ROC.

Understandably, the argument for a "distinct feminism" stems, in part, from the need for a common front to preserve nat-cult specificity. Fragmentation due to internal divisions and struggles would threaten the nat-cult project. It should be noted that the "anti-confrontational" argument is not specific to feminism's role in Québec's political history. Rather, this contention often arises in nat-cult movements around the world, when feminists challenge the subordinate role of women in such struggles. Like other nationalist movements, Québec's nat-cult suffers from a general subordination of most grassroots progressive political struggles to the state-building project.

Many feminists rightly argue that Québec women have been heavily involved in the nat-cult project since its inception. However, the projection and dismissal of a perhaps mythic "confrontational" Anglo-Saxon feminist tradition risks missing important emancipatory strategies. In addition, an anticonfrontational approach risks underestimating the potentially nonoptimal tactics of women's subtle—even if persuasive—manner in Québec. Strategic thinking implies staying clear of reductionist projections of feminist "false consciousness" and "aggressivity," as well as of "the united front" of nat-cult.

Subordination and Dissociation

Many feminists argue that the radical feminist analysis of women's subordination does not correspond to Québec's culture and history. According to this argument, Québec men, more than—or at least as much as—women, have suffered from the "historical disadvantages" related to the "male" English conquest. The effects of conquest, the argument continues, have produced a hierarchy between the conquerors and the conquered deeply internalized by Québec men. The serious wounds inflicted on men by conquest would thus have significantly affected the patriarchal hierarchy between men and women in Québec society. This argument is also often raised in nat-cult struggles around the world and often expresses some profound truths.

In Québec, this argument opposes the Anglo-Saxon conception of women's exclusion and inferiority in patriarchal societies to the classic nat-cult ideal of partnership between men and women to overcome the effects of conquest. Implicitly, this appeal evokes the nat-cult gender identity myths of the Québec matriarch and her somewhat meek consort, contemporarily designated as *l'homme rose* (the pink man). Simultaneously, it conjures the stereotypes of the "Latin" relations between men and women defined in terms of seductiveness, sexiness, and desire, a set of attitudes that do not fit the combative cadre of Anglo-feminist battlefields.

Québec feminists make the strategic claim of a "distinct feminism" through their projection of a "confrontational" Anglo-feminist identity. They dissociate themselves from this Anglo image using nat-cult rhetoric and a complex sense of belonging to the Latin cultural family. Québec women embrace "Latin" stereotypes of "femininity" partly out of a still vivid, if diminishing, allegiance to a distant French past, and partly out of a desire to assert their distinctiveness in North America. At the same time, they reject the blatant sexism associated with French and other Latin cultures. In addition, the hold of the "French past" decreases as the proportion of Québec women without any historical or "ethnic" ties to France increases; moreover, this "French past" never had any positive meaning for first nations women. Thus, the same projection and dissociation mechanisms that operate towards Anglo-feminism also operate in relation to French and other Latin cultures. The North American influence makes Québec women critical of the blatant sexism prevalent in these "sister" cultures. By dissociating themselves from both Anglo-feminism and Latin-femininity, Québec women and feminists attempt to construct a sense of their own intersectional identity.

I stress that I celebrate and embrace these strategic efforts of projection, dissociation, and distinction that succeed in creating a sense of feminist identity fitted to the Québec context. However, these projection, dissociation, and distinction moves should be viewed for what they are: strategies.

Conclusion

Writing this chapter in English constitutes one more example of strategic intersectionality, entailing many risks. On the one hand, my efforts may be appropriated by those seeking arguments against feminism—either of Québec or of the ROC—and/or nat-cult. On the other hand, my feminist and nat-cult colleagues from all parts of Canada may feel disturbed by my desire to focus on strategic approaches. I have attempted to position myself delicately in the intersection between my own feminist and nat-cult loyalties.

Focusing separately on traditional gender or national boundaries risks either subordinating feminist struggles to nat-cult battles or claims to feminist demands. Subordination occurs because one struggle's borders hide or render invisible demands made in the name of the other struggle. For example, nat-cult claims may be ignored by transnational feminist analysis. Conversely, nat-cult struggles have often "postponed" feminist demands to the postliberation period rather than fully integrating them in the emancipatory process—a "postponement" that may last forever.[3] Failing to account for the impact of double allegiances on Québec and ROC feminists also limits the potential of constructive dialogues and coalitions. However, strategic thinking does not imply that a consensus on goals will necessarily be reached. Distinct strategies are unavoidable, as well as political and ideological disagreements about which tactics to adopt in different settings. Yet such conflicts may lead to imagining and deploying even more creative and original intersectional strategies because of the struggles and coalitions they will compel.

Notes

1. I would like to thank especially Nathaniel Berman but also Brenda Cossman, Diane Lamoureux, Louise Langevin, Teresa Scassa and my research assistants, Johanne Carrier and Marie-France Fortin. A more elaborate version of this study has been published in Belleau, Marie-Claire, "'L'intersectionnalité': Feminisms in a Divided World (Québec-Canada)" in Dany Lacombe and Dorothy Chunn eds., *Law as a Gendering Practice* (London: Oxford University Press), 1999, pp. 19–37.

2. I have coined the expression "nat-cult" to avoid making a statement about the nationalist or cultural component of Québec's emancipatory struggle. I use the hyphen (-) to refer to the idea of the alternative as well as the combination of a proportion of both.

3. However, sometimes, the same phenomenon operates in a reverse way. Women are given more rights and power during the nat-cult emancipatory struggle that they are denied after liberation.

Bibliography

Belleau, Marie-Claire. "Les Théories Féministes: Droit et Différence Sexuelle." In *Revue Trimestrielle de Droit Civil*, (2001): 1–39.

Boivin, Michelle. "*In Memoriam* Marlène Cano." *Les Cahiers de Droit* 36 (1995a): 3–4.

———. "Les Acquis du Féminisme en Droit: Reconceptualisation de la Représentation des Femmes et de Leur Place dans la Société Canadienne." *Les Cahiers de droit* 36 (1995b): 27–59.

———. "Le Féminisme en Capsule: Un Aperçu Critique du Droit." *Revue Femmes et Droit* 5 (1992): 357–410.

Bottomley, Ann, ed. *Feminist Perspectives on the Foundational Subjects of Law*. London: Cavendish, 1996.

Bouchard, Josée. "L'indemnisation des Victimes de Harcèlement sexuel au Québec." In *Cahiers de Droit* 36 (1995): 125–160.

Brockman, Joan. "Bias in the Legal Profession: Perceptions and Experiences." *Alberta Law Review* 30 (1992): 747–808.

Bunting, Annie. "Feminism, Foucault, and Law as Power/Knowledge." *Alberta Law Review* 30 (1992): 829–842.

Canadian Bar Association. *Les Assises de la Réforme: Égalité, Diversité et Responsabilité. Un Rapport du Groupe de Travail de l'Association du Barreau Canadien sur l'Égalité des Sexes dans la Profession Juridique.* Ottawa: Canadian Bar Association, 1993.

Cipriani, Lucille. "La Justice Matrimoniale à l'Heure du Féminisme: Analyse Critique de la Jurisprudence Québécoise sur la Prestation Compensatoire, 1983–1991." *Les Cahiers de Droit* 36 (1995): 209–243.

Cornell, Drucilla. *Transformations: Recollective Imagination and Sexual Difference.* New York: Routledge, 1993.

———. *Beyond Accommodation: Ethical Feminism, Deconstruction, and the Law.* New York: Routledge, 1991.

Crenshaw, Kimberle, "Mapping the Margins: Intersectionality, Identity Politics, and Violence Against Women of Color." *Stanford Law Review* 43 (1991): 1241–1299.

———. "Demarginalizing the Intersection of Race and Sex: A Black Feminist Critique of Antidiscrimination Doctrine, Feminist Theory and Antiracist Politics." *University of Chicago Law Forum* (1989): 139–167.

De Beauvoir, Simone. *Le Deuxième Sexe.* Paris: Éditions Gallimard, 1949.

De Sève, Micheline. "The Perspectives of Québec Feminists." In Constance Backhouse and David H. Flaherty, eds., *Challenging Times: The Women's Movement in Canada and the United States,* 110–116. Montréal: McGill-Queen's University Press, 1992.

Des Rosiers, Nathalie. "La Responsabilité de la Mère pour le Préjudice Causé par son Enfant." *Les Cahiers de droit* 36 (1995): 61–98.

Dhavernas, Odile. *Droits des Femmes, Pouvoirs des Hommes.* Paris: Éditions du Seuil, 1978.

Dumont, Hélène, ed. *Femmes et Droit: 50 Ans de Vie Commune . . . et Tout un Avenir.* Montréal: Thémis, 1993.

Frug, Mary Joe. *Postmodern Legal Feminism.* New York: Routledge, 1992.

Gény, François. *Méthode d'Interprétation et Sources en Droit Privé Positif: Essai Critique,* 2nd ed. Paris: Pichon & Durand-Auzias, 1919.

Hodgson, Ellen E. "Equal Pay for Work of Equal Value in Ontario and Great Britain: A Comparison." *Alberta Law Review* 30 (1992): 926–987.

Horwitz, Morton. *The Transformation of American Law, 1870–1960: The Crisis of Legal Orthodoxy.* New York: Oxford University Press, 1992.

Kennedy, Duncan, *A Critique of Adjudication: fin de siècle.* Cambridge: Harvard University Press, 1997.

Kobly, Peggy, "Rape Shield Legislation: Relevance, Prejudice and Judicial Discretion." *Alberta Law Review* 30 (1992): 988–1017.

Lacroix v. Valois [1990] 2 S.C.R. 1259.

Langevin, Louise. "Avant-propos." *Les Cahiers de droit* 36 (1995a): 5–8.

———. "Responsabilité Extracontractuelle et Harcèlement sexuel: le modèle d'évaluation peut-il être neutre? " *Les Cahiers de Droit* 36 (1995b): 99–123.

Lippel, Katherine, and Bienvenu, Claudyne. "Les Dommages Fantômes: L'indemnisation des Victimes de Lésions Professionnelles pour l'Incapacité d'Effectuer le Travail Domestique." *Les Cahiers de Droit* 36 (1995): 161–208.

Loi Modifiant le Code Civil du Québec et d'Autres Dispositions Législatives afin de Favoriser l'Égalité Économique des Époux, L.Q. 1989, c. 55, modified by L.Q. 1990, c. 5.

MacDonald, Lois G. "The Violation of Women: Towards a Clearer Consciousness." In *Alberta Law Review* 30 (1992): 900–925.

MacKinnon, Catharine. "Reflections on Sex Equality Under Law." *Yale Law Journal* 100 (1991): 1281–1328.

———. *Towards a Feminist Theory of the State*. Cambridge: Harvard University Press, 1989.

———. *Feminism Unmodified, Discourses on Life and Law*. Cambridge: Harvard University Press, 1987.

———. "Feminist Discourse, Moral Values, and the Law: A Conversation." *Buffalo Law Review* 34 (1985): 11–87.

———. "Feminism, Marxism, Method, and the State: Toward a Feminist Jurisprudence." In *Signs* 8 (1983): 635–658.

———. "Feminism, Marxism, Method, and the State: An Agenda for Theory." *Signs* 7 (1982): 515–544.

———. *Sexual Harassment of Working Women: A Case of Sex Discirimination*. New Haven: Yale University Press, 1979.

Martin, Sheilah L. "Women as Lawmakers." *Alberta Law Review* 30 (1992): 738–746.

Munro, Karen M. "The Inapplicability of Rights Analysis in Post-Divorce Child Custody Decision Making." *Alberta Law Review* 30 (1992): 852–899.

Néron, Josée. "Foucault, l'Histoire de la Sexualité et la Condition des Femmes dans l'Antiquité." *Les Cahiers de Droit* 36 (1995): 245–291.

Noonan, Sheila. "Theorizing Connection." *Alberta Law Review* 30 (1992): 719–737.

Olsen, Frances. "The Family and the Market: A Study of Ideology and Legal Reform." *Harvard Law Review* 96 (1983): 1497–1578.

Parent, France, and Postolec, Geneviève. "Quand Thémis Rencontre Clio: Les Femmes et le Droit en Nouvelle France." *Les Cahiers de droit* 36 (1995): 293–318.

Ross, June, et al. "Women in the Class of 1979: Thirteen Years Later." *Alberta Law Review* 30 (1992): 843–851.

Scassa, Teresa. "Violence against Women in Law Schools." *Alberta Law Review* 30 (1992): 809–828.

Stoddart, Jennifer. "Des Lois et des Droits. Considérations à Propos d'un Cheminement Distinct." *Les Cahiers de Droit* 36 (1995): 9–26.

Stychin, Carl F. "Queer Nations: Nationalism, Sexuality and the Discourse of Rights in Québec." *Feminist Legal Studies* 5 (1997): 3–34.

Williams, Patricia. *The Alchemy of Race and Rights*. Cambridge: Harvard University Press, 1991.

CHAPTER FIVE

~

Feminism Under Fire[1]

Sigal Ben-Porath

In a talk in a Jerusalem high school a few years ago, a lieutenant-general in the Israeli Army was presenting military opportunities to the soon-to-be soldiers. "From time immemorial," he said "men have been warriors, and women—prostitutes." Apparently he was clumsily trying to encourage the young men in the audience to volunteer to serve as combat soldiers, by referring to the importance of men's service as warriors, and the benefits that come along with it, including easy access to sexual favors.

In the relatively liberal, relatively equal American public sphere, such a comment seems entirely out of place. Can women be dismissed as merely giving sexual and other services to men, in a military or other context? Not when the national security advisor is a woman, Americans can reassure themselves. Not when women have made so much progress in the military, the workforce, and many other practical and conceptual levels of the public sphere. On a second thought, ethnic minorities like Arab Americans may have had the same liberal vision of the American public sphere, but after September 11 were confronted with a more intolerant public and a changing balance in the political and legal systems between civil liberties and security concerns (Hardin 2004). The tension around security issues is bound to have an echoing effect on a vast array of perspectives and conceptions, from human rights to legitimized government intervention, to public priorities.

Could women's rights and other feminist causes take a toll too? Can the public realm retreat to the conservative stance of expecting women to care for the homes while the men protect their country? I suggest that these questions cannot be carelessly dismissed by those of us who care for democracy. Discussing them, in the American and comparative context, can offer some important insights into the mutual construction of gender and war; this discussion can simultaneously serve as a preemptive action to some worrisome changes in the public discourse on both topics.

I start this chapter from the widely acknowledged suggestion that militarism and patriarchalism are closely related social phenomena, which together feed undemocratic public inclinations (Isaksson 1988; Enloe 1989; Nordstrom 1991; Cooke and Woollacott 1993; Vickers 1993; Warren and Cady 1996). Societies enduring a protracted conflict, such as the war on terror, tend to reconceptualize citizenship as a narrow notion, which I call "belligerent citizenship." Along with other democratic commitments, gender equality withers in the face of the conservative security state that ensues. In such social circumstances, the more a public domain is preoccupied with security issues, the more it is inclined to move toward conservative conceptions of gender roles (see an Israeli perspective in Abdo and Lentin 2002). Women's lives as well as their social perceptions are negatively affected by the war system, making the war an important social and feminist point of interest. The first part of this chapter is focused on examining the links between gender and war, mainly for the purpose of identifying the unique challenges that women face in a society plagued by conflict. I begin by illustrating how conflict and the changes in the conceptualization of citizenship it entails influence the civic standing of women, including its impact on the public education system. This impact is the focal point of the second section. The argument I make is motivated by the suggestion that the education system has a crucial role in strengthening democracy, particularly in challenging times. Thus in the last part I outline theoretical perspectives and feminist pedagogies that can contribute to civic education as a main tool for maintaining democratic attitudes in wartime.[2]

Women and War: Framing the Connections

On October 31, 2000, the United Nations Security Council unanimously adopted Resolution 1325 on women, peace, and security. It states on the outset that "Resolution 1325 marks the first time the Security Council addressed the disproportionate and unique impact of armed conflict on women, recognized the under-valued and under-utilized contributions women make to conflict prevention, peacekeeping, conflict resolution and peace-building, and stressed the importance of their equal and full participation as active agents in peace and security." (www.un.org) The gendered perspective on armed conflicts offers numerous viewpoints on the plight and role of women in the context of war. First, the unique plight of women as victims is the focus of many works: as men fight wars, women are usually the civilians who are hit first and hardest by the direct consequences of war, such as poverty, expatriation, rape, and destruction (Bergoffen 2003; Franks 2003). Many feminist authors pursue this line of analysis when considering the relations of gender and war, mostly regarding the fact that men have been the main planners and executors of military violence as mere contingency or social construction. Another gendered perspective on war is the role women serve in the armed forces, which is an ongoing debate within feminist circles for the past two decades (Feinman 2000). A third and less commonly acknowledged aspect, which will be the focus of this section, is the civic (including educational) consequences of a security-dominated public sphere. The effects of belligerent citizenship on the public standing of women are often intense, rendering their interests marginal and their actual voices faintly heard in the public realm.

The exploration of the consequences of conflict on women's social roles is based on an understanding of both gender and war as social constructs. This suggestion contradicts earlier feminist contentions that women are more peaceful by nature, that femininity is essentially tied to nurturing, or that women are morally superior to men. Goldstein (2001) combines research from a variety of disciplines to conclude that gender and war are mutually constructed. Common Western perceptions of gender and war grow each in the shadow of the other, and the two are inseparable as social entities. Masculinity is defined in the context of war, and war—in the context of manifesting masculinity. This mutual influence explicates both the near-total exclusion of women from the combat forces and their near-equal performance as soldiers when they are given the opportunity to fight. The construction of war as a masculine ideal excludes women from fighting in most instances of war, but still women can and do excel in these socially constructed masculine activities when they manage to fight their way into the armed forces.

The relations of gender and war are deeply connected to basic perceptions about what it means to be a man or a woman; what it means to be a social creature; and what is the basis for social relations (care or aggression? desire or hierarchy? reproduction or domination?). This mutual conceptual construction underlies the fact that some of the civic implications of living in a state of conflict pertain particularly to women. Because women are socially staged in opposition to both masculinity and war, they are readily marginalized in wartime. Gender-related issues lose standing in the public discourse, as a result of the centrality of security issues. The move toward conservatism, which is a common response to perceived threats, negatively affects the social standing of women. In the educational realm the combination of these two elements creates a shift toward reflecting the culture of war that among its other disadvantages, offers marginalized portrayals of and opportunities for women.

In a country in a state of war, security issues tend to surmount most other political matters (Barzilai 1992; Kimmerling 1993; Levi 2003). References to the acute requirements generated by the war permeate discussions on budget, civil rights, and education. The lion's share of these issues is diverted to the private sphere, to be solved (or neglected) there. The farther away a question is from the pressing issues of security, the more superficial the public debate about it becomes. Women and their interests are marginalized as well by the militarized public sphere.

In wartime, politicians, the media and large parts of society tend to be enchanted by the heroism and sacrifice that are generally associated with the military and come to the fore during wartime. In a theoretical discussion it is easier to remember that "War is destruction, pain, separation, gore and savagery as well as strength, courage and heroism." (Noddings 1984, 183) During actual wartime, however, perceptions shift and the general trend is to associate glory with military activities and their outcomes. The struggle to cope with the destruction and pain that are a constant reality in wartime necessitates a stronger public emphasis on the more compelling—heroic, victorious—aspects of war. The cultivation of a noncritical perspective is sometimes portrayed as the duty of the home front in honoring those in combat. Even in times of a controversial conflict, while criticism is expressed, attention is focused on the destruction and pain caused by war, and the public agenda is overtaken by the responses to war, whether derogatory or laudatory. The glorification of war, along with the centrality of male-dominated security issues in the public debate, create a national ethos in which women (like other groups and issues less directly related to the conflict) have little room.

The public debate thus narrows down, focusing on the state's role to protect its citizens. In a short and insightful response to the aftermath of the September 11 attacks, Iris Marion Young criticizes the benign portrayal of the state as protector of the vulnerable (2003). In the post-September 11 United States, she claims, the security aspect that characterizes every state took over large parts of the public discourse. The state turned into a security regime: "In the security regime, the state and its officials assume the role of protector toward its citizens, and the citizens become positioned as subordinates, grateful for the protection afforded them." (2003, 224) This is an apparently benign description of the masculine role of the state (or of a head of household who is assuming the role of the protector). Masculinity here is not portrayed as aggression, but rather as chivalry. The citizenry, like the vulnerable members of the household, are thankful for the protection. However, its cost is the unequal relations, the loss of autonomy and voice in decision making, and a broad authoritarian turn that leaves citizens, like women in the household, protected, but also subordinate and committed to obedience.

Moreover, the separation of public from private becomes more apparent and more widely endorsed in times of a protracted conflict. The conservative public conceptions of the private sphere and of gender roles are evident in the common depiction of the family in the Israeli debate as well (Izraeli, 1999). The basic presumption concerning the Israeli family is one which Okin famously criticized: "that families operate with benignity never expected of . . . the sphere of politics." (1998, 36) The misconception of a strict differentiation between the family and the sphere of politics is intensified when the latter is preoccupied mostly with war and terrorism. Compared with the vehement public sphere of a country under fire, the family seems to glow with tenderness and care. The public conceptualization of the family in Israel strives to keep this sentimental portrayal intact. The correlation of war with masculinity, and of caring for the home front and the wounded with femininity, generates a public sphere in which femininity is secondary to masculinity, where women serve the causes that men actively pursue. Thus the family in its classic or conservative form is safeguarded in the public's mind; within it, as well as in the public sphere, women are regarded mainly as mothers and wives. They are expected to keep warm homes for their soldiers— even during more peaceful times, even when the men are not coming home from war but merely from work. In the post-September 11 United States, the convergence of conservatism and militarism turned into a driving force for much of the public agenda as well as some administration policies. One of its most striking intellectual manifestations is William Bennett's *Why We Fight*, which is an elaborate attempt to reconstruct anger as a driving force for justified male aggression in the service of patriotism (2002; see critique in Bar-On 2003). The protection of the home as a motivation and justification for supporting the military struggle provides context for the war. In ancient Greece only citizens who owned land were called upon to protect their country from invasion or to serve in the military during times of war. The rationale for this rule was clear to the ancient Greeks as it is to modern governments—the good soldier is one who has someone and something to protect. Israeli soldiers, who are not paid for their years of compulsory service, will be motivated as long as they feel they are personally protecting their own homes and families. To promote this attitude, the homes, and the mothers who are to keep them, are idolized. Does women's behavior support this notion of femininity, in the battlefield and beyond?

When women serve in military posts, they are not proven more merciful than men. Jean Elshtain (1995) offers a detailed account of women and war, describing both the "ferocious few" and the "noncombatant many," as well as the support for various wars by organized and sporadic women's activities. Women cannot be considered peaceful by nature, as we can see from Elshtain's evidence, as well as from contemporary examples of women's participation in, and support for, military actions. In Israel the military was forced by the High Court to admit women to combat positions, and consequently a growing number of young women volunteer to serve in various front line units (although they are still a minority there). Women soldiers have since been charged with what feminist philosophers call "gratuitous cruelty," (Ruddick 2003) pointing to the fact that evils associated with masculinity can easily be performed by women in the relevant positions (Alon and Harel 2003).

Even suicide attacks are not a men-only domain any more, with a number of young Palestinian women perpetrating such attacks against Israeli civilians. Israeli women soldiers have been participating in some of the dehumanizing routines of the occupation, sometimes demonstrating, like their male counterparts, the corruption and cruelty that the occupation generates. In the Iraqi prison abuse scandal in Abu Ghraib, where military wardens seemed to take pleasure in humiliating and torturing their Iraqi prisoners, one of the main alleged perpetrators was a woman. It seems that in past generations women seldom took part in military operations simply because they were denied the opportunity to do so. Women apparently share with men the ability to dehumanize the other and to act forcefully when persuaded that this is the right thing to do. Goldstein, too, like Elshtain and others (Brock-Utne 1985; Enloe 2000), offers ample evidence that "when women have found their way into combat, they have generally performed about as well as most men have." (2001, 127)

What, then, is the unique significance of women's contributions—beyond their equal standing as citizens—to the public debate in times of conflict?

Wartime affects the agencies from which we learn our gendered roles, by encouraging the depiction of gender as related to a more traditional division of labor. Unfortunately, the public education system tends to contribute to the perpetuation of traditionally gendered social roles; it does so even more rigorously in times of war and in the context of a protracted conflict. The public education system is justified as a publicly funded institution only inasmuch as it realizes its main aim, namely, the preservation and promotion of democratic affiliations (skills, attitudes, behaviors) in the next generation of citizens. It is thus the education system's responsibility to maintain or resume its democratic and civic role by opposing undemocratic social tendencies, one of which is the hierarchical gender differentiation. Feminist pedagogic tools can offer proper responses to the narrowing perceptions of citizenship and to the traditional dichotomous conceptualization of gender roles, both of which characterizes societies at war. Let us then turn to look at the gendered effects of war on the education system, and at some suggested critical feminist responses to war in the educational context.

Learning to Be a Man: Education, Gender, and War

The effects of a protracted conflict and a militarized public sphere on the education system are manifold. Public pressure, and the constitution of the teachers and administrative bodies, redirects the education system into compliance with the public's expectations of creating citizens. In wartime these pressures push in the direction of unified patriotism, suppression of dissent, and support for the military effort.

The effects of this tendency on women's social standing are evident on the administrative as well as the curricular level. One such affect that is uniquely Israeli is the parachuting of retired military officers to lucrative principal positions in the public education system (mainly in high schools). In addition to blocking the paths of promotion to individuals—mostly women—who have devoted their careers to education, this phenomenon also sends a conspicuous public message about social order. Men manage, women are their subordinates, even in those professions where women are a wide majority.

Broader gendered consequences of the endorsement of belligerent citizenship by the education system can be found in the curriculum itself. The first and most obvious aspect of the curriculum affected is the history studies. The emphasis on military history and on militarized national narratives of nation building leaves little room for presenting historical contributions of women. This problem, evident in more tranquil countries as well, worsens when a protracted conflict takes its toll on the curricular emphases. The presentation of an occasional woman who was allowed to serve and excelled, volunteered to do crucial paramilitary work, or was a devoted nurse, only serves to highlight the absence of women from the curriculum and from the militarized version of national history.

Another problematic affect of belligerent citizenship on schools, from the gendered perspective, is the differentiated socialization of men and women. In Israel, a democracy that mandates service to both men and women, the effects of the militarized culture on public schooling are mostly evident in the future-oriented socialization of boys and girls. Boys and girls anticipate a different future, with most boys (and very few girls) aspiring from a very young age to serve in combat positions. A considerable part of youth socialization toward their roles is correspondingly split.

In a democratic society that does not practice universal draft and has a narrower gender differentiation in military roles, like the United States, the effects of actual military roles on civic socialization of young people are more subtle. The gendered culture of war, however, has its differentiated effect on young men and women (Enloe 1988). Belligerent citizenship relies on a positive conception of war as a necessity, even a virtue, of political action. Both Israel's and the contemporary United States' common depiction of the conflict in which they are engaged are focused on describing it as one that was forced upon them. The necessity of going to war, however, turns into a virtue from the civic perspective, with belligerent forms of citizenship striving to express support for the causes of war as a unified form of patriotism, which involves an endorsement of the gendered characterization of war. The heroism being heralded is mostly a masculine one, with an occasional heroine (like the fictional, mythic aspects of the story of Jessica Lynch during the Iraq war) whose story nourishes the masculine glory of the fight. This view of civic virtue as militaristic and thus masculine carries belligerent qualities over into the public conception of the Good Citizen, which grows to accommodate the combat soldier as the embodiment of good citizenship (along with other visions of good citizenship, but still with significant weight). This conceptualization, along with the reorganization of notions of patriotism and national identity, have an impact on schools almost immediately after the beginning of an armed conflict, through ad hoc lesson plans as well as "hidden curricula" materials. Later on it infiltrates the public education system through history books, civic studies curricula, and other standardized forms of learning. Some evidence to valuing patriotic unity over free speech could be traced in the post-9/11 American academic world. In January 2003 (Murphy 2003) the University of California, Berkeley refused to allow a fundraising appeal for the Emma Goldman Papers Project, because the appeal quoted Goldman on the suppression of free speech and her opposition to war (writing during the first World War, and before she was deported to Russia). Even before the war in Iraq began, the winds of war created much caution on various educational forums, as CNN reported: "After complaints that the children of soldiers were upset by anti-war comments at school, Maine's top education official warned teachers to be careful of what they say in class about a possible invasion of Iraq." (cnn.com 2003)

The feminist critique of the education system in times of a protracted conflict thus points out the portrayal of women as occupying traditional roles, and the emphasis on men's heroism, as main aspects that require attention in the context of belligerent citizenship. What constructive suggestions can be found in feminist literature from which such responses can be developed? To answer this question I turn to the examination of feminist pedagogical contributions to peace education.

Women as Peacemakers? An Educational Perspective

The feminist literature has long been suggesting that women's experiences, and specifically mothers' experiences, offer an interesting and productive basis for a philosophy of peace. Much as patriarchalism and war seem to have significant relations of mutual reinforcement, so do feminism—or femininity, or motherhood, or simply women—and peace (Eaker-Rich and Van Galen 1994; Reardon and Nordland 1994; Oliner and Oliner 1995).

The opposition of care and justice—and thus of women's and men's moral perspectives—serves as background for various feminist political theories, among them "maternal thinking." Since Sarah Ruddick's groundbreaking book (1989), the practice of motherhood has been considered by many feminist philosophers and educators as a benchmark of peacemaking politics. According to Ruddick, mothers are concerned with preserving the life of the child, fostering her growth, and training her for social acceptability. They use analytic as well as emotional work toward these goals and toward overcoming violence, including their own. Under this description, motherhood provides tools for a peaceful resolution of conflicts on the personal and political levels. Ruddick's account of maternal work and its significance to peace politics derives much of its force from the reference to the perception of the masculinity of war, and of women's peacefulness. In a paraphrase on de Beauvoir she says: "A boy is not born, but rather becomes, a soldier." (1989, 145)

Ruddick was not the first to examine philosophically the connection between women's lives and peace. Back in the 1920s Virginia Woolf devoted her essay *Three Guineas* to the exploration of the relations between the two, with a substantial discussion of related educational matters. Woolf regards the poverty of women, and their lack of formal education in her time, as one of the causes for the prevalence of war. She calls for more and better education for women, suggesting that their inclusion in the public world of politics will result in more peaceful policies.

These perspectives, though revolutionary for their times and providing important insight to the research of gender, are the context of criticism for feminist and other authors who resist the plain association of an individual's gender with her or his moral affiliation. Gender and morality (much like the narrower relations of gender and war, or women's supposed alternative managerial style) mutually construct each other; there are various characteristics that can be attributed to one gender more than the other, but the correlation should be interpreted in social construction terms rather than as essential components of each gender.

If indeed women do not have essential moral perspectives that are alternative to the dominant male morality, if they (we) do not indeed harbor a tendency to peaceful social relations, whether as women or as mothers, why is it still worth discussing education and war in a feminist context? What is the relevance of the feminist educational perspective to the debate about citizenship and war, and why is it interesting or productive to suggest, as I do, that feminist pedagogical practices should be integrated into a broader conception of civic education in wartime (which I develop elsewhere).

Women have a unique contribution to make in the field of education generally, and peace education specifically, because of their (our) disproportional contribution to the education of children, both their own children—as mothers—and other people's children—as teachers. The socialization of children into their roles as citizens, family members, and public actors has been the role of women for many generations, in their capacity as caregivers at home and by their function as an overwhelming majority among educators in recent generations. Despite this fact there are various masculinist tendencies in the formal education system, even in peaceful times, and some trends in feminist theory have suggested pedagogical ways to incorporate feminist insights into the structure and content of the education system (Noddings 1984, 1992). As I suggested, male-dominated tendencies in the public sphere generally, and in public education specifically, surge during wartime. Educators working in this context of the social circumstances of conflict should be aware that among other impacts of war on the education system, the security-dominated public sphere can push the curriculum and other educational practices in the direction of less recognition, space, and voice for women. Feminist pedagogy can aide in constructing a nuanced response to this challenge.

Feminist pedagogy offers guidelines for education for positive recognition of the gendered, racial, ethnic, and national "other." It provides guidelines and tools for overcoming oppression and expanding the social sphere to include a diverse citizenry. As such, it offers an invaluable instrument for education in wartime. Wartime Education, in its effort to oppose the attenuating public sphere, can use lessons drawn from feminist pedagogies, lessons that were often developed through struggle against narrow social conception that failed to accommodate women's perspectives.

The most influential and effective feminist perspective on education was offered by bell hooks (1989), in her direct manner: "talk back." This simple phrase symbolizes the main cause of feminist, as well as other radical and critical trends of education. The critical response to the social mainstream, both by analysis and by political activism, is the crux of any educational approach that trusts education to be an anchor for social change.

Engaged Pedagogy is used by bell hooks to describe a holistic approach to teaching and learning. It values students and teachers' expressions, risk-taking, recognizing, and challenging of power issues. As a student of Paulo Freire, hooks values the mutual work of students and teachers in opposing the social mainstream.

In 1977 Adrianne Rich called women students to claim their education, not wait to receive it. The general sense evidence from Rich, hooks, and other radical feminist authors is that education can serve as a woman's ticket out of the social oppression and discrimination that usually awaits them. Feminist theory often regards education as a crucial step in the road to gender equality (however that notion is conceived). Beyond demands for equal access to educational resources, which are less consequential to the discussion of education in wartime, there are a number of tools which feminist theory can contribute to the educational effort to achieve peace.

Nonviolence

Contrary to Just War theorists, Sara Ruddick (in Cooke and Woollacott 1993, 109) claims that she is "not preoccupied with the question, When, if ever, is it right to kill?" Rather she "seeks to expose the multiple costs of violence and to disrupt the plans of those who organize it." (1993, 109) Ruddick construes feminist peace politics as a subversive activity that is wary of organized violence, discloses hidden violences, and invents strategies and ideals of nonviolence.

Much feminist scholarly work has been devoted to teaching strategies for defying violence and affirming peacefulness. Consequently there is a vast pool of social and educational materials within feminist thought to be taken into account when working toward civic education for peace. Some authors, such as Brock-Utne and Reardon, investigate the peace education realm through a gender lens; Brock-Utne's broad definition of war as any situation involving breech of human rights, inequality, poverty and violence on the personal or public level, leads her to the claim that "peace starts in the minds of women." (1985, 73) Other authors offer pedagogical tools that can enhance skills and attitudes necessary for building a peaceful class climate or a peaceful community. Thus Nel Noddings suggests a pedagogy of care that is designed to encourage humane and cooperative rather than competitive and aggressive interaction in school (and beyond). Still other authors (Diller, Houston, Morgan, and Ayim 1996), employing a gender-sensitive approach, provide tools for dealing with the structural violence of gender oppression, as well as the practical violence in the form of harassment of physical attacks against women in and outside the educational realm. These feminist tools combine cognitive and emotional perspectives toward the goal of learning new ways of perceiving the "other" as well as new, nonviolent modes of expressing one's views. Although a description of all those tools is beyond the scope of this work, it is worth mentioning their common structure, which they share with the Expansive Education approach. The struggle against the exclusion which characterizes existing social perception, which is made by peaceful means and as part of an attempt not to conquer social constructions but to expand them so that they include further perspectives, is characteristic of both feminist pedagogies and Expansive Education. The message of non-violence is crucial in itself in a public realm that is enchanted by the heroic perception of war. In addition it supports the further aims of feminist peace education, and particularly the struggle for recognition.

Recognition
Feminist literature has long claimed that women are commonly identified as the "other" within the social order. Feminist theorists provide strategies for learning to overcome alienation, to recognize and respect the other, and create common grounds beyond differences. One such tool for generating and reinforcing recognition is through dialogue, which is a tool employed by various radical, postcolonial, antiracist, and poststructural pedagogies. Generating recognition through establishing a meaningful dialogue among teachers and students, and within a diverse group of students, is a means to overcoming stereotypes and animosity (Freire and Shor 1987; Fuss 1989). The recognition of difference is considered a valuable tool for beginning to consider different needs and interests on the policy level, as well as for learning to respect other perspectives and values on the social level. The recognition of difference is a good in itself, as well as a tool for the purpose of diversifying the voices heard in public. Hearing more voices in the public realm works against the current of focusing the public debate on security issues; it also serves to empower members of groups, including women, who manage to represent their perspectives in the public debate.

Resistance

Feminist pedagogy emphasizes the counteractive ways of educating against widespread social perceptions. Where women are conceived of as vulnerable, voiceless, or unworthy, education can empower them, give them voice, and foster their differences, and sameness, in ways that can change their self- and social perception. Resisting widely held social prejudices and opposing an oppressive social mainstream have been key goals of feminist pedagogy for decades. By using methods such as questioning basic assumptions, presenting students with unconventional role models, and encouraging them to think critically about the construction and content of their social beliefs, feminists have managed to push forward the social recognition of women as equal members of society.

This educational process needs to engage both the cognitive critical abilities of students and teachers, and their emotional affinity. Feminist pedagogy at its best challenges a multiplicity of widely accepted dichotomies, including the cognition/emotion one. Hence a feminist pedagogy offers educational tools that engage the students' feelings, beliefs, and knowledge with a critical consideration of current social practices. Much like peace pedagogies at their best, the process of change and growth that takes place through feminist pedagogy involves the individual as a human being, respecting her complexity. Fear, hate, and misconceptions must be present in the classroom, acknowledged, and dealt with rather than dismissed. For students to be able to reconceptualize notions of gender, of nationalism, or patriotic commitments (as well as of race, class, and other social matters), their initial perceptions on these topics must be recognized in class. This learning process thus is a mutual one, involving the teacher who has to learn and respond to the students' conceptual world, and the students who may learn to overcome misconceptions and grow to think about themselves and others in fresh, broader ways.

In times of war, this tool becomes even more valuable. As Ruddick suggests (in Cooke and Woollacott 1993, 122), "Obedience is the handmaid of war, resistance the prerequisite of peace." Being able to resist the temptation of unity and solidarity offered by the belligerent form of citizenship is easier for women, for to a large extent they are not invited to equally share its rites or its benefits. Since the war culture in its civic manifestation continues to discriminate against women, they are in a better position to oppose it and thus to offer society as a whole an alternative vision of the future.

Positive Self-conception

When looking for ways to teach peace and democracy against a rising tide of unifying patriotism and erosion of democratic commitments, the forms of resistance suggested by feminist radical and poststructural pedagogy are particularly helpful. As in the case of dialogical pedagogy from the Freire School, which informs trends in feminist pedagogy, this emancipation is manifested through strengthening the positive self-conception of the learners. The empowerment of learners, a distinctive aim of all radical pedagogies, expresses itself in the case of feminist pedagogy also in the form of creating a positive conception of the future self. Nel Noddings notes that the teacher must offer confirmation to the student by attributing to her the most positive motives possible; by this and other ways she can support the student's confidence and help her build a conception of herself as a positive person in the present and in the future.

Helping a student establish a positive future self-conception is arguably the most important, if not widely discussed, contribution that a teacher can have in a student's life. Being able to imagine oneself as a positive person, as having a positive or desirable future, is a crucial aspect of overcoming present time difficulties, peer pressures, self-doubt, and actual failure. How this goal can be achieved is a question that hardly has a simple answer, and this is not the place to discuss the many aspects of personal and social affirmation, empowerment, and expectation that make up the environment suitable for developing such self-conception. The reason this notion is stressed here is because it carries much significance to the question at hand, namely the feminist educational and pedagogic ways of promoting peace. For this important lesson regarding positive future self-conception to pertain to civic education for peace, it has to be expanded to the social arena. A main aim of civic education for peace is to enable the formation of a positive vision of the future, a positive communal self-conception that incorporates the role of the nation in the region and world. Regarding oneself as an American, Palestinian, Iraqi, or Israeli and finding a nonmilitaristic form of pride in this identification can contribute to the emergence of an expanded form of patriotism that does not necessarily include belligerent aspects of nationalism. Envisioning a different future for the country one identifies with depends upon a host of variables, some of which can be addressed in the school setting. Students get their information from the news and other media, from possible engagement with the political world, from their family members and their communities. Schools, however, can offer a perspective that goes beyond what many children learn in other settings. School can work with the students, engaging their critical capacities and their imagination, to envision alternative possible futures other than the grim ones that a country engaged in a protracted conflict tends to generate.

These approaches and tools are of immense importance to civic education, particularly in times of a protracted conflict when the possibility of gender equality diminishes, along with other democratic attitudes and perspectives. They can serve the goal of overcoming past differences and learning to live alongside the former adversary as neighbor or fellow citizen, as well as serve to support the nation itself in the transition toward peace, which is a demanding and sometimes divisive project. Seyla Benhabib (1992, 192) suggests that engaging in a democratic discourse in a diverse society requires a capacity for "enlarged thought." Melissa Williams (2003, 237) takes up this contention in her discussion of citizenship as shared fate by asserting the requirement for democratic citizenship under conditions of "sometimes-unwelcome diversity." Enlarged thought's emphasis on the importance of diversity, recognition of the other, and learning through exercise, echoes the feminist commitments to preserving and expanding democratic equality. Enlarged thought relies on the substantial usage of classroom diversity through curricular and other activities. This use is made to support the ability of students to put themselves in the position of the "other" and to share the other's experiences. Some of the most productive curricular and pedagogic tools of endorsing and encouraging diversity are adapted from feminist (as well as multicultural) literature. These perspectives are focused on expanding the knowledge of students (and teachers) beyond their immediate environment and beyond the formal academic knowledge, to know people and cultures different than themselves. Employing diversity in positive ways can help celebrate it in the ethnic and cultural sense, and support democracy in a society that does not always welcome all forms of diversity. This use of diversity to develop the students' minds and hearts in democratically oriented ways embodies the endorsement of descriptive (ethnic, cultural, religious) diversity while encouraging the development of diversity in ideological stances and in conceptions of the political. The positive employment of diversity in this dual sense is tied to learning to acknowledge both differences and similarities among people of various backgrounds of viewpoints. A complementing form of learning to acknowledge the other is through generating dialogue among rival groups, whether through actual meetings or through learning about them, and creating a shared and equal dialogue among them. As Giroux (2002, 1155) reminds us, it is the role of educators to "provide spaces of resistance within the public schools . . . while simultaneously providing the knowledge and skills that enlarge their sense of the social and their possibilities as viable agents capable of expanding and deepening democratic public life." Actively supporting the expression of a variety of standpoints, rather than plainly responding to their implied existence in the public and educational arenas, would be an effective practice of manifesting the students' civic equality. It would demonstrate a resistance to the exclusion of individuals and groups by the security-dominated, solidarity-oriented public sphere.

Working with feminist pedagogic tools to oppose the educational aspects of belligerent citizenship can empower women, and consequently society as a whole, to learn to question the alleged advantages, or inevitability, of war. It can suggest to all students that the patriotic unity expected of them is not truly inclusive; it can teach them to critically engage with the political and social questions that the conflict raises. At minimum, students can learn to consider how belligerent citizenship is aimed to shape their political perceptions; they can thus learn to autonomously reassess their acceptance of the social norms and values tied to belligerent citizenship. The mere infusion of the public discourse—or its miniature educational equivalent—with the silenced voices of women, can serve the aim of expansive education to diversify the public sphere and thus to offer further options, further visions, and further voices beyond the oppressive unity of belligerent citizenship.

Notes

1. A much earlier version of this chapter was presented at the 1998 International Association of Women Philosophers meeting in Boston. I thank the participants, and particularly James Sterba, for their valuable comments. I have since developed my thoughts about the topic into a chapter in my book *Citizenship Under Fire: Democratic Education in Times of Conflict* (Princeton University Press, 2006). This revised version is printed here with permission from Princeton University Press. For their comments on various versions I thank Eran Ben-Porath, Harry Brighouse, Suzanne Dovi, Meira Levinson, and Rob Reich. Deborah Orr provided valuable advice in the final stages of writing.

2. These are part of a broader educational approach, dubbed "Expansive Education," which I develop in *Citizenship Under Fire: Democratic Education in Times of Conflict*.

Bibliography

Abdo, Nahla, and Ronit Lentin, eds. *Women and the Politics of Military Confrontation: Palestinian and Israeli Gendered Narratives of Dislocation*. New York: Berghahn Books, 2002.

Alon, Gideon, and Amos Harel. "Female Soldier Charged with Making Palestinian Woman Drink Poison." *Ha'aretz*, June 23, 2003, A4.

Bar-On, Bat-ami. "Manly After-Effects of September 11, 2001." *International Journal of Feminist Politics* 5, no. 3 (November 2003): 456–458.

Barzilai Gad. *Demokratia be-milhamet: Mahloket ve-consensus be-Israel* [*Democracy in Time of War: Conflict and Consensus in Israel*; in Hebrew] Tel Aviv: Sifriat Poalim, 1992.

Benhabib, Seyla. *Situating the Self: Gender, Community and Postmodernism in Contemporary Ethics*. New York: Routledge, 1992.

Bennett, William J. *Why We Fight: Moral Clarity and the War on Terrorism*. New York: Doubleday, 2002.

Bergoffen, Debra. "February 22, 2001: Toward a Politics of the Vulnerable Body." *Hypatia* 18, no. 1 (2003): 116–134.

Brock-Utne, Birgit. *Educating for Peace: A Feminist Perspective*. New York: Pergamon Press, 1985. cnn.com, February 28, 2003.

Cooke, Miriam, and Angela Woollacott, eds. *Gendering War Talk*. Princeton, NJ: Princeton University Press, 1993.

Diller, Ann, Barbara Houston, Kathryn Pauly Morgan, and Maryann Ayim, eds. *The Gender Question in Education: Theory, Pedagogy and Politics*. Boulder, CO: Westview, 1996.

Eaker-Rich, Deborah, and Jane Van Galen, eds. *Caring in an Unjust World: Negotiating Barriers in Schools*. Albany: State University of New York Press, 1994.

Elshtain, Jean. *Women and War*. Chicago: University of Chicago Press, 1995.

Enloe, Cynthia. "Beyond 'Rambo': Women and the Varieties of Militarized Masculinity." In *Women and the Military System*, edited by Eva Isaksson. London: Harvester, 1988.

———. *Bananas, Beaches and Bases: Making Feminist Sense of International Politics*. London: Pandora, 1989.

———. *Maneuvers: The International Politics of Militarizing Women's Lives*. Berkeley: University of California Press, 2000.

Feinman, Ilene Rose. *Citizenship Rites: Feminist Soldiers and Feminist Antimilitarists*. New York: New York University Press, 2000.

Franks, Mary Anne. "Obscene Undersides: Women and Evil between the Taliban and the United States." *Hypatia* 18, no. 1 (2003): 135–156.

Freire, Paulo, and Ira Shor. *A Pedagogy of Liberation*. London: Palgrave Macmillan, 1987.

Fuss, Diana. *Essentially Speaking: Feminism, Nature and Difference*. New York: Routledge, 1989.

Giroux, Henry A. "Democracy, Freedom, and Justice after September 11th: Rethinking the Role of Educators and the Politics of Schooling." *The Teachers College Record* 104, no. 6 (2002): 1138–1162.

Goldstein, Joshua S. *War and Gender: How Gender Shapes the War System and Vice Versa*. Cambridge and New York: Cambridge University Press, 2001.

Hardin, Russell. "Civil Liberties in an Era of Mass Terrorism." *The Journal of Ethics* 8, no. 1 (2004): 77–95.

hooks, bell. *Talking Back: Thinking Feminist, Thinking Black*. Boston: South End Press, 1989.

Isaksson, Eva, ed. *Women and the Military System*. London: Harvester, 1988.

Izraeli, Dafna, et al. *Min, Migdar, Politika [Sex, Gender, Politics*; in Hebrew]. Tel-Aviv: Hakibutz Hameuhad, 1999.

Kimmerling, Baruch. *The Interrupted System: Israeli Civilians in War and Routine Times*. New Brunswick, NJ: Transaction Books, 1993.

Levi, Yagil. *Zava Aher le-Israel [A Different Army to Israeli: Materialistic Militarism in Israel*; in Hebrew]. Yedioth Aharonot, 2003.

Murphy, Dean. "Old Words on War Stirring a New Dispute." *New York Times*, January 14, 2003, A1.

Noddings, Nel. *Caring, a Feminine Approach to Ethics and Moral Education*. Berkeley: University of California Press, 1984.

———. "The Challenge to Care in Schools: An Alternative Approach to Education." In *Advances in Contemporary Educational Thought series*. Vol. 8. New York: Teachers College Press, 1992.

———. "An Ethics of Care and Its Implications for Instructional Arrangements." In *The Education Feminism Reader*, edited by Lynda Stone. Routledge, 1994.

Nordstrom, Carolyn. "Women and War: Observations from the Field." *Minerva: Quarterly Report on Women and the Military* 9, no. 1 (Spring 1991).

Okin, Susan Moller. "Feminism, Women's Human Rights, and Cultural Differences." *Hypatia* 13, no. 3 (1998): 32–52.

Oliner, Pearl M., and Samuel P. Oliner. *Toward a Caring Society: Ideas into Action*. Westport, CT: Praeger, 1995.

Reardon, Betty, and Eva Nordland, eds. *Learning Peace: The Promise of Ecological and Cooperative Education*. Albany: State University of New York Press, 1994.

Ruddick, Sara. *Maternal Thinking: Toward a Politics of Peace*. Boston: Beacon Press, 1989.

———. "Notes toward a Feminist Peace Politics." In *Gendering War Talk*, edited by Miriam Cooke and Angela Woollacott, 109–127. Princeton, NJ: Princeton University Press, 1993.

———. "The Moral Horror of the September Attacks." *Hypatia* 18, no. 1 (2003): 212–222.

Vickers, Jeanne. *Women and War*. London: Zed Books, 1993.

Warren, Karen J., and Duane L. Cady, eds. *Bringing Peace Home: Feminism, Violence and Nature*. Bloomington: Indiana University Press, 1996.

Williams, Melissa S. "Citizenship as Identity, Citizenship as Shared Fate, and the Functions of Multicultural Education." In *Citizenship and Education in Liberal-Democratic Societies*, edited by Kevin McDonough and Walter Feinberg, 208–247. New York: Oxford University Press, 2003. www.un.org, accessed September 14, 2005.

Young, Iris Marion. "Feminist Reactions to the Contemporary Security Regime." *Hypatia* 18, no. 1 (2003): 223–231.

CHAPTER SIX

~

When Girls Just Wanna Have Fun: Third-wave Cultural Engagement as Political Activism

Cathryn Bailey

"In some of the most crucial ways, the political battles fought today are battles of representation, struggles for control of the mass media, definitions and terminology. As the site where third wave identities are most actively forged, the activism that most engages the question of representation will be definitive." (Heywood and Drake 1997, 102)

One criticism of so-called third-wave feminists is that they are not activists in ways that are politically meaningful. Although there have been no highly visible grassroots groundswells of younger women as in past decades, younger feminists are active, primarily engaging with cultural images of women, both in the critique of such images and in the creation of new ones, especially the production of music, zines,[1] and websites. As one observer puts it: "Where are the younger generations of feminists? people often ask me. Have we lost them? My answer is always the same: 'You're looking in the wrong places. There is a strong anti-sexist and anti-racist manifesto present in today's music. . . . It's where the pulse of young feminism beats." (Saraco 1996, 26) These cultural productions and critiques constitute meaningful feminist activism primarily as resistance to the cultural forces that shape their development as subjects. Young women are taking some control over the forces that shape their identities. However, given the very nature of this type of activism, especially its potential for cooptation, it cannot supplant the need to seek other, more traditional sorts of political change.

The use of cultural critique, especially that of popular culture for political aims, is not new to feminism. Some of the most visible and memorable second-wave feminist protests were challenges to how women were represented in the media, for example, the protest against the 1968 Miss America Pageant. Feminists have long understood the importance of popular culture. What is different today is many young feminists' almost exclusive focus on cultural rather than traditional political life as well as the prevalence of a peculiarly postmodern style of expression, one which often emphasizes the reclamation and performance (often to the point of parody) of previously disparaged aspects of gender.

This intense focus on popular culture is one of the aspects of third-wave feminism that helps make it appropriate to call it a "postmodern" movement. It is one of the themes of postmodernism that almost anything can be treated as a "text," and, in this respect, expressions are on par, and that the hierarchy of "high" over "low" culture and "nonfiction" over "fiction" has been toppled. The emphasis ceases to be on whether or not a text reflects reality or not (such a reflection is regarded as ultimately impossible), but is to explore the multiple meanings, constructions, and interpretations the text makes possible. Thus, the critic informed by postmodernism is comfortable talking about a political speech in one breath and dialogue from a situation comedy in the next; the question isn't whether one is real and the other one isn't but *how* each is real. This activism, instead of focusing on the old strategies of grassroots organization and agitation, focuses on such texts and their relationships to each other and the social and material world.

There are many reasons why younger feminists are emphasizing cultural strategies rather than more obviously political ones. One is an increased disenchantment and alienation from political life in general. For the post-Watergate "Monica-gate" generation, no optimistic pretense about politics is even possible. Americans of all ages may be troubled by the likelihood that the current President Bush lied about weapons of mass destruction, but younger voters cannot even remember a time when political leaders and political processes were regarded with anything close to respect. Another is that the distinction between the political and the cultural really has become increasingly blurred to the point that younger people do not feel a need to make a sharp distinction between the two in their analyses and creations. Both in terms of style and content, what counts as politics and what counts as popular culture are harder to tell apart.

An especially pessimistic conclusion to draw is that, in reducing politics to pop culture, younger people are no longer taking political reality seriously. And there is certainly reason to worry that this is the case. After all, there *are* important differences between a real senator casting a vote and an actor playing a senator who casts a vote in a film. But a converse emphasis is just as important: Younger people are taking cultural images *more* seriously than they used to; at least they are more self-conscious about doing so. Thus, for example, a feminist group called the "Barbie Liberation Organization" may alternately be criticized for its triviality and praised for its appreciation of the ways in which subjects are socially constructed according to images like Barbie, to an extent never before imagined (VE 1997).

In short, that younger feminists have focused so much on cultural images need not be seen as representing a retreat from reality as much as an appreciation for how much of our reality is mediated through such images. In fact, this is exactly what some third-wave feminists imply. As one feminist puts it, "Our hybrid engagement with culture and/as politics sometimes looks problematic to second wave activists, who might accuse us of exchanging engagement with institutional and economic inequities for a self-referential politics that overestimates the power of critiquing, reworking, and producing pop- and subcultural images and narratives. But, as third wave activists, we contest a politics of purity that would separate political activism from cultural production. We acknowledge the tension between criticism and the pleasures of consumption, and we work the border between a critical, even cynical, questioning of things-as-they-are and a motivation to do something anyway, without the 'support' of a utopian vision." (Heywood and Drake 1997, 52)

Academic courses that teach popular cultural criticism reflect the perceived legitimacy of the connection between popular culture and feminist politics. Here, the relevance of popular culture to political life is established in historical and philosophical studies of the construction and control of women through popular culture. This cultural/political work involves the development of critical skills, for example, the ability to offer "resistant readings" in which politics are explicitly brought to bear on the consumption of popular culture, as well as the production of new images, for example, the creation of music, zines, websites, or video. It is the first and second of these that I focus on most specifically, that is, the role of cultural criticism and cultural production, focusing especially on the examples of television criticism, and music and zine production.

"Resistant reading" involves transforming the intended meanings of a text or uncovering its hidden ideological functions, for example, analyses of women's soap operas, ones that emphasize, for example, how the repetitive nature of the soap narrative reinforces the repetitive nature of women's housework (Modleski 1997, 36). Bell hooks makes it clear that resistant reading is not just a new preoccupation of younger people. She explains,

"Cultural criticism has historically functioned in black life as a force promoting critical resistance, one that enabled black folks to cultivate in everyday life a practice of critique and analysis that would disrupt and even deconstruct those cultural productions that were designed to promote and reinforce domination." (1990, 3) What is frequently thought of as the quintessential pastime of the apathetic quietest becomes reinterpreted as a site of political engagement. As hooks claims, "The screen was not a place of escape. It was a place of confrontation and encounter." (1990, 4)

One of the concerns about considering resistant reading to be political action is that it seems to involve a conflation of the fictitious with the real, of the word with the action. For example, Joy James worries that some so-called progressive intellectuals are substituting words about texts for calls for action: "If there is a distinction between speech that calls for action and text that is insular and rhetorical, then some writing offers specificity and strategies in their analyses of oppression while others produce liberation rhetoric." (1997, 137) Although James is right to demand accountability from those who would retreat from concrete reality to hide behind the text, it is one of the virtues of cultural studies to emphasize the connections between the two realms.

In fact, it is misleading to simply say that one realm represents the real and the other does not. Texts and their characters have a certain kind of reality, the proof of which is often in the effects they have on other aspects of reality. For example, one television critic urges that we take seriously the influence that some fictional characters have had on the earlier development of current feminists and antifeminists, claiming "that one of the ways that programs such as Mary Tyler Moore and Murphy Brown function politically is that they offer visions of what feminism 'means.' They are fictional, to be sure, and to some extent we are aware of their artificiality. However, to deny that they influence our thinking about women, women's roles, and the impact of social change is, it seems to me, to be dangerously naïve." (Dow 1996, 5) Television images are certainly real in that masses of people actually experience them and are influenced by them. For countless women and men, "feminism" itself became defined by how they were able to relate to such fictional characters. There is little doubt that something similar has happened with characters such as Ally McBeal and Buffy the Vampire Slayer.

The female President Allen, played by Geena Davis on the current series *Commander in Chief*, is an especially noteworthy character in this respect. On the one hand, political writer Katha Pollitt has warned against taking this television character too seriously in terms of its impact on future elections. According to her, "The substantial minority of voters who, according to polls, wouldn't vote for a woman nominated by their own party probably aren't watching the show, and besides, they're most likely Republicans . . . who would sooner admit the Earth is more than 10,000 years old than vote for Hillary." (2005, 10) However, Pollitt clearly uses her praise of this strong, fictional female character to chastise real people. "As the backlash gets daily more open and absurd," she claims, "our real-life female politicians seem paralyzed. It's up to television now: Run, Geena, run!" She challenges real people to live up to a standard set by a fictional character. Pollitt makes her point tongue in cheek, but it is the seriousness with which we have come to regard the characters of popular culture that permits her to make it at all.

Part of the difficulty of appreciating the value of cultural protest is that we are so used to focusing on the negative instances of the blurring of the cultural with the political. Although this blurring may have begun in earnest with the almost surreal reign of actor-president Ronald Reagan, it has intensified in the years since. This is true both in terms of how politicians package themselves for sale and how they position themselves in reaction to figures of popular culture. Former vice president Dan Quayle's vilification of the television character Murphy Brown was the quintessential example of the latter. Increasingly, "real" politicians and political issues are harder to distinguish from the pretend ones intended for our entertainment, a fact exploited by the election of Arnold Schwarzenegger and the film *Wag the Dog*. Revelations that the current Bush administration paid journalists to write favorably about its policies (in the United States and in Iraq) raise eyebrows, but hardly shock, partly because such actions are a predictable extension of a phenomenon to which we have grown accustomed.[2]

One of the difficulties of assessing the activist potential of "resistant reading" is in trying to figure out exactly what is involved in it. Certainly, in order for something to qualify as political activism it must involve some attempt to alter the power relations within a society, not merely to comment upon them. The word "active" is defined in part in opposition to mere "contemplation" or "speculation." Hooks certainly uses activist rhetoric to talk about the process of resistant reading as enabling "colonized folks to decolonize their minds and actions, thereby promoting the insurrection of subjugated knowledge." (1990, 10) Hooks uses the language of the revolutionary, but what does it mean to "decolonize" the mind? Apparently, it involves, at least in part, stepping outside of the dominant worldview, for example, to escape from seeing a production merely as innocuous, popular entertainment and instead see the pernicious ways that it reinscribes sexism, racism, and heterosexism. Alternately, it may involve progressive interpretations of material, the superficial message of which is repressive.

Although resistant reading isn't the same type of activism as political demonstration, it isn't mere contemplation or speculation either, the supposed opposite of "activism." One of the functions of popular culture is not merely to entertain, but to construct social subjects. Many of the ways in which this is accomplished are obviously oppressive. For example, the overriding intent of commercial television must be to produce audiences for advertisers; television is better able to do this to the extent that it influences viewers to become consumers, for example, producing shows with characters who spend a great deal of money on clothes encourages viewers to do the same. As has been amply documented, this social construction occurs at the conscious and unconscious levels. Increasingly, we are steeped in images from every aspect of media until it may be impossible to distinguish what is "really me" from what TV, film, and radio have made me be.

The construction of subjects, as consumers, as men, as women, is not easily definable (no visible hands emerge from televisions and radios to mold us), but it is pervasive. To borrow from Sandra Bartky's reading of Foucault, the very invisibility and anonymity of the process through which subjects are produced helps to explain its success. She explains that "the disciplinary power that is increasingly charged with the production of a properly embodied femininity is dispersed and anonymous; there are no individuals formally empowered to wield it; it is, as we have seen, invested in everyone and in no one in particular." (1998, 41) It is to be expected that challenges to that subjectification process would also be dispersed and hard to pinpoint. In the case of resistant readings, those who experience the images and messages of the media are simultaneously altering them as they are receiving them, as, for example, when TV viewers altered their perspective on *Xena: Warrior Princess* to exploit the homoerotic potential between Xena and her sidekick, Gabriella. The film *Brokeback Mountain*, a tale of gay cowboys, may be seen as a kind of culmination of this tendency; the long suppressed, hidden, homoerotic subtext has, at long last, been transformed into the main story line.

Resistant reading strategies are a way of taking some control over the media forces that shape one's subjectivity. Bonnie Dow considers this strategy in relation to the television sitcom *Murphy Brown*, a show noteworthy for its influence on popular definitions of feminism, definitions which are still operative. Although Dow characterizes the show primarily as exemplifying so-called post feminist values, she acknowledges that some viewers "constructed" readings of the main character as a feminist, "filling in a context that the sitcom's narrative does not provide. . . . As is always the case, the possibility of such a reading of Murphy Brown depends upon the experiences a viewer brings to a text as well as on the work s/he is willing to do in decoding it." (1996, 150) Pollitt intentionally does a similar revisionary reading of *Commander in Chief*, focusing on the character's feminist strengths, suggesting that the impoverished landscapes of television and reality license her to find feminist models where she can.

But to what extent is it really possible to resist the intended messages of culture, especially when these messages are pervasive? Is, for example, bell hooks' belief in her family's ability to overcome racist messages an example of false consciousness, or were they genuinely able to transform racist entertainment into antiracist education? Although disagreements about the extent of peoples' capacities to resist ideology have been around since Marx, and seem no closer to resolution, it is evident that at some level, at least some people sometimes reshape the meaning of what they are experiencing. Given the impossibility of making a definitive empirical determination about peoples' genuine capacity to resist (for denial is said to be one of the symptoms of false consciousness), a decision has to be made. Because I am not willing to dismiss all cultural consumers as hopelessly duped and victimized, I have to admit that many people (and not just myself and a few other "sophisticated" scholars) have some capacity to resist.

However, it is just as important not to underestimate the ideological effects of popular images. This is especially true in an era of mass communication that employs psychologically sophisticated methods to shape consumers. The use of product placement, for example, of a particular brand of cigarettes, in movies, is a good example. Even more pernicious is the increasing tendency of the media to advertise products, for example, the release of a new product, in the form of a news story. Still, as mass media's methods have become more effective, so has the critical potential of the viewer. In an era when the media have been transformed from an invisible, almost magically anonymous producer of images to a subject of scrutiny in their own right, as evidenced, for example, by the many ways the media have become their own favorite topic, there is every reason to suspect that viewers, too, are more aware of media as media.

Part of the test for how genuinely political a cultural critique or product may be is how closely it proceeds from or relates to a *particular*, concrete, social context. Some cultural agents such as Camryn Manheim, who played a defense lawyer on the TV show *The Practice*, provided rich material for the cultural critic. Manheim, who openly celebrated the size of her body, describing herself as "one of Rubens' girls," accepted an Emmy award by holding her trophy high and proclaiming: "This is for all the fat girls!" (Hutchings 1999, 287) She is a cultural agent who is so unambiguously connected to "real-life" social values that she invites the kind of analysis of her performance that can be expected to transform subjectivities. Similarly, by playing an out lesbian, Ellen DeGeneres produced a cultural product that unmistakably mirrored specific social and political values. Unfortunately, this may also help to explain why DeGeneres' show was so short lived and why, in her successful current role as television host, the "l-word" is rarely, if ever, uttered. At the end of the day, it seems, it is capitalist interests that hold sway.

Certainly it is critical that cultural critiques and productions be critical of the capitalist forces underlying their own production. Genuinely political cultural products must contain at least an implicit critique of consumer capitalism as a matrix in which the new critiques and products are always already implicated. Nowhere is an awareness of capitalism's coopting danger more important than in the production of music and zines. While the mainstream versions of both become consolidated in fewer and fewer corporate hands, technology allows individuals to create and disseminate their work in ways that may bypass much of the capitalist machinery.

Consider, for example, the feminist albums produced by primarily female musicians and composers such as Ani DiFranco, Le Tigre, and Tribe 8. A quick perusal of some of the lyrics testifies to their feminist messages. DiFranco's lyrics are clearly intended to be antisexist, antiracist, and antiheterosexist. For example, in "The Story" she sings: "I would have returned your greeting / if it weren't for the way you were looking at me / this street is not a market / and I am not a commodity / don't you find it sad that we can't even say hello / because you're a man and I'm a woman / and the sun is getting low / there are some places that I can't go / as a woman I can't go there." (1992) Le Tigre's song "Dykemarch 2001" couldn't be more straightforwardly political: "I like going to the dyke march because I like to be surrounded with women. Marching naked ladies. We recruit, we recruit. . . . There's no one tellin' us where to stand or where to be. . . . Resist. Shout it out. Resist, Resist, Shout it out . . . Feminist fury. Feminist fury." (2002) Similarly outspoken, Tribe 8 seems to shy away from nothing, addressing gang rape in one song: "frat pig / it's called gang rape / we're gonna play a game / called gang castrate." (Tribe 8, 1995)

Bands such as Tribe 8 and 7 Year Bitch are decidedly edgy, a quality described by one third-wave feminist as "a postmodern focus on contradiction and duality, on the reclamation of terms. S-M, pornography, the words cunt and queer and pussy and girl—are all things to be reexamined or reclaimed. In terms of gender, our rebellion is to make it camp. The underground music community has served as a particularly fertile breeding ground for redefining a feminism to fit our lives." (Klein 1997, 208) Although very different from the "women's music" of decades past, this music is similar in terms of what it can do politically.[3] Not only are the words empowering to many women who hear them, but "there is something about the mere image of a woman playing guitar that is thrilling, that gives me the same impression as the painting of Rosie the Riveter on my kitchen wall—a strong woman with a power tool waiting to be bent to her will." (p. 215) In addition, these music communities are sites for political organization "like the antiwar and civil rights movements before it . . . a place where young women learned or solidified radical means of analyzing the world and then applied these powers of analysis to their own lives, only to realize that, as girls, they felt disenfranchised within their own supposedly 'alternative' community." (p. 211) Not incidentally the Riot Grrrl Convention in Washington, D.C., featured music as well as workshops on issues such as sexuality, rape, racism, and domestic violence (p. 214).

The images and meanings produced in the music are political and the act of producing such images can politicize, a process that also occurs in the creation of zines and blogs. As one feminist explains, "Like other means of expression, fanzines [zines with an initial focus on specific musicians, bands, or other popular personality] embodied an attempt to process a wide variety of past and present images of femininity. . . . Fanzines helped girls form a network with each other, not only between towns such as Olympia, D.C., and San Francisco, but also among other places, smaller places, suburbs." (Klein 1997, 217) The very nature of the medium, small-scale, and technologically accessible can be significant. A third-wave feminist explains that "maybe creating a fanzine is cathartic to one young girl alone in her bedroom. Maybe it helps another young girl, reading it alone in her bedroom, come out or speak out or just feel less alone. And if these things are true, then that fanzine has fulfilled its fundamental task of fostering creativity and communication." (p. 217)

The general question about the music and the zines, "Do they qualify as feminist activism?" breaks into the questions: "Do they qualify as feminist *activism?*" and "Do they qualify as *feminist* activism?" First, as with resistant reading, there is a style of activism here that depends upon an appreciation of the collapsing distinction between the political and the cultural. Insofar as modern social inequity is produced and maintained not merely (or even primarily) by simple, visible coercive power, but through the production of subjects who effectively construct themselves, visible cultural images are simultaneously politically significant. The guitar- or pen-wielding woman (or the image produced through the song lyric or the zine article) becomes part of the cultural currency through which other women are able to imagine their own possibilities. In fact, the link between cultural imagery and politically engaged subjects may be a very tight one. Again, an appreciation of this link is not only an insight of younger feminists. As hooks suggests, "It is no mere accident of fate that the ground of current discourse on black subjectivity is cultural terrain. Art remains that site of imaginative possibility where 'anything goes,' particularly if one is not seeking to create a hot commodity for the marketplace. Black folks' inability to envision liberatory paradigms of black subjectivity in a purely political sense is in part a failure of critical imagination." (1990, 18–19)

The question of how *feminist* some of these third-wave images are is another matter. Some clearly intend to be more feminist than others, but cultural images are vulnerable to capitalistic cooptation in a way that may be both more direct and more complete than other forms of political activism. First, once one produces and disseminates an image, one "loses control" of the meanings the image comes to have for people. For example, the lead singer of Tribe 8 may intend the bare-chested, dildo-wearing image she presents on stage and in promotional materials to be one of empowerment for women, but in a capitalist and pornographic society, the meanings are easily appropriated into standard ones of female perversion. In short, recontextualized images are easily separated from their original politics. Consider the lyrics to a Tribe 8 song that one commentator described as "savagely satiric": "Patriarchal standards of beauty / is what my p.c. girlfriend would have me refuting / she's got a great mind and an even better booty / it makes me feel like raping and looting . . . neanderthal dyke / neanderthal dyke / I never read dworkin / I ride a big bike / feminist theory gets me uptight / get in some heels and lipstick / and I'll spend the night." (Saraco 1996, 26)

It isn't difficult to imagine how one might miss the "satirical" aspect of these lyrics, understanding them simply as misogynistic reflections of the backlash. An analogous, although politically reversed, situation occurred in the case of the 1970s television sitcom *All in the Family*: "Archie was the repository for the conservative bigotry that Norman Lear wished to attack. Poking fun at Archie was a way to debunk the ideology he represented. However, audience interpretation of this strategy is unpredictable. . . . Research shows that many viewers loved Archie *because of* his contentious conservatism." (Dow 1996, 149; emphasis in original) Part of the point here is that because cultural images are usually meant to be artistically motivated, their messages are typically not as didactic as, say, those of political columnists. While this fluidity is part of what makes artistic images powerful, it also makes them more vulnerable to being misused.

It is also clear that modern capitalism has shown itself to be remarkably adept at coopting feminist messages in order to profit from their appeal while neutralizing their import. Consider, for example, the Disney animated film

Mulan, in which some consumers' desire for a strong, independent female character is addressed even as that character is ultimately funneled into the role that more reactionary consumers expect, compliant daughter and future wife. Similarly, the character of Carrie Bradshaw, of the television series *Sex and the City*, expresses values that are superficially feminist, but ultimately reinforce stereotypes. On the one hand, Bradshaw demonstrates sexual agency and an admirable frankness about it. On the other hand, she is presented as a man-obsessed shopoholic.

Ani DiFranco is a more hopeful example. Although she has retained her independent label, DiFranco has appeared on numerous television shows and magazine covers, including *Spin*. That her image is something not fully in her control is something DiFranco is apparently aware of. As she sings: "People talk / about my image / like I come in two dimensions / like lipstick is a sign of my declining mind / like what I happen to be wearing / the day that someone takes a picture / is my new statement for all of womankind." (DiFranco 1998) DiFranco shows a savvy sensitivity not only to the dangers of becoming an icon for the mass media, but also to criticism from a constituency that values her, in part, precisely for her outspokenness, individuality, and unwillingness to be coopted.

But even DiFranco's concern for how her image is misused cannot keep that from happening. The surest way to ward off the capitalist perversion and dilution of one's political message may be to tie that message as specifically and unequivocally as possible to a political context. For example, songs that mention actual names and events are much less cooptable than those that deal in generalities and platitudes. Fanon describes this as the strategy of revolutionary poet Keita Fodeba, whose "constant desire to define accurately the historic moments of the struggle" result in a poem that is "a true invitation to thought, to de-mystification, and to battle." (Fanon 1963, 227) Unfortunately, even in the most overtly political music from young women that I have heard, this rarely occurs. Although it is true that the more specifically an image is tied to a particular political context, the less likely it is that mass capitalistic forces will want to appropriate it, it also seems to be that mass appeal (even at the small scale most alternative artists are aiming for) is best achieved by avoiding real social and political specificity. It underscores the point I am making that there is probably much specifically political music out there that I have missed because it has not become popular.

As Fanon suggests, political cultural products can also serve as calls for more traditional, proven forms of action. For example, for decades, Sweet Honey in the Rock has made political music, including the song "Are My Hands Clean," "which argues that women who consume have connections to women who produce," (Scanlon 1996, 177) offering a not-so-subtle challenge to women to be politically responsible consumers. Cultural products such as this one are especially interesting in that they circulate within the capitalist machine in order to challenge it, not unlike a virus that both is and is not a part of the very body it inhabits and may potentially destroy.

The practice of transforming the very strategies and concepts that define the system is challenging and prevalent in third-wave cultural production. This is a generation of feminists that has taken to heart the postmodern celebration of parodied performances of gender and irreverence and playfulness with language. Consider, for example, the punk-based Riot Grrrls' "fierce reclaiming of things girlish" (Klein 1993, 7) and the claim from one Riot Grrrl that "We DO want to take over the world, PAD POWER—LET THE BLOOD FLOW!" (Green and Taormino 1997, 185) or some of the titles of recent zines including "Diabolical Clits," "Pasty," "Hey There, Barbie Girl," and "Cupsize." (Green and Taormino 1997) The suggestion is that such works transcend sexist values by embracing and pushing them to extreme limits. Such values are transformed and transvalued, it is thought, by twisting them into previously unimagined shapes.

A genuine transvaluation is one that transcends the evaluative framework provided, one that questions the legitimacy of the entire scheme.[4] So, for example, a transvaluative perspective on gender in an androcentric society doesn't merely affirm the female but upsets the gender dichotomy. As Kathleen Hanna of the band Le Tigre (formerly of Bikini Kill) explains: "I don't believe in the concept of positive and negative in the first place. I don't believe that, okay, there are all these really sexist representations of women in the media and they're really negative and therefore I'm going to create positive ones. The way that I feel is that I'm going to create other ones." (Klein 1993, 7) Explicit rejections of any evaluative standards make it especially hard to tell where pushing aesthetic and conceptual limits has become a performance intended merely to shock. Consider, for example, article entitled "Why I Play with My Cunt" from a zine called Brat Attack that responds to the title's question with answers that range from the innocuously empowering: "Because it feels good," to the intentionally disturbing: "Because I want to be gang-banged by female inmates." (Green and Taormino 1997, 95–96) The second response strikes me not as pushing the limits of a framework that expresses repression, but as complicit with it in that it represents a mere reversal, an affirmation of that which the dominant culture despises.

Although there is tremendous variety in the third-wave material, one of the most problematic features of the music, zines, and blogs is the tendency to focus on a narrowly construed type of individual expression without drawing out deeper political implications. This tendency reflects one of the most insidious strategies of patriarchy, that of acknowledging feminist insights only to reinscribe them as individual women's problems to solve rather than as societal ones. A good example is the framing of women's overwork as a problem in which the onus is on her to balance impossible demands, a strategy that deflects attention from the responsibility to move society beyond traditional family and work structures.

One of the primary virtues of these alternative third-wave media is often said to be precisely that they are especially individualistic modes of expression, ones that bypass "the cooptiveness of the mainstream media and corporate world through an attitude of self-sufficiency." (Klein 1993, 7) However, self-publishing a zine or blog, or self-producing a compact disc, with no emphasis on any politically situated collective, invites the artist to escape attaching her message to collective social agendas that may be politically liberatory. As an interviewee in an electronic zine put it: "There is that sexy sort of appeal of the Internet. You're all alone in your house, nobody's supposed to be watching you, and you can do anything you want." (VE 1997) So, although there is a wealth of personal experience in much of this material, the intentional informality of the process (for example, many zines read almost like letters from the author), can permit one to avoid making connections between her voice and those of others. Such a feature may also be a part of the fact that these are meant to be entertaining as well, and one aspect of the sort of popular entertainment we are accustomed to is a focus on the individual.

It is important to keep in mind, however, that the risk of focusing solely on the *personal* in "The personal is political" is one with which second-wave feminism has also had to contend. For example, the question of when consciousness raising degenerates solely into group therapy, with no clear connection to the transformation of society, is one that the very innovation of consciousness raising raised. In other words, the strength of the method is also its point of greatest potential weakness. Similarly, although it is a strength of new publishing techniques that a lone individual can express herself relatively easily to a large audience, the very ease may loosen standards of accountability to others and perpetuate the illusion that one woman's problems with sexism are only personal. This is a danger that is reinscribed by descriptions like the following: "Some zines have a political nature, focusing on feminist issues, such as race, gender and class. Some are strictly personal, with revelations about self-esteem, relationships, growth, and pain." (Green and Taormino 1997, xii) Instead, these editors might have emphasized the connections between the personal and the political in the zines they have compiled.

Still, many young feminists show a sophisticated understanding of the need to balance the personal with the political. Barb Howe critiques traditional objectivity and explicitly defends the personal slant of her blog. "I shouldn't feel guilty about not forcing myself into a style that's not my own and that in some sense is a very masculine style anyway, one that's based on certain assumptions about the nature of knowledge," she claims. Howe clearly appreciates the feminist understanding of the connections between the personal and political, adding that "I shouldn't feel badly about 'not being able to make up my mind about whether this is a political blog that should leave the personal out or a personal blog that should leave the political out' because it's neither of those." (2006)

Clearly, third-wave activism does exist but tends to focus more immediately on popular culture than on the traditionally political. In light of the genuine conflation that has occurred between the two realms, it just makes sense that much third-wave material would take cultural expressions more seriously than have past generations. In fact, handled in a way that is self-consciously connected to actual political events or values (the more directly the better) and to a critique of the consumerism that underlies the production and cooptation of cultural products of late capitalist society, there is no question but that such cultural expressions constitute genuine political activism. This is an activism, the relevance of which is especially apparent when one considers the increasing influence of cultural images on the production of social and political subjects. However, there remains an important distinction between cultural images, real as they are, and other sorts of political realities even if we may not always easily be able to tell the difference. It has become increasingly difficult to make traditional political gains as the political climate has grown more and more conservative and corporate, and this can make activism through cultural media much more appealing than traditional activism. But cultural engagement, no matter how closely it is tied to "real life" events, is no substitute for more traditional forms of political change. The critique and creation of new images, images that encourage the development of progressive social subjects, is vital but, by itself, incomplete. To appreciate this point, we need only remember that in an extremely oppressive society such images would never even find their way to an audience.

A failure to appreciate the significance of basic civil liberties may be a consequence of what younger feminists have been able to take for granted in the political background. Older feminists had to create the political framework and consciousness that argued for such mundane things as women's equality in education and the workforce. Younger feminists, whatever the material reality, came of age in a social and political milieu that, at least at a rhetorical level, assumed such equality. Increased awareness of the genuine inequities in the material reality and of such crisis issues as the lack of abortion practitioners may challenge the assumption that cultural engagement is "political enough" to replace traditional forms of resistance.

Thus, I agree with the quote with which I began this chapter. It is true that "the activism that most engages the question of representation will be definitive," but "representation" should be taken in more of its senses than that author intends. It is right and appropriate that feminists of all ages be concerned with media representations, especially as they are implicated in racism, sexism, heterosexism, and the overthrow of these injustices. The third-wave focus on this material should be a lesson for older feminists who may have been ignoring it. It no longer makes sense, if it ever did, to say, "It's just a TV show." Still, we must continue to be concerned about traditional political change, too, which will involve supporting women and men who will express these progressive values in courtrooms, council halls, and congress as well as coming up with some creative new ways to make real change. After all, the kind of freedom we are fighting for is not just a freedom of imagination, a freedom to dream of the kind of identities we want to develop. It is a freedom to become those people, imaginatively *and* materially.

Notes

1. Zines range "anywhere from Xeroxed handwritten rants and cut-and-paste collages to professional design and offset printing" according to Karen Green and Tristan Taormino, p. xi.

2. Boehlert (2005) and Kurtz (2005) describe two such cases in which the Bush administration paid journalists.

3. I am referring to the sort of music one finds in the "folk" category at music stores, for example, Chris Williamson, Holly Near, and Meg Christian, much of which sounds like an extension of cultural feminism's celebration of things feminine and female.

4. I am using "transvaluation" in a Nietzschean sense, as a strategy that he sometimes describes as the "noble mode of valuation" that "acts and grows spontaneously" and "seeks its opposite only so as to affirm itself more gratefully and triumphantly." (Nietzsche, 37)

Bibliography

Bartky, Sandra Lee. "Foucault, Femininity, and the Modernization of Patriarchal Power." In *The Politics of Women's Bodies*, edited by Rose Weitz, 25–45. New York: Oxford University Press, 1998.

Boehlert, Eric. "Third Columnist Caught with Hand in the Bush Till." *Salon*, January 25, 2005. www.salon.com/news/feature/2005/01/27/mcmanus/index_np.html.

Brunsdon, Charlotte, Julie D'Acci, and Lynn Spigel, eds. *Feminist Television Criticism: A Reader*. Oxford: Clarendon Press, 1997.

DiFranco, Ani. "The Story." *Ani DiFranco (The First Album)*. Righteous Babe Music, 1992.

———. "Little Plastic Castle." *Little Plastic Castle*. Righteous Babe Music, 1998.

Dow, Bonnie J. *Prime-Time Feminism: Television, Media Culture, and the Women's Movement Since 1970*. Philadelphia: University of Pennsylvania Press, 1996.

Fanon, Frantz. *The Wretched of the Earth*. New York: Grove Press, 1963.

Green, Karen, and Tristan Taormino, eds. *A Girl's Guide to Taking Over the World: Writings from the Girl Zine Revolution*. New York: St. Martin's Griffin, 1997.

Heywood, Leslie, and Jennifer Drake, eds. *Third Wave Agenda: Being Feminist, Doing Feminism*. Minneapolis: University of Minnesota Press, 1997.

hooks, bell. *Yearning: Race, Gender, and Cultural Politics*. Boston: South End Press, 1990.

Howe, Barb. "Feminist Blogs and Storytelling." *Lucky White Girl*, January 6, 2006. http://barbhowe.typepad.com/lucky/2006/01/feminist_blogs_.html.

Hutchings, David. Where the Defense Rests. *InStyle*, June 1999, 282–287.

James, Joy. *Transcending the Talented Tenth: Black Leaders and American Intellectuals*. New York: Routledge, 1997.

Klein, Melissa. "Interview Grrrl Style: Kathleen Hanna of Bikini Kill." *Off Our Backs* 23, no. 2 (February 1993): 6–12.

———. "Duality and Redefinition: Young Feminism and the Alternative Music Community." In *Third Wave Agenda: Being Feminist, Doing Feminism*, edited by Leslie Heywood and Jennifer Drake. Minneapolis: University of Minnesota Press, 1997.

Kurtz, Howard. "Administration Paid Commentator." *Washington Post*, January 8, 2005, A01.

Le Tigre. "Dykemarch 2001." *Remix*. Mr. Lady Records, 2002.

Lovechild. "Why I Play with My Cunt." In *A Girl's Guide to Taking Over the World: Writings from the Girl Zine Revolution*, edited by Karen Green and Tristan Taormino, 96–96. New York: St. Martin's Griffin, 1997.

Modleski, Tania. "The Search for Tomorrow in Today's Soap Operas: Notes on a Feminine Narrative Form." In *Feminist Television Criticism: A Reader*, edited by Charlotte Brunsdon, Julie D'Acci, and Lynn Spigel, 36–47. Oxford: Clarendon Press, 1997.

Nietzsche, Friedrich. *On the Genealogy of Morals and Ecce Homo*, edited and translated by Walter Kaufmann. New York: Random House, Inc., 1967.

Pollitt, Katha. "Madam President, Madam President." *The Nation*, November 14, 2005, 10.

Reed, Jennifer. "Roseanne: A 'Killer Bitch' for Generation X." In *Third Wave Agenda: Being Feminist, Doing Feminism*, edited by Leslie Heywood and Jennifer Drake, 122–133. Minneapolis: University of Minnesota Press, 1997.

Saraco, Margaret R. "Where Feminism Rocks." *On the Issues*, Spring 1996, 26.

Scanlon, Jennifer. "Material, Girls: Women and Popular Culture in the Twentieth Century." *Radical History Review* 66 (1996): 172–177.

Tribe 8. "Frat Pig." Fist City. *Alternative Tentacles Records*, 1995.

VE. "Hacking Barbie with the Barbie Liberation Organization." *Brillo* (electronic zine), 1997.

~

CHAPTER SEVEN

My Once and Future Self

Marlene Benjamin

Twenty years ago, I began graduate work at Brandeis University. These were my daily habits: I would start with five cups of coffee before my first morning class; take a couple of diet pills throughout the day; smoke—more or less—two packs of cigarettes; have donuts for breakfast, at least one Mars Bar at lunch, and a meat-and-potatoes supper, no veggies. At registration, I had tested positive for TB and was put on a year-long course of medication and bimonthly check-ups. I objected to all exercise, on the grounds that it would use up precious study-time, and was not in the least troubled that my heartbeats were unusually fast, even when at rest. At one of my regular check-ins with the university physician, my intransigence, or stupidity, finally got to him. "No," I had never meditated, as he had suggested. "Yes," I had tried yoga, but it was "too slow." Failing to make his point by the weight of repetition, in barely concealed exasperation, he fell back on a rhetorical question. "Don't you know that your body is a temple?" he asked. "Maybe," I said, "but I worship elsewhere."

Sometimes a cigar *is* just a cigar. The body, however, is never *just* a body. The body is material and real, and yet is also constructed in discourse that is always socially and politically located in time and space. In such discourse, the body is both tied to, and separate from, the self.[1]

Because I *felt* fine, none of the scientific reports about my body—not the clinical news that my lungs showed serious scars; not the gathering public evidence that what I put into my body did, in fact, have an influence on my future health—carried any meaning for me. Like most people my age, lucky in the graces of youth, I had never paid any deep or careful *attention* to my body. Mostly, it *worked*; what more did I need to know?

This chapter is about a future self—*my* future self—shaped by catastrophic illness. In equal measure, it's a chapter about language and experience, their connections and confusions, and about my search to find a language adequate to the task of accurately *describing* my future self as it has been shaped by both the presence *and* the prospect of catastrophic illness. In parts of this chapter, I try to *do* what I *talk* about doing in other parts. It's a "show-and-tell" sort of project, a "stop-and-start" project, and I have imagined several audiences: professional philosophers, of course; literary critics of certain inclinations; novelists. But most important, people *without* their professional hats on: just people going about their daily lives faced with questions about living and dying, and doing it in everyday, *common* language.

More on this later, but it's important to say up front that until cancer barreled its way into my life, I did all my scholarship in the traditions of Anglo-American analytic philosophy.[2] Neither philosophy nor I were up to the tasks cancer set. Thus, one of the central questions in my life became: "What were the inadequacies—in the discipline and in myself—that were at fault?" This project doesn't do what professional philosophers, or literary critics, or novelists, *do* when they are practicing their professions in accepted, traditional ways.[3]

This has meaning for the content of what I explore, because form and content are not accidentally connected. But so much for prologue. Back to my body.

Mostly, my body *worked*; what more did I need to know? Using my body to carry out my daily activities, not having any subjectively recognized signs of body inadequacy to the tasks I set myself, clinical reports were literally beyond my ken. I could make no subjective sense of them. The absence of fit between subjective and objective senses of the body has an ancient history. Language itself is complicit in the divide. As soon as I begin to think, or speak, about my body, I am thrown back upon a language of parts: body parts related to, but distinct from, each other; all body parts related to, yet somehow distinct from, my "self;" the two words "my" and "self" already in revolt from the single word "myself"—something that *is* me; something that is also *mine*. It is impossible to entirely ignore such quirks of language, which are, in any event, used both in, and outside of, philosophy's investigations.

But where to start? Assume, for the sake of brevity, and perhaps even sanity, that the "chicken/egg" "language/object of language" question is not, or is not primarily, at issue. Assume only that we are trying to get some generally useful idea of the distinction and relation between "my body" and "my/self," between objective and subjective, between parts and whole. Then, as Iris Marion Young points out, it will be helpful to remember that

> The unique contribution of . . . certain . . . existential phenomenologists to the Western philosophical tradition has consisted in locating consciousness and subjectivity *in* the body itself. This move to situate subjectivity *in* the lived body jeopardizes dualistic metaphysics altogether. There remains no basis for preserving the mutual exclusivity of the categories subject and object, inner and outer, I and world.[4]

This move, however, is not entirely successful, in large part because "antidualist philosophers still tend to operate with a dualist language, this time distinguishing two forms of experiencing the body itself, as subject and as object."[5]

I know something about this, both as subject and object, and as antidualist philosopher bound by dualistic paradigms in the very framework of Western philosophy. The diagnosis and subsequent treatment of TB should have been an early introduction to the issues. It wasn't. It took the diagnosis and treatment of cancer to finally get my attention. And even then, it was difficult to concentrate. Experience, and the language available for its expression, were a source of constant confusion.

Why should this be so? Obviously, much has to do with the prospect of death. In my case, a lack of clarity about this prospect constantly undid my best efforts at understanding. Unlike some women with breast cancer, in my case, my doctors said, the prospect of death was not high on the probability charts. This has to do with statistics. Women with early stage breast cancer and noninvolved lymph nodes are in "the best possible statistical profile."

Statistics persuade people. In certain moods, from certain vantage points, they persuade me. Or rather, some part of my self is persuaded. Call this the "objective" self, who allies herself with her doctors and acknowledges empirical data as possessing some sort of predictive power. In this mood, with this angle of vision, it was enough to repeat to myself the litany of empiricism and scientific method I learned from my doctors: "There is a very strong likelihood that the lumpectomy and the radiation were curative; but if these procedures have missed some free-floating sub-microscopic cells, the systemic hormone therapy will likely do the trick." This is as far as my doctors would go. The objective self was satisfied.

But there was another self in all of this, a self who took no comfort from the data. This self resonated to a fact that the objective self was not much troubled by: According to current medical research, my doctors could not, and still cannot, say that I won't confound the data; that I won't number among the small percentage of women who, even while being in the best statistical profile, will nevertheless suffer a recurrence of the disease.

Call this the "subjective self," who lives her life from the inside, for whom "the best possible statistical profile" means nothing, an incomprehensible phrase in an impenetrable foreign language. In this mood, with this angle of vision, the litany of empiricism and scientific method fails completely to account for the larger metaphysical question that asks how to reconcile—for my self that is (somehow) *not* split, but whole—the objective and subjective perspectives on the experience of cancer.

I wanted to shatter time and resurrect another, synergistic self. Waiting for the anesthetic to take hold, astonished and still in a room full of green-cottoned doctors, reconciliation of perspectives wasn't a problem. Fear and surprise wonderfully concentrated my mind. I wanted, I still want, that clarity again. Without the fear or the surprise, I want to be that woman again.

But you see how language itself is problematic. Even so, common sense definitions do well enough. "Objective" means "seen from the outside," an overview not limited to the viewpoint of any one person, but necessarily inclusive of many (perhaps all?) individual viewpoints or experiences. Thomas Nagel called this "the view from nowhere,"[6] a view, as some have pointed out, that is, paradoxically, "both 'here' and 'now.'"[7] The *presence and pressure* of the present time and place cannot be ignored. Thus, I take Nagel's "subjective" counterpart (to his "objective-seen-from-the-outside" language) like this: "subjective" means "seen from the inside," from the vantage point of one individual person, though not necessarily exclusive of objective perspectives, since these may be part of any given subjective point of view.[8]

Some, like Anthony Kenny, warn that there is a kind of "mental vertigo which all this is likely to induce in the reader."[9] For me, the mental vertigo went further than mere dizziness; I felt positively schizophrenic from unrelenting exposure—both *in* my mind and *in* my body—to the so-called "mind-body problem." The most well-known philosophical progenitor of this schizophrenic response and position is Descartes. From the moment of diagnosis, through surgery and radiation; through hormonal therapy, infections, and treatments; I could not get away from Cartesian dualism and its metaphysically monstrous demands upon my reason. Riddled with logical conundrums, Descartes' epistemological project is nevertheless inescapably seductive. It is also a project well suited to medical scenarios of various sorts.[10] Medical statistics were confusing enough in the face of *existing* catastrophic illness and its *curative* surgeries and treatments. In the face of *probable* catastrophic illness and its *prophylactic* surgeries and treatments, medical statistics are crazy making.

By the time I went in for my second, and then my third, major cancer-related surgeries, my body had been well and truly partitioned by the medical profession and its Cartesian language, and by my easy acceptance of that language.

There is a reason for this: The Cartesian split-self arises *out of* our lived experience. In *The Absent Body*, Drew Leder does a wonderful job explaining how this happens. His explanation is part of a project aimed at both breaking the "conceptual hegemony" of Cartesian dualism "while simultaneously reclaiming its experiential truths."[11] "*Absence* . . . refers to all the ways in which the body can be away from itself. One manner is simply through disappearing from self-awareness,"[12] of which focal, background, and depth disappearance are three subcategories. This sort of absence occurs when the body parts at issue disappear from our cognitive radar, as it were, because they are functioning *properly*.

There is another sort of absence: the body in dysfunctional modes, when some body part or ability *fails*, through illness, disease, or accident, to meet its assigned responsibilities in the otherwise finely tuned workings of the whole organism. This kind of absence, in which the body is dysfunctional in some way, is difficult enough to grasp in cases of *curative* surgery because the technologically advanced state of our medical professions leads us, foolishly, to doubt our mortality. But the question of dysfunction in relation to *prophylactic* surgery is even more difficult to grasp, because medicine is telling us that no part of our body is *at present* failing, but if we wait, and perhaps not too long, some part will almost certainly dysfunction in a most spectacular way. In such cases, the dualism of *having* a body and *being* a body are confounded in the extreme.

In such cases, it becomes a question of avoidable contamination of parts. This is what Leder means when he talks about the Cartesian split-self arising *out of* our lived experiences. This is why he says it makes sense to think in Cartesian terms, to use the mechanical language of pieces and parts. It's hard to resist such thinking when *the body itself* offers us our own experiences in often discreet pieces and parts.

But the logic of Cartesianism comes at the price of split-self confusions. Leder has some suggestions about how to overcome the damaging dualisms of Cartesian thought. Remember that the body is an object *in* the world and that "the body-*as*-experiencer" is also the medium through which our world comes into being.[13] It is worthwhile quoting Leder at length here. As he reminds us,

> In articulating this dual perspective, philosophers have often utilized the distinction within the German language between *Korper* (physical body), and *Leib* (living [or lived] body). Cartesianism tends to entrap the human body in the image of *Korper*, treating it as one instance of the general class of physical things. Yet the body understood as *Leib* . . . provides a potential mode of escape from cognitive habits of dualism deeply entrenched in our culture. Insofar as the body is restricted to its causal-physicalistic description, those aspects of self involving cognition and intentionality are commonly relegated to a substance called "mind." This division of labor between *res extensa* and *res cogitans*, between the scientific and the humanistic domains, is the very basis of Cartesian ontology. Yet this is precisely what the concept of the lived body subverts. If the body as lived structure is a locus of experience, then one need not ascribe this capability to a decorporealized mind. The self is viewed as an integrated being.[14]

This is what I am after: an integrated sense of self. But Cartesian dualism is so embedded in the Western psyche, in my psyche, that I have not been able to overcome its schizophrenic temptations. Leder suggests that a *broad* concept of the lived body can protect against these temptations and their consequent confusions. He locates this broadened concept with "the embodied self that lives and breathes, perceives and acts, speaks and reasons."[15] This is, *by definition*, an integrated self, inclusive of all aspects of both *Korper*, and *Leib*. "These are not two different bodies. *Korper* is itself an aspect of *Leib*, one manner in which the lived body shows itself."[16]

This incorporation of both concepts is important, because the temptations of dualism are profoundly insistent, and Leder wants to avoid any further dualistic traps lying in wait for those who rely too heavily on the distinction between *Korper* and *Leib*. I am sympathetic to Leder's concerns; I know from experience how easily such dualisms arise, and how damaging they are to the sense of an integrated self. I have long been trying to speak *from* the lived body, from the body that is both *Korper* and *Leib*, rather than *about* the lived body. More importantly, I have been trying to speak *from* my lived, and living, body.

But the language of analytic philosophy doesn't give me a way to speak *from* an integrated self. Language and experience are mutually informing. This is true of any language, but particularly significant in the language of analytic philosophy. This is because the dualism of language reflective of our lived experience is heightened in the discourse of analytic philosophy, in which Cartesian rationality is valued above embodied experience. Such valuing deprives me of language adequate to the task of expressing body-knowledge because body-knowledge is *by definition* suspect in Cartesian understanding. Recall that *dis*-appearance is one form of absence, one way in which the body can be away from itself. It is not accidental that analytic philosophy—with its emphasis on the *dis*-passionate—compromises, if not actually prevents, having the experience of an integrated self.[17] Even when analytic philosophy uses what it calls the "essential indexical" and speaks about those instances when the indexical "I" is indispensable to analysis, its appropriation of the first-person indexical "I" is a "place-holder" in a dispassionate linguistic statement, as in "I am in pain."[18]

For this reason, another sort of language is necessary, a language that, even as it may also suffer from the dualisms inherent in Western thinking, nevertheless values body-knowledge *and* emotional knowledge, as analytic philosophy does not. Martha Nussbaum often explores these issues. She would have us remember that "certain truths about human life can only be fittingly and accurately stated in the language and forms characteristic of the narrative artist."[19] But, as she notes, the "predominant tendency in Anglo-American philosophy has been either to ignore the relation between form and content altogether, or, when not ignoring it, to . . . [treat] style as largely decorative—as irrelevant to the stating of content, and neutral among the contents that must be conveyed."[20] Like Nussbaum, I don't want to *dismiss* Western philosophical traditions of inquiry and *replace* them with the works of literature.[21] However, the style and form of drama and narrative offer structural invitations to *enter into* the lived experience of characters and narrator in ways not offered even by the "essential indexical" of analytic philosophy.[22]

The raw and messy immediacy of narrative, tragedy, and drama—in their lush, sensuous, details—evoke both passional *and* intellectual responses, and deliver us up to the power of experience, which is *itself*, as Nussbaum argues, a form of knowledge.[23]

Interestingly, the language of the courts also fails. Not even the language of the courts captures the "essential indexical 'I.'"[24] As Alan Hyde points out in *Bodies of Law*, legal language is remarkable in its profoundly cold constructions of body experiences.[25] In fact, reading Hyde, it is striking how legal language is very like the language of analytic philosophy: a language of Cartesian pieces and parts.[26] In law's discourse, the body is always fragmented.[27]

As in Cartesian discourse—philosophical, legal, or medical—I was fragmented for a long time. It made me hysterical. Hysteria, no longer listed as a disease, remains built into our social language about sex and gender.[28] Even when young, this language told me that *something* was "wrong" with my body.

Only recently have I come to know that this "wrongness" kept me always *away* from my body, and featured large in my hysterics. Maybe I've always been hysterical. Maybe part of why I took up philosophy was because I wanted to leave hysteria behind; to be cool, calm, and rational.[29]

But it didn't work that way, at least not for me. This is how it was: "Philosophy begins in wonder" was, for me, the truly subversive Platonic come-on; that, and the system's disembodied comforts. Wonder, and bodily deceptions, have never been in short supply for me; Plato's seductions were irresistible. It took me years to realize that philosophy probably ends in wonder, too.

Of course, it takes two to tango, and perhaps I was more susceptible to the more corrupting aspects of its charms. To those of a certain feverish disposition, philosophy offers a particular sort of intellectual adventure, a kind of high and inspirited eroticism that Plato attaches to the ascent up the dialectical ladder. Like Thrasymachus, whose coltish spirits require the patient, purposeful training of Socratic inquiry, we need reigning in. Perhaps my disposition was not just spirited, but "hysterical." Anyway, there was a *physical* heat to it all. It's what philosophy used to *feel* like. But I worked hard, and reigned in that heated feeling. Hard work pays. But sometimes, it pays in ways not imagined.

This is how it has been with philosophy and me. That kind of inspirited eroticism that Plato attaches to the ascent up the dialectical ladder came back; doing philosophy feels as it once did. Or rather the same, but also different, because now I'm older, and things have happened. Ten years ago, breast cancer beat me up pretty good. Eight years ago, and then eighteen months ago, prophylactic surgery for ovarian, and then uterine, cancer beat me up even more. In between, and since, my mother, and friends, and colleagues, dying and dead.

Philosophy seduces again, but it no longer corrupts: Like falling in love the second time around, I feel less spiteful about philosophy's betrayals. Also, I know more about its inadequacies, and that—as with the frailties of a beloved—makes me more generous. Generosity like this, however, isn't easily had, especially when your own body and future prospects mix it up with medical statistics based on Cartesian metaphysics. Ovarian cancer, particularly in *prospect*, is a perfect precipitating event example of what it means to fall out of love with philosophy, and then be seduced again.

In a terrible California heat wave, in 1990—twenty-one years after her sister, my favorite aunt, died young of ovarian cancer—my mother was diagnosed with the same disease. This was very hard on Mom. My recent breast cancer had made fresh again her own mother's death from breast cancer and complications of a bloody mastectomy at the age of thirty-eight; and the deaths of *her* two favorite aunts, also gone young, from breast cancer.[30] This, it turns out, is a history worth noting.[31]

The history is worth noting, but ovarian cancer is different from breast cancer in several ways.[32] Ovarian cancer remains hidden deep inside the body, protected from exposure by the very depth of its origins, and by the absence of diagnostic tools comparable in effectiveness to that of mammography. Recall Leder's explication of Cartesian categories, themselves a direct response to the body's lived experiences: This is an instance of both depth disappearance and depth dysfunction, in which internal organs disappear when functioning properly, and "appear" to the body and the experiencing self when dysfunction brings them forward to our conscious attention.[33] By the time symptoms of ovarian cancer are suspected for what they really are, the disease has usually metastasized beyond the ovaries.[34]

Mom's ovarian cancer was diagnosed at Stage III. This is very bad, but at least, her surgeon told my sister Mal and me when he came out of surgery, it wasn't Stage IV; at least it hadn't metastasized to her liver. The cancer was like salt granules, liberally poured over Mom's pelvic and abdominal cavities. When Mom was forty-something, her uterus was removed.[35] Now, the surgeon removed her ovaries and fallopian tubes, and her stomach lining and appendix, and as many of the granules as he could see. Prognosis in such cases is eighteen months.

The analogy and prognosis took about ten minutes in the telling. He shuffled his feet. Because history mattered. Now, he said, he understood our genetic tree. As if still in the O.R., with quick, efficient strokes of language, he said that *both* of us "*absolutely*" had to have total hysterectomies with bilateral salpingo-oopherectomies." We must have looked stupid, so he broke it down into language, he seemed sure, we could understand: "You must clean yourselves out." Also: "Don't wait too long; it's wise to move quickly." Here, he stared at me for a moment, and left.

We called our brothers with the news, and went for pastry, since the comforts of philosophy were nowhere to be found. Two months later, Mal gave herself up to the technical wizardry of Mom's famous gynecological surgeon. I resisted everything. It took eight different doctors, all telling me to "clean myself out, and fast" to wear me down. This was obscene; I wasn't dirty. I did my own research; relevant literature was actually inconclusive and variously disputed. No one listened, until I literally *did* go flaming, spectacularly hysterical, barging into my oncologist's office with what I knew. He promised to do more research. Two days later he called and agreed that, given my youth and the nature of the competing risks in different surgeries and after-care, I *wasn't* being irrational in arguing to keep my uterus, at least for now, not irrational in arguing for hormone replacement therapy. He would speak with my surgeon.

Where were the comforts of philosophy when I needed them? I had been in love with philosophy, and breast cancer put me wise to my lover's flaws, and so I fell out of love. And then, I came back. But ovarian cancer, present *and* in prospect, slapped me around again, as if to say: "OK, here's another chance to get it right, to avoid the Cartesian dualisms so damaging to the sense of an integrated self. Don't mess up."

So I tried, as Leder advises, to see that there "are not two different bodies. *Korper* is itself an aspect of *Leib*, one manner in which the lived body shows itself."[36]

This isn't ever easy, but I had a head start. Experience kept hitting me over the head, and it was beginning to get through to me: *experience matters*.[37] And this is where I think biology comes in. Consider Leder when he notes that it is "only adult males in the middle years who experience health as an unchanging state. From this standpoint any noticeable changes do indeed signal disruption and dysfunction. However, for the young and the aged, for adult women as opposed to men, normal body functioning includes regular and even extreme bodily shifts."[38] Things can, and usually do, just *happen* to women because of their biology; and things can, and often do, *go wrong* for women simply *because* of their biology. These ongoing body experiences can, and often do, make women more conscious of issues of embodiment. But men, simply because of *their* biology, generally have less experience with bodily *disappearances* because they *generally* have (once having grown past adolescence and into old or late-middle age) less experiences with bodily *dysfunctions*. For it is *dysfunction* that gets our attention in the first place, and makes us aware of the other possible forms of absence.[39]

Probably, this is problematic, perhaps on certain narrowly conceived views of biology, perhaps even imbued with antifeminist possibilities.[40] But I need help getting out of a conundrum. The following points, taken together, are what constitute a significant part of the conundrum all feminists face when thinking about how to value female body experience without falling into the trap of making such experience the single, or primary, standard by which the whole of a lived life is appropriately judged. First, as I've said, I agree with Young that "The unique contribution of . . . certain . . . existential phenomenologists . . . has consisted in locating consciousness and subjectivity in the body itself . . . [which] jeopardizes dualistic metaphysics."[41] And I have, in my own lived body, been literally bloodied and irrevocably changed by the medical consequences of those metaphysics. Second, I also agree with Young that there remains a problem with the move to escape the binds of Cartesian metaphysics by situating subjectivity *in* the lived body, because "antidualist philosophers still . . . operate with a dualist language."[42] But, third, Leder's advice on how to rectify this problem, by recourse to a broad concept of *Leib*, is also problematic. Thus, given the amount and kind of exposure to bodily changes women have as compared to men, it seems hard to avoid that such exposure must have at least *some* very important influence on the way men and women view and inhabit their bodies, and the worlds in which those bodies exist.

And thus, in important, gender-specific ways, the body's violated promises, the presence of its "empty" spaces, irrevocably alter how one lives in the world. And because of the important, gender-specific connections between language and experience, the *manner* of how one thinks and speaks about these alterations influences the content of what is thought, and thus the "how" of how one lives. It is now commonplace to note that traditional, analytic philosophy (long caricatured as "male"), and personal, or literary, narrative (long dismissed as "female"), are distinct modes of inquiry, each offering their own particular lessons, each suffering from methodologically specific limitations.

Does any of this lead to a sensible position on the issues involved? I don't claim that men will always use the dispassionate descriptions available in the language of philosophy, or that women will always use the passionate/passional language available in narrative's various forms. But I *do* think that the language chosen to speak about some question will be connected to how *separate* the speaker aims to be, consciously or unconsciously, from the question raised. Methodologies and animating questions of analytic philosophy don't easily combine with the immediately pressing, and sometimes dangerously revealing, emotions of narrative. Yet combined use can lead to interesting speculations.[43]

Here is a piece of speculation about empty spaces and *my* future self gone before my time: I don't have a uterus. Among other things, a uterus is a vessel; it holds things: fetuses, future babies,[44] fibroids, cancer. I can't hold any of these things. What shall I, or should I, carry in that empty space? Can air be pumped into me, into the space of absence? Can my belly get balloon big? What would that feel like? How should I think and speak about that space? And what about a man? What would, what should, he think and feel about his own future self cut out, cut off, before its time? What about the prospect of cancer in both testicles (in both "balls" he might say, though perhaps not to me, if I am a stranger)? How does castration fit your future self? Or penile cancer? He could live without a penis, but that is something different than living without a uterus: the absence of a uterus need not erase the possibility of "normal" sex.[45] As my belly might get balloon big from pumping my empty space with air, could he then rig up some inflatable substitute organ and *feel* its extensive properties and activities. Does it matter? He and I have many organs in common, both ecstatic and recessive. But some, both surface and internal, belong to us only by sex, tied in various ways to reproduction, both biologically and in social construction. Now that my body has been cut up according to notions of parts and pieces, I know in a *passional way—in a way that analytic philosophy cannot fully access*—that absence matters. But some men, men I know and care for, know—seem sometimes *aiming* to know, inadequately. Some with, but most without, formal training in philosophy, they are caught in the temptations of Cartesian dualism and the protections of analytic philosophy against the pressing and dangerously revealing emotions of narrative.

Beyond speculation is an unexamined intuition: that the prospect of future selves altered by necessary *curative* surgery is equally difficult to grasp and live for both men and women. But the prospect of future selves altered by the necessity of *prophylactic* surgery is, in some ways I don't yet understand, significantly different for men and women, particularly around sex specific organs.

This is what I understand so far: *I want to find the truths that value the experiences I have*; truths expressed in language that makes real and immediate the experience of lying spread-eagled on the examining table, feet up in stirrups, radiologist swinging a camera on a stick between my lifted legs around in circles in my uterus and talking about me in the third person to his medical assistant, saying: "Look, she has a perfectly formed uterus," and measuring it off in centimeters on the screen, and paying no attention to the fact that the sheet has fallen off my belly and a real person is there; paying no attention to the fact that *I* am there. So far, analytic philosophy on its own somehow misses *me* on that table, misses the truth of my experience. The cold language of analytic philosophy often tramples on, rather than elicits, nuanced moral response. By definition and purpose, the cold language of analytic philosophy doesn't offer the power and importance of experiential truth, and thus fails to value what it felt like, and meant, to be sick at my stomach four days after the oopherectomy and hear my surgeon babbling into the phone, happy as a lark, telling me that pathology reports show that I had "perfectly healthy ovaries: no sign of cancer anywhere." I want more. I want to find truth like this, from Scott Bradfield's *History of Luminous Motion*:

> The body, I have often thought, is like a promise. You keep things in it. Those things are covert, immediate, yours. There is something lustrous about them.

They emit energy, like radium, or appliances. They can be replaced, repaired, or simply discarded. The promise of the body is very firm and intact. It's the only promise we can count on, and we can't really count on it very much.[46]

Notes

1. For a moment, as an infant perhaps, I had a self that was wholly my body, and a body that was wholly my "self." But growing up in Western culture, the distinction and division between my "body" and my "self" was early made, and, from all quarters, continuously reinforced. My body and my self—in discourse, in meaning, even in materiality—could, and often did, go separate ways.

2. I mean here the general sorts of *linguistic* analysis at the base of current Anglo-American analytic philosophy (Peter Angeles, *Dictionary of Philosophy*, New York, 1981, p. 11) and the wider range of schools which cares deeply about analysis of language and the definitions of words but emphasizes the *role* of analysis rather than that which is being analyzed. (Simon Blackburn, *The Oxford Dictionary of Philosophy*, Oxford, 1994, 14) On this view, the term "analytic philosophy" is perhaps too wide, indeed, able to accommodate any particular school of Western philosophy: say, existentialism, Marxism, hermeneutics. This definitional breadth is intentional, not only because the borders between philosophical schools are never clearly drawn (Anthony Kenny, *Oxford History of Western Philosophy*, Oxford, 1994, 365–366), but also because the *role and activity* of analysis have always been central to all philosophizing. Each school has "simply" put forward its own set of terms as those most important to the philosophizing project. For this reason, it might be better to speak about "the various technical languages and procedures of the philosophy profession," but this is, while more accurate, too cumbersome. Thus I rely on "analytic philosophy" as a stand-in for this more complicated explanation.

3. One of the problems in holding the interests of such varied audiences, professional and nonprofessional alike, is itself a philosophical puzzle. I think there is a kind of language that can encompass and make accessible to all audiences the issues at stake. I haven't mastered it yet; this chapter is part of a continuing effort at making the words fit the meaning. It is, again, a question about audience, about form-and-content. As I said, I want to keep all of my imagined audiences, and if philosophy's *instrumentality* (not to mention its inherent value) is worth anything, it ought to be able to communicate its insights into living and dying to as wide a population as possible. This doesn't mean that philosophy ought to become anything other than what it is. You have the right to wonder why, at a conference of and for philosophers, I bother to imagine interested, nonprofessional, philosophically minded listeners. The brief answer is that I believe philosophy—particularly moral philosophy, the kind I do for a living—is both inherently *and* instrumentally valuable, but that we professional philosophers—oddly enough—often forget one of its most important, if not central, instrumental uses: its explicit aim at helping us discover what is, and how to live, the "good life." Because the human good life is clearly more various than that

lived in the philosophy profession, it seems—as I get older—more than mere myopic vision to limit philosophical investigations to the technical language of the profession, but actually to do positive harm to the philosophic enterprise when our professional projects, and we as individuals, could benefit by more regular intellectual exchange with those whose experience and language are outside our more formal modes of communication. This issue is itself part of the larger project of which today's remarks are constitutive. I welcome help sorting out the "where" and the "why" of certain boundaries. My prologue is less a set of caveats about, and more a petition for, that necessary help.

4. Iris Marion Young, "Pregnant Embodiment," in *Body and Flesh*, ed. Donn Welton (Oxford, 1998), 275.

5. Ibid.

6. Thomas Nagel, *The View from Nowhere* (New York and Oxford, 1986).

7. Stephen Darwell, review of *The View from Nowhere*, *Ethics* (October 1987): 137.

8. Nagel, "Mind and Body" and "The Objective Self," in *The View from Nowhere*, especially pages 32–42 and 60–64.

9. See Anthony Kenny, "The Self" (The Aquinas Lecture, Milwaukee, 1988) 19–20. Kenny lets Nagel speak for those "very intelligent and sophisticated philosophers of our own day" who know the flaws of Cartesian rationalism and British empiricism, but nevertheless make the same mistakes (p. 17).

10. See, for example, Roy Porter, *The Greatest Benefit to Mankind* (New York and London, 1997), 217–219 and 226–228. Porter tells the story of how Harvey's circulation system found favor with the "new philosophers" who promoted "mechanical philosophy, chief among them Descartes and Hobbes, and who viewed the body as a machine, with parts that became fatigued, worn down, and were sometimes replaceable." See also notes on works by Drew Leder and Alan Hyde, below.

11. Drew Leder, *The Absent Body* (Chicago, 1990), 3.

12. Ibid., 26.

13. Ibid., 5.

14. Ibid., 5.

15. Ibid., 6

16. Ibid., 6

17. The technical language of analytic philosophy, which in some cases cannot be sharply distinguished from even the formal, mathematical language of linguistic philosophy is far more constrained and constraining in the expression of our lived experiences than other forms of language. Angeles, *Dictionary of Philosophy*, 11.

18. John Perry, "The Problem of the Essential Indexical," *NOUS* 13 (1979): 3–21. Here is Perry's own abstract of his paper: "Beliefs about where we are, who we are, and what time it is, seem to be essentially indexical; we cannot express them by following the words 'I believe that' with *context insensitive sentences* [my emphasis]. I argue that traditional theories of belief cannot account for this fact, and that to do so we must make a sharp distinction between belief-states and objects of belief, and

realize that there is not a one-to-one correspondence between them." I have no quarrel with this, except for the important fact of Perry's choice of language to talk about the essential indexical, which, I believe, addresses only one part of human knowing—the intellectual—and thus effectively undercuts the context-sensitive descriptions that he argues are part and parcel of the use of the essential indexical "I." Such language is itself an example of how traditional analytic philosophy carves up the self into Cartesian pieces and values only the traditionally recognized "thinking" aspects, not the passionate ways of knowing. Even the first-person experience with which Perry begins his essay—following a sugar trail in a supermarket not realizing that his own cart is the culprit—lacks the heat of *felt* experience, as if the dominant form of language (analytic philosophy) dictated the sorts of experience available as illustration of the claims being made. It is impossible for me, the reader of such a claim, *to enter into* the lived world of the indexical "I" who speaks, except to engage in the same sort of dispassionate "analysis," an analysis that is *away from* the passions being assigned a place in the analysis. In the absence of this possibility, whatever understanding I may have of the pain of which the indexical "I" speaks is sorely limited. As Nussbaum argues (see below), style is not neutral, and rational human understanding requires more than is available in the style and language of analytic philosophy, for lived experience is not, as analytic philosophy *of necessity* would have us believe, so radically truncated and split.

19. Martha Nussbaum, *Love's Knowledge: Essays on Philosophy and Literature* (Oxford, 1990), 5.

20. Ibid., 8.

21. Ibid., 27.

22. Interestingly, even Nussbaum's use of the indexical "I" in "Love and the Individual" (in *Love's Knowledge*), as is her use in *Therapy of Desire* (Princeton, 1994), is essentially of the analytically philosophical form. In *Therapy*, we have a fictional character thinking and feeling her way through various philosophies in an attempt to see which one is most medicinally useful for treating certain illnesses, or problems, of human living, with Nussbaum as author "documenting" and examining the character's search. This sort of conceit keeps the author *separate* from the experiences being documented. *Therapy* pretends nothing other; that is, it is a piece of analytic philosophy doing analytic philosophy's job. But in "Love and The Individual," we have a "literary conceit" of a narrator *and* Nussbaum herself as author. This conceit posits both an author and someone very like the author whose experiences provoke the philosophical reflections of the author (Nussbaum). But why not just *speak* in the first person indexical with no recourse to an imagined character; why rely on an imagined other teacher with the interests of Nussbaum (and even some of her experiences)? Why not just *do* philosophy in the first person? Is an attempt closer to the storytelling of first-person narrative found in both fictional and real-life accounts of experience? However, the very conceit relied upon, of a character similar to the author, juxtaposed with the analysis of philosophy, maintains a barrier between Nussbaum and the experiences she reports.

23. Martha Nussbaum, *The Fragility of Goodness: Luck and Ethics in Greek Tragedy and Philosophy* (Cambridge, 1986), 45.

24. See John Perry, "The Problem of the Essential Indexical."

25. Alan Hyde, *Bodies of Law* (Princeton, 1997), passim.

26. Though Hyde doesn't, to my memory, use the term "*analytic* philosophy," he does talk about the connections between the languages of law and philosophy, and gives a fascinating example of the way in which the law, in appropriating the Cartesian language of philosophy, constructs—in discourse about privacy and related subjects—the "legal penis" and the "legal breast," both of which are oddly separate from the actual persons whose "privacy interests" are being discussed. And, of course, the difference in sex matters. See Hyde, *Bodies of Law,* chapters 9 and 10.

27. What can help undo such fragmentation, help reintegrate the self? Narrative, tragedy, and drama offer an invitation to break down barriers *built into* Cartesianism's dualistic conception of the self. This explicit invitation to *enter into* the lived experience of another is one of the hallmarks of drama and narrative. It is not always successful. However, when the narrative does not restrict the lived experience to the narrowly conceived notion of subjective, but also includes—as my earlier definition suggested—a conception of objective perspectives (often simultaneously held within any given subjective point of view), the invitation to *enter into* the lived experience of another person—be that person character or narrator, real or fictional—captures the imagination of more people, is more *philosophically* instructive, than any of the temptations of Descartes' dualism. This is attested to in various ways. For example, Joan W. Scott, in "The Evidence of Experience" (*Critical Inquiry* [Summer 1991]: 773–797), talking about "the importance of 'the literary' to the historical project," points us to the way in which we all construct "parallel narratives" about our public/political and private/individual "sides," failing to recognize that both "sides" are "imbricated in one another and that both are historically variable." She wants us to realize that language and the understanding of the self are not independent and that by "contextualizing language . . . one . . . historicizes experience itself." This is important for a number of reasons, not least of which is that recognition of this fact allows us to appreciate that "if it is the split . . . that constitutes the subject, it is only after the Roman *inflation of the private into the subjective*." (pp. 794–795; my emphasis) I aim to avoid such inflation with my definitions of the "objective" and "subjective" selves. Similarly, in *The Absent Body* (p. 6), Leder describes how too heavy a reliance on the distinction between *Korper* and *Leib* results in the sorts of Cartesian dualism it is invoked to correct. The problematic dualism can arise "when we identify the lived body solely with the first-person perspective, the body lived-from-within, as opposed to the 'object body' seen from without." And Nussbaum, in *The Therapy of Desire* (pp. 486–487), raises the same sorts of issues about "objective/subjective," and "public/private" categories.

28. Two very different, but equally excellent, sources on this subject are Mark S. Micale, *Approaching Hysteria* (Princeton, 1995) and Judith Herman, M.D., *Trauma and Recovery* (New York, 1992), especially chapter 1, "A Forgotten History."

29. It took a long time for me to realize that philosophy does a decent job of keeping hysterics at bay, but forever is out of the question; philosophy can't *eradicate* hysterics, not unless one relinquishes a significant part of one's humanity, the part that reacts spontaneously, that comes *fresh* to each day's experiences. See Nussbaum, *Love's Knowledge* (especially chapter 1, "Form and Content, Philosophy and Literature"). Nussbaum also deals with these questions throughout *The Therapy of Desire*, especially chapter 10, "The Stoics on the Extirpation of the Passions."

30. Again, see Nussbaum, *The Therapy of Desire*, 486.

31. Yet not until very recently have some doctors taken notice of the importance of family history, in part because ovarian cancer fails to *show* itself in expected ways. Such failure complicates the picture. Ovarian cancer is a relatively rare disease: only about 1.4 percent of women will get it—or one in seventy—as compared to the significantly higher one in nine women who get breast cancer (or, one in seven women, depending on whose newscast is quoting which body of research). But even these statistics are misleading, because breast cancer numbers reflect the percentage of women as the population ages, but ovarian cancer statistics do not yet reflect that variable. Because of this, physicians are less likely to speculate that a woman's vague stomach complaints import anything life threatening. Why employ the big guns of cancer diagnosis—MRI, or ultra-sound, or even X-rays—for a tummy ache? The recently much-touted CA-125 blood test has a high rate of false positives, and without something like a mass (either palpable upon rectal examination or technologically imaged) susceptible to biopsy (the only *definitive* diagnostic procedure), ovarian cancer, in the vast majority of cases, escapes early detection. Also see Susan Sherwin, *No Longer Patient: Feminist Ethics and Health Care* (Philadelphia, 1992), especially chapter 9, "Ascriptions of Illness," and chapter 10, "Medical Constructions of Sexuality."

32. One of the most important differences between breast and ovarian cancer has to do with diagnosis, which significantly affects prognosis. Unlike breast cancer, which usually presents itself, even early on, as palpable lumps in the breast (most breast cancer is discovered by the woman herself), or is discovered as minute spots on mammograms, ovarian cancer is neither palpable early on nor seen early on even if the big guns of diagnosis *were* to be called in for the early minor bloating and stomach aches (see above).

33. See Leder, *The Absent Body.*

34. Metastasis spreads to the uterus or fallopian tubes; or invades the stomach wall and regional lymph nodes, with surface invasion of the abdominal cavity and its organs such as the liver and the intestine; or, in the worst case scenario, the cancer has invaded the liver and/or spread to a distant site such as the lungs.

35. This was, and is, an extremely popular operation among many gynecologists. I have heard gynecological surgeons themselves refer to hysterectomies as their "bread and butter" income.

36. Leder, *The Absent Body*, 6.

37. Exactly how it matters is, of course, the further, and essential, question. Derek Parfit's *Reasons and Persons* (Oxford, 1984) can be helpful here.

38. Leder, *The Absent Body*, 44.

39. Menstruation is a good example. Menstruation is not dysfunction. In fact, in women of ovulating age, the uterus's fluctuating and recurrent *dis*appearance demonstrates the organ's proper functioning. On the other hand, a cessation of menstruation altogether during the ovulating years, or an excessive amount or duration of bleeding during any years at all, demonstrates the organ's *dys*function.

40. In my current thinking, however, I believe that antifeminist implications and consequences arise only if the concept of "biology" is narrowly construed. (I am grateful to an audience member at the Eighth International Conference of Women Philosophers, where this chapter was first delivered, for pointing out that this area deserves more attention.) The exact shape of such a narrow construction isn't yet clear to me, except that it would probably limit the understanding of "biology" to definitions of materiality. I point here only to the fact that I am aware that some may take my claims where I do not intend them to go, and that I intend to work more on this piece of the puzzle. For example, some questions worth pursuing include these: Are we who we are, as Jean Bethke Elshtain claims, *because* of our sex? And if so, what does this mean for our participation in both public and private spheres? I worry about her conclusions because I believe her arguments are based on faulty premises, and share the same sort of preconceived notions about gender that Rousseau and Aristotle share (on whom she is easier than on Mill and Plato, explicit advocates of admitting women into the public arena on the grounds that they do possess the necessary rationality). Still, it is difficult to dismiss the insight that experience matters, that body experience is a large part of experience, even though socially constructed, and that body experience is in large part as result of biology. All of this is difficult stuff, precisely because there is a germ of truth in her claims. What happens with that "truth" in her book, however queasy it makes me, stimulates the sort of discussion all people should be having about the issues raised. See *Public Man, Private Woman* (Princeton, 1981).

41. See Iris Marion Young, "Pregnant Embodiment," in *Body and Flesh*, 275.

42. Ibid.

43. I have come to believe that that isn't necessarily a bad thing: *in* their tensions, combined use of both sorts of inquiry forces us to explore in remarkable ways some of the male and female gender-specific alterations that come with bodily promises violated, with the powerfully felt presence of "empty" spaces, and leads us to speculate about some of their moral implications and consequences from another standpoint.

44. The loss of reproductive capacities occurs in many ways. None is *necessarily* more or less important in its influence on women's thinking and/or feeling of, and about, the loss. All vary from woman to woman, and all experiences are worthy of attention.

45. This subject is another rife with language constructions and implications for how we experience our empty spaces. I simply raise the point, and leave discussion for another time.

46. Scott Bradfield, *The History of Luminous Motion* (New York, 1989).

PART II

PUTTING IDENTITY
BACK INTO POLITICS

~

CHAPTER EIGHT

Keeping Authenticity in Play— Or Being Naughty to Be Good

Morwenna Griffiths

To be authentic is to be true to oneself in how one conducts oneself. Thus authenticity—being authentic—is a serious business: a matter of high moral purpose and integrity. It is lucky for those of us who aspire to seriousness and high moral purpose, but who do not wish to be stuck with solemnity and earnestness, that the achievement (and continued reachievement) of authenticity can be found in playfulness. This is the suggestion made in this chapter.

Achieving authenticity is difficult. Finding it may be the product of some earlier pain. Indeed, difficulty and pain are often felt precisely as a result of being forced to be inauthentic: to play false by oneself; to play out a part instead of being open. At the same time, an individual can use her difficulty and pain to come to authenticity through an ability to be playful when playing false, and to take playing a part as role-play. This play is naughty, rather than innocent.

In the course of a struggle for justice, urgent questions for us women (in all our political and personal variety) are related to individual and collective changes of identity. This is equally true for groups distinguished by race, disabilities, sexuality, and so on, most of which include women. As individuals change, they are faced with questions, "Can this really still be me, after such changes in my feelings, and changes in my ways of understanding and reacting to them?" and "As I change, am I being true to myself?" The first of these questions is from a more passive position: The individual observes changes in herself. The second is from a more active one: The individual wonders about the directions of change that she has some choice about. Activist groups, organized by gender (or gender and race, or race and class, etc.), face similar questions, but with the added complication that in the process of developing a group identity that identity must change, if only in the fact that it is now possible to see it as a group with members and to act collectively. Moreover, each group member will then have individual changes to cope with, simply as a result of being part of the (changing) group.

In this chapter I explore how a nonunitary self may come to authenticity. I begin by outlining some different feminist ontologies of self in order to trace how they each relate to the idea of authenticity. Using a model of a patchwork self, I then go on to look at autobiographical narratives of change, and how the themes of continuity and connection shed light on the achievement of "authenticity." I use some suggestions from María Lugones (1989) about possible links between playfulness and the changing self to argue that playfulness, especially naughty playfulness, is helpful in coming to authenticity. I end by giving some examples using Fatima Mernissi's *Dreams of Trespass* (1994).

Method: Critical Autobiography— Using Autobiographies and Theories

I call the method I use in this chapter "critical autobiography." It draws on autobiographical narratives while maintaining a reflexive, critical distance from them. I developed this method within a larger, epistemological, methodological framework, as I explained in my book, *Educational Research for Social Justice* (Griffiths 1998). In that book I make a link between feminist approaches and methodologies for social justice. There are a number of different "feminist epistemologies," often strongly critical of each other (see, for instance, Stanley and Wise 1990). On the other hand, various common threads in the different epistemologies can be found, as I have argued in more detail elsewhere (Griffiths 1995). I distinguish three such links: the significance for (most) feminists of (1) the perspective of women, whether that is expressed in terms of "experience," the "subject," "subjectivity," or "position in a discourse;" (2) politics and/or values; and (3) theorizing and reflection undertaken in collaboration with others.

The method of critical autobiography is responsive to all three of these threads in feminist epistemologies. It is predicated on attention being paid to the voices of personal experience, the politics of whose voice gets heard (and then becomes woven into large-scale theories), and the importance of weaving personal accounts into a perspective capable of challenging coercive orthodoxies of the mainstream. The method depends on an iterative process of using two sources in conversation with each other: These two sources are autobiographical narratives and academic theories. Central to the method is the use of autobiographical material. This is chosen to include material written from a number of different political positions, for instance in relation to race, class, sexuality, nationality, religion, ethnicity, disability, and age. These are all factors that might affect the relative power of individuals to contribute to public debates and theory making. However, there is no attempt to try and listen to everyone. To attempt to do so, I argue, leads to what I have called "cultural tourism," which leaves the listener unchanged by the encounter. Thus the method entails that all knowledge gained is subject to change from as yet unheard perspectives and so is provisional: It is reliable but revisable. I say more about this in Griffiths (1998) and again in Griffiths (2003).

I have used the term "autobiography," since I am referring to the stories people tell of their own lives. However, the term autobiography needs to be used with caution, since we of the West have developed a view of autobiography as individualistic, confessional, truthful, and unframed by theories or political considerations. In his series of books on the history of sexuality, Foucault has traced the rise of the "obligation to confess," and the way that such confession is increasingly taken as a direct expression of experience, truth, and self-knowledge. All this is culturally specific, as is shown by the explicitly political Latin American testimonies, by the explicitly political and religious American slave narratives, and by life-history work with people from nonliterate cultures. Autobiographical material is represented in a wide range of genres.

Critical autobiography was not invented by me. It is not even new. Indeed, I would argue that Augustine's *Confessions* is one example of a work that uses experience to reflect and re-think, using theory, and with a clear political intent in relation to the power struggles surrounding religious and philosophical positions in the fifth century. However, he would not have liked my description of his work. Carolyn Steedman's autobiographical writing on the other hand, is explicitly used in the way I characterize as "critical autobiography." In her book, *Landscape for a Good Woman*, she uses autobiographical material (about herself, and her mother) to reflect on what she calls "the official interpretative devices of a culture" regarding both class and gender. As she puts it, the past can be "re-used through the agency of social information":

> It matters then, whether one reshapes past time, re-uses the ordinary exigencies and crises of all childhoods whilst looking down from the curtainless windows of a terraced house . . . or sees at that moment the long view stretching away from the big house in some richer and more detailed landscape. (1986, 5)

I use autobiographies, including my own, to challenge and develop theories, and so to create new knowledge. The use I make of them is critical and it is not dependent on the reasons that particular autobiographical stories were told. I am, in a way, proceeding by the well-known philosophical method of the use of example and counter-example. The argument is iterative. I begin with theorization by outlining some feminist ontologies of the self in relation to change and authenticity. I then go on to tell some of my own autobiographies of self changing over time, and to summarize three others. These then feed into the next section, in which I continue to theorize processes of change.

Feminist Ontologies of Self

Feminists are, for the most part, agreed that women's selves and identities are affected by their sex and gender, that is, by the social and cultural consequences of being female. There is serious disagreement about what those consequences are, in particular with regard to the relation between the social construction of the self and its subjectivity on the one hand, and the agency of any individual in the creation of her own gendered, racialized (and so on) identity. These are ontological disagreements at root: about what *is* being a self, a subjectivity, or female. A number of feminist theorists do not use the term "self" because of its association with humanist theory, preferring to work with notions of subjectivity and the subject. I prefer to use the term self, rather than surrender this useful term to a particular school of thought.

Three ontologies of feminist self have no problems with authenticity. Firstly, there are those who espouse a kind of essentialism: the idea that there is a real core self. In this case authenticity (finding a real self) is only to be achieved by undoing the adverse effects of conditioning on the core self. If the active core is essentially female, then, as the radical feminist Mary Daly so memorably put it, the need is to get women unwinding the shrouds of conditioning to get at the real, wild, untrammeled, lusty self underneath (Daly 1979, 1984). Or, in a more liberal mode, an essentially androgynous (human) core with individual needs and desires is what would flourish if the unfortunate effects of society were undone. Martha Nussbaum comes close to this position in Nussbaum and Glover (1995). Secondly, there are opposing ontologies that self (or more usually, "subject position") is the result of social construction, through social behavior, in some versions or, in others, through immersion in discourse. Such ontologies leave no logical space for authenticity, since there can be no "doer behind the deed"—

or sayer behind the saying. Rather an "authentic self" is seen as a damaging fiction of humanism or liberalism (Hartsock 1990). A third ontology derives from a politics of identity based on experience. This view has its origins in the politics of identity developed in early feminist struggles and in the black civil rights movements. A stress on experience as a source of political action ("the personal is political") means that there was pressure to conform to group norms. Consequently, there are moral obligations on individuals from marginalized groups to behave in accordance with their group norms. For instance, a woman can stand accused of behaving, inauthentically, like a man, or a black person of "acting white."

Against these ontologies are those that argue for a nonunitary self. It is variously conceptualized as fluid, fragmented, multiple, shifting, and border crossing. There are a number of these ontologies, often bitterly disagreeing with each other about the details. It is not always clear how much agency is included, that is, whether a particular version should be included as one of the constructivist selves (subject positions) of the previous paragraph. The discussion between Seyla Benhabib and Judith Butler is an example of how difficult it is to be clear about this, as Moya Lloyd's useful summary demonstrates (Benhabib 1995; Butler 1995; Lloyd 2005). For my purposes in this chapter, it is enough that there exist ontologies that allow both fluidity (or fragmentation) and also agency. Valerie Walkerdine warns that the discourse of humanist individualism has harmful effects because, she argues, there is no lone individual, but rather multiple subjectivities. At the same time, she suggests how "subjects created in multiple causality, shifting, at relay points of dynamic intersection" can contribute to struggles for "transformation of that sociality, those practices and of the subject-positions produced within them." (1990, 57) Similarly, Jane Flax says that "a unitary self is unnecessary, impossible, and a dangerous illusion." (1993, 93) But she also argues,

> The ability to tolerate and the will to encourage fluid and multiple forms of subjectivity are imperative and fully ethical positions. The unitary self is an effect of many kinds of relations of domination. . . . Only multiple and fluid subjects can develop a strong enough aversion to domination to struggle against its always present and endlessly seductive temptations. (pp. 109–110)

A theory of self used in this chapter is of the kind described in the previous paragraph. Briefly summarized here, it was developed in my book, *Feminisms and the Self* (Griffiths 1995). I have named it a patchwork self. It is a construction, but one that is influenced by the whole to date. A self has some influence on the deployment of patches, as it draws on previous states and builds on them. As Young says about (what she prefers to call) subjects:

> Subjects are not only conditioned by their positions in structured social relations; subjects are also agents. To be an agent means that you can take the constraints and possibilities that condition your life and make something of them in your own way. (2000, 101)

Therefore the self is neither fixed nor fragmented. Here I agree with Flax that in trying to become clearer about (what she prefers to call) subjectivity,

> our imaginations are too often imprisoned by an inability to think about subjectivity as multiplicities that are neither fixed nor fragmented. (1993, 93)

However the patchwork self differs from the subjectivity Flax describes, which struggles with its own dichotomies. Often theorists posit an apparently dichotomous choice between two ideas of subjectivity:

> Subjectivity is depicted either as a coherent entity or as formerly solid ones that have (or should) split into fragments. (1993, 93)

It can achieve "coherence or long-term stability," but it is always liable to fall into being "the instrumental, split subject" on the one hand, or, on the other hand, sliding into "the endless terror, emptiness, desolate loneliness and fear of annihilation" that pervade a subjectivity fluctuating wildly between affective states (Flax 1993, 102–103). By contrast the patchwork self is not a delicate balancing act between one (and split) or many (and incoherent) as Flax seems to suggest. Rather it is the delicate balancing act of members of a set adjusting to each other, each one with its purposes etc, and each one influencing the others. This could be a group of people or a parallel distributed processing network as described by Margaret Boden (2004, chapter 5).

The patchwork self begins with the material circumstances of particular bodies, born into a particular set of family attachments and marked by sex, race, abilities, energies, and sexual pleasures, growing up in material circumstances such as riches or poverty. These material conditions interact with social and political circumstances over lifetimes, which begin in babyhood and go through the changes of a long adulthood. Thus it is a patchwork in which new patches join, adjoin, or obscure what is already there, changing it in the process. It is never possible to throw away the whole construction and start again. Thus I argue that a socially constructed self is sewn together using fabric from political formations of gender, race, disability, social class, sexuality, and so on, but that there is more than one cloth that can be made from the patches. This patchwork self has agency and connection, which implies that there is a sense in which there is a self, persisting over a lifetime, although that self need not be the single, unitary subject of standard philosophy. It is always under construction. To summarize,

1. The self I am—the identity I have—is shaped and controlled by the politics surrounding factors such as gender, which are sites of struggle about oppression and liberation.
2. Such shaping and control are not absolute, or fixed, or deterministic. I have an influence over such forces—some agency—even though the "I" in question is to some extent a product of them.
3. This is a unified though nonunitary self, since the connections imply that there could be sense in which a (changing) self persists over a lifetime.

Stories of Selves That Change

In this section I draw on autobiography. I begin with myself and pieces of my own autobiography. These are pieces of autobiography that are told at this particular time in my life, against an understanding of my life and how incidents in it fit into the whole. The other autobiographical narratives have been chosen partly because their subjects are not full members of the (relatively more male, more rich, more white) groups that give rise to the mainstream voices of orthodox theory. They have also been chosen because they give an account of constructing a self over time, in conditions of change—changing and so reconstructing, changing in response to undergoing reconstruction. Most obviously, the choice has been theoretically informed by the arguments I develop in this chapter, arguments that are themselves informed by these narratives. This is well explained by Maggie MacLure:

> They involve a kind of retrospective search for the prospective significance of events and decisions, in which the seemingly innocent temporal relationship between past, present and future is confounded and displaced. (1996, 280)

Citing Ricoeur, she explains,

> The parts advance cumulatively, towards the whole; but the whole (that does not yet exist) tells you "in advance" how to read the parts. (1996, 280)

Migration—Morwenna Griffiths

Let me tell you where I come from. When I was a child I lived in East Africa in the country now called Tanzania. It was a colonial childhood. My father was in the British administration of the country. I was the third generation on my father's side, and the second on my mother's, to be born out of England, and to be born in a different country from my grandparents. My mother and father were born in South Africa and my paternal grandfather in India. To continue this story of migration, my paternal grandmother was from Scotland, my paternal great-grandfather from Wales. Only my mother's parents were born and raised in England, the country I have always regarded as my own—although I have a Welsh name and now call myself British. Recently I made a brief visit to East Africa. I "came home" to the sights and smells of my childhood—but I was not at home. But nor am I at home in England, at least not compared to English friends (white and black) who are inclined to argue passionately about which part of England is theirs (is this an English obsession? It is not mine!) or compared to those whose siblings, aunts, uncles and cousins are mostly in England, not, like mine, in three other continents.

This is not just a story of geography or citizenship. It is also a story of different migrant cultures and the movement from one to the other. I notice that as a small child of four of five I must have been actively working to understand the social position of my family in my world of colonial administrators, in spite of my parents' principled resistance to the enterprise. I asked my mother "Who is higher, Daddy or Mr. Clarke?" My mother, understanding very well what I meant, tried to head me off by answering in terms of physical height. I relapsed into silence, wondering why she couldn't understand such an obvious question. I wondered: Had I perhaps misphrased it? When I was ten I moved to England. Not surprisingly, I did not understand the class system very well, nor the politics it engendered. Here my parents were of limited help because they did not relate to it particularly clearly either. In fact British politics in general were not of great interest in our household. On the other hand, for me as a young teenager, South African politics had a peculiar salience. My mother expressed horror at Sharpeville and admiration of Mandela, and did so with a feeling that British politics did not arouse.

I also had to learn a new everyday culture: What was Wimbledon? What was the top ten? I pretended interest and kept my mouth shut until I gained enough knowledge to pass. Much of my own childhood culture of, for instance, turning pumice stone fragments into boats in the irrigation furrows or exploring the coffee plantations, became something peculiar to me, which bore little relation to life in England. I don't remember missing all that earlier life; it was, rather, that it became irrelevant, out of place and unspoken.

For a short time, I invented a more exotic set of stories to please my new friends, who expected Africa to be more extraordinary. Then I "became" English. It was much later that I learned to acknowledge and use this past (as I am doing now, writing this chapter).

Changing Self-understanding—Morwenna Griffiths[1]

I took a degree in physics, but I did not enjoy it very much. I found that my interests were more philosophical, and, moreover, I did not much fancy the kinds of employment open to me as a scientist. I moved into primary education, and then went back to university to study the philosophy of emotions and their relevance to education. By then I was in my early thirties, and was, for the first time, becoming increasingly involved in feminism as I came to see the relevance of emotion to how girls and women related to computer technology. I submitted a paper on the subject to the first international Girls and Science and Technology Conference.

It was the first time that I had attended a conference at which women were in the majority. At the suggestion of the facilitator, the seminar group in which I found myself began the session with introductions. Each of us was to explain why we were at the conference, and something about our personal or professional interest in the area. I was very anxious indeed. Now, I thought, I would be found out. My credentials for attending such a conference were shaky, I thought. I was not longer "in" science. I had no history of activism in feminist politics. I would be shown up as an outsider, as a charlatan, even. I was not a real scientist, a real feminist, or even a real philosopher.

There was no escape. I explained myself to the other women. I found that they were listening with interest and respect. The facilitator smiled. "A typical women's career," she said. With an intense relief I realized that I was all right. I did not need to pretend. It turned out that the other members were no more typical of my imagined ideal conference-goer than I was. I was a bit of a scientist, a bit of a feminist, and a bit of a philosopher, and that was all right.

Migration—Eva Hoffman

Eva Hoffman's lovely book, *Lost in Translation* (1991), describes her transition to "life in a new language" when she emigrated as a girl of thirteen from Poland to Canada. So happy are her memories of her Polish childhood that she entitles this section of the book "Paradise." The rest of the book traces her movement from exile to living in a new world (though this is New York, not Canada): a mode of living with which she is comfortable, but which includes her continuing ambivalence about it; about her family home in Vancouver; about Poland when she goes there; and about her own life in more

than one language. In writing a self-analytic book about her identity she includes the puzzlement of her Polish émigré friends in New York with the obsession Americans have with self-analysis and identity. Ironically, she records
that this puzzlement is also her own, is also her own minority, migrant voice.

Migration—Grace Nichols

Grace Nichols' collections of poems (1984, 1989) draw on her emigration to
England from Guyana when she was already in her late twenties. In turns
ironic and serious, and sometimes both together, she uses everyday images
with both Guyanean and British overtones (of food, supermarket trolleys,
bubble baths) to talk of (1984)

> the power to be what I am / a woman
> charting my own futures / a woman
> holding my beads in my hand

Against—or perhaps with—this comment, she talks of how (1989)

> the women in me
> slip free
> of the charmed circle
> of my moulding

Like Hoffman she is concerned with language, especially with the language—tongue—of exiles (1984):

> from the root of the old one
> a new one has sprung.

Migration—María Lugones

A piece of autobiography that I have found particularly helpful is Lugones
(1989) article about what she terms "world-traveling." Lugones writes from
her position as a Hispanic American philosopher. In this article she explores her own coming to consciousness as a daughter and as a woman of
color. As part of the exploration she introduces her concept of a world: "a
real place inhabited at present by some flesh and blood people," including
"the description and construction of life" of the people in it (1989, 281).
She analyzes what it is that makes her at ease in the different worlds she inhabits, some of them Latin American and some of them Anglo-American;

some of them female, some of them mixed sex. She notes that in some of them she is a serious person, while in others she is playful. And it is this, the personal characteristic of being playful or not, which is center-stage of her story (1989, 286):

> My problem is not one of lack of ease. I am suggesting that I can understand my confusion about whether I am or am not playful by saying that I am both and that I am different persons in different worlds and can remember myself in both as I am in the other. I am a plurality of selves.

Later in the article she describes how changing her self-understanding changed her approach to life. She claims that she lives in a Latino world. However, this world is not the world of her childhood, for the very reason that she now understands it differently. Her article chronicles how Marion Frye's article on loving perception has helped her understand her position as a woman, both object and subject of arrogant perceiving, this being something that is common to Anglo and Latino worlds. She also chronicles how she has learned not to be an arrogant perceiver, especially in relation to her mother. To this extent her world has changed. To use her own terminology she now inhabits a society given a nondominant rather than a dominant construction: she has traveled to a different world.

Common Threads

As with any personal account, my autobiography of migration is unique. At the same time, it is commonplace. Aspects of it are shared by Hoffman and Nichols. Migration across countries, societies, and continents is ordinary. For centuries Europeans and others have migrated across the world, conquering and colonizing. In the last century, poor people were encouraged to migrate to countries with fast-growing economies. They were joined by refugees from wars and cold wars. Although immigration controls have tightened, migrationary pressures of war and poverty ensure that the peoples of the world continue to move across it. Visible minorities can be seen in most Australian, European, and North American cities, many of them born in the region as a result of their parents or grandparents having migrated there. Alongside them are the less visible minorities from Australia, Europe, New Zealand, and North America. A marker of this in England, for instance, is that in many inner-city London primary schools, the English language is used alongside twenty or thirty other languages, including Polish and Greek as well as Hindi and Yoruba.

Theorizing Change in a Self

The autobiographical pieces I have described may be used to criticize, extend, and work with Lugones' theory of world-traveling, in order to gain a better understanding of a patchwork self and the possibility of authenticity. While I find her term "world"-traveling useful, I also find that her conceptualization of worlds is too narrow. She does not take account of disappearing worlds, and she focuses on real material contexts rather than on perceptions as creating a world. I shall take each one in turn, showing that the idea of world-traveling is strengthened by attending to these two points.

Lugones talks only of persisting worlds. However, my narrative was one of a disappearing world. Worlds change, and they can—and do—disappear. Sometimes they change, but do so while we, ourselves, are not inhabiting them. The autobiographical accounts speak of moving from one physical and social context to another and the adjustments of losing one and gaining another in the movement. Lugones gives an account of the Latino world as if it encompasses both her childhood in Argentina and aspects of her present life in the United States. She remains a member of both this world and of the Anglo world where she is a producer of feminist philosophy. She can move back and forth between them. In contrast to this is my own colonial childhood world, which has gone completely, living on only in memories and history books. (I would not, of course, wish it back!) Hoffman's paradisical Poland has also gone, but not completely. She describes returning to Poland, and her reaction to what it has now become: something that she still recognizes, but that is not quite the world of her childhood. Both of us describe how our lost worlds continue to affect the threads of our new worlds. We do not have the selves we had then, but neither are the selves of our new worlds unrelated to those lost ones, springing from the roots of the old.

There is another way in which Lugones' idea is too narrow. She fails to acknowledge how far the existence of worlds is dependent on perceptions as well as on material existence. Self-perceptions and perceptions of the world can alter without any other changes of history, geography, or other material circumstances. This process irrevocably changes the world that is lived in. The old world can go as completely as colonial Africa or it may remain, in some form, like the Poland of Hoffman's childhood. My account of the Girls and Science and Technology Conference shows another way in which a world could disappear. I described how I moved to perceiving myself and my world as one in which I was "a bit of a scientist, a feminist, and a philosopher," rather than "not a real scientist, feminist or philosopher."

At the same time, I adjusted my view of a career, the place of women in the world of paid employment, and my relationship to other women. All these things happened simultaneously. In terms of worlds and of world-traveling, I had moved from one world to another, keeping not only memories, but also some reactions (and skills, emotional habits, pleasures, associations) from the old one, which was now lost to me. The new one was my world, even if nothing material had changed. Moreover, this episode could be told as part of a longer story, in which I became feminist. By stages my understanding of the world changed, and so my world changed. Indeed, my world changed so much that I, like other women who had made the same journey, wondered how we had ever lived in the old one. This is part of a story that has taken place in stages, and at least partly with a sense of my own agency in how far, how fast, and in which direction I move. The same process can be seen in Lugones' account of loving perception. The world now appears to her in terms of arrogant perceiving and the old one without that perception has gone.

The autobiographies and their theorization can be understood as ways of achieving narrative continuity. At this stage I draw on an article by Maggie MacLure that uses life histories told to her that focus on the move from being a teacher to an academic. The article is itself an example of theorizing based on critical (auto)biography. Her article includes a discussion of transitions in life stories. She discusses the tensions evident in the descriptions between accounting for change while at the same time both preserving narrative continuity and also sustaining a notion of a core or essential self. On the one hand, the accounts show a kind of "looking back" for "overarching themes and explanatory links," which "grounds the sense of what remains constant in the journey of the self." (1996, 275) On the other hand, the transitions are often told as being moments of transformation, of new insight and excitement. She says that people both "become" and in a sense were "always already" their new, more academic selves. They describe the seduction of the intellectual life or of leaving the contained world of teaching as it begins to feel a trap in comparison to the world outside. This leads them to make an exit from their old selves from "speaking of teachers as 'us' to—however benevolently—as 'them.'" (1996, 276)

These are stories that are told very differently from the ones told by Lugones. The people interviewed by MacLure do not use the terminology of world-traveling, although that is what they have done. More significantly they do not see themselves as a plurality of selves as Lugones does. Rather, as MacLure points out they appear to be searching for connections that will allow them to demonstrate the continuation of a constant, single self between the different worlds they have inhabited. Lugones' theory is am-biguous about the degree of distinctness of the different selves that form the plurality. The two selves she describes could be seen as distinct frag-ments. In one world she is playful, and in the other she is not. Using the metaphor of strands, rather than of fragments, she begins the article claim-ing that the paper weaves two aspects of her life together, and that this weaving "reveals and affirms the plurality in each of us and among us as richness." (1989, 275) Her arguments indicate that the weaving metaphor is an appropriate one for her theory, because the strands connect but do not merge. The connections between them are made only by memory. She talks for instance of having memories in one world of her playfulness in the other. Further, she points out that it is in the world where she is not play-ful that she is writing about and advocating playfulness. Thus she seems to be arguing that memory connects the strands, but they remain little changed by the encounter. If these strands are as separate as she describes, with only memory joining them, the weave will be one that could, in prin-ciple, unravel in order to be rewoven. This is in contrast to my own model of the construction of self, which is a much more layered, connected affair. In my model, the effects of living in the Latino world, where she is playful, persist and continue into the Anglo world, where she is not, and would do so, even if the Latino world disappeared. Or vice versa. The patches may start separate, but as they become sewn together, they form new patterns, sometimes making each of the original pieces appear in a new light.

How to tell these narratives is a matter of judgment. All these narratives can be read as similar to the others described in this chapter: my own, Lu-gones, Hoffman, Nichols. We all search for similarities and differences be-tween different worlds in our lives. We all demonstrate connections and overarching themes from one world to another. Choosing a form for the nar-rative is to make judgments about how to understand agency and structure in conditions of becoming and being. These are judgments about how to un-derstand self, identity, and the achievement of authenticity.

These searches are made in response to the kinds of questions noted at the beginning of this chapter, as being questions that arise with a particular ur-gency in a struggle for justice. At the same time, I want to emphasize here how much these are also everyday questions (for instance for school teachers turned academic), which feel highly significant to the people who tell the stories. In more abstract terms, as human beings we all struggle to resolve questions about our place in different worlds and what to do about it. This is a point at which the framing of key questions for women puts a new per-spective on current orthodoxies about the "universal" of human beings.

Change, Connection, and Continuity

It is the argument of this section that the theory of a patchwork self allows the possibility of understanding how to achieve the kind of coherence that leads to authenticity. This is in contrast to more usual strategies from other theories of self. MacLure argues that her respondents tell the story of their lives as tales of victory and redemption. This is a narrative that arises out of the unitary theory of the self. However, she argues convincingly that people using this mode are doomed to disappointment as they find that the boundaries refuse to remain safely crossed. This is reminiscent of the dilemma faced by Flax's or Lugones' plural selves, which face the continuing problem of how to get this plurality to stay connected, but not too connected: neither immured in a unitary world, nor afloat like flotsam in a sea of fragments.

The patchwork self does not face the problem of staying connected. It does, however, face the problem of how to keep the different patches in a unified (though not unitary) whole: that is, authentically itself. The changing self is marked by its history. It is a patchwork, made over time, of patches upon patches, continually worked over, but with no possibility of any of it being thrown out or erased in order to start afresh. On the other hand it is lived now, not across a life. Spontaneity and "how I feel" is significant in assessing "Is this me?" Phrases like "This is really me" typically get their purchase in situations where the experience of individuality and spontaneity of feeling is important. However the experience of immediacy and individuality cannot possibly be giving the whole story, since it masks the process of construction, of being and becoming over time. A complication is that if the self is a patchwork, then *each* patch is marked like this, just as the whole set is. Further, the way the patches are constructed *with* and *over* each other may—and does—mask the processes of construction.

Standard accounts of authenticity by Martin Heidegger (1962) and Charles Taylor (1991) discuss ways of resolving the issues of agency and structure. Heidegger discussed the idea that there is a possibility of release from "thrownness" into authenticity. Thrownness is a term coined by Heidegger that expresses that Dasein has being-in-the-world as its way of being. The world is not external to, and added on to Dasein (1962, 174). He argues that: "Thrown into its 'there,' every Dasein has been factically submitted to a definite 'world'—its 'world.'" (p. 344) For him, the conscience attests that authenticity is possible. It also indicates that authenticity is "uncanny"—a state of mind of anxiety (or "anxiety of conscience"). "Being-guilty" (p. 325ff.) indicates that one's own Dasein has been disclosed in the uncanniness of its individualisation (p. 342). In this way, "the Self is brought back from the loud idle talk which goes with the common sense of the 'they.'" (p. 342)

For Taylor, too, there is a tension between authenticity as an ideal of self-determination and acknowledgement that the construction of self depends on circumstances. He argues that the ideal of authenticity in modern times is an ideal of individuality transcending social roles:

> As this [ideal of authenticity] emerges, for instance with Herder, it calls on me to discover my own original way of being. By definition, this cannot be socially derived but must be inwardly generated. (1991, 47)

These useful accounts fall short in that they do not appear to include attention to the complexity introduced by patchwork. Compare Heidegger's definite world with my small lost world of childhood—and the multiplicity of worlds I have lived in since. Or compare it with Lugones' (allied) notion of a world, in which she travels from one (not very definite one) to another. Taylor does not appear to notice this multiplicity of worlds either, nor that roles may be—often are—deeply incoherent or even conflicting. Yet the complexity is not hard to see, as I have shown, especially for those who are not of the mainstream. There are patches in the self that coexist without any trouble. There are others that give more trouble. Lugones' chapter is partly about the tensions of being a Hispanic American feminist philosopher. There are patches that only coexist happily in certain circumstances, but when those circumstances change, they are in tension. (Consider the case of a small boy who likes wearing dresses: no problem until he goes to kindergarten.) Sometimes the arrival of a new patch affects others that used to be stable. Hoffman's new life as a Polish Canadian affected her old life simply as Polish. Or consider the domino effect of my self-definition moving from "not a real feminist" to "a bit of a feminist"—to writing articles as a feminist philosopher.

Playing and Achieving Authenticity

I am indebted to Lugones' article not just because it introduces the idea of world-traveling, but also because it introduces the idea of play that I work with in this chapter. At the beginning of her article Lugones says that she recommends shifting across contexts, what she calls "this willful exercise":

> I recommend this willful exercise, which I call "world-traveling," and I also recommend that the willful exercise be animated by an attitude that I describe as playful. (1989)

I want to criticize and extend Lugones analysis of play, as I did for the concept of world-traveling. I think she is implicitly working with two ideas of play, even though she only acknowledges one of them as valuable, and is, I argue, working with an unacknowledged ambiguity in the concept of play as, on the one hand the play of good children, playing by the rules, under the benign and protective care of adults. On the other, people at play are imaginative and creative. So it is not surprising that they seek out what is new, strange, secret, forbidden, defiant of authority: in a word, what is naughty.

Lugones advocates playfulness as an attitude that should animate world-traveling. She describes playfulness as fun, not necessarily rule-governed, undertaken in a spirit of "openness to surprise," to "being a fool," to "not worrying about competence, not being self-important, not taking norms as sacred and finding ambiguity and double edges a source of wisdom and delight." (1989, 288) This is where her argument begins to go wrong. This carefree attitude was not possible in the very case she began by considering traveling to the world of Anglo academic philosophy. That was an episode of world-traveling to a place where such lighthearted playfulness was not a good idea.

However her argument works better for naughtier playfulness. Consider the examples that she uses. These examples do not fit her descriptions of carefree ease and health. She talks of how women of color refer "half jokingly" to schizophrenia in traveling between worlds. She describes how the ambiguity inherent in an intentional animation of a Latin American stereotype is funny and is also survival rich:

> So we know truths that only the fool can speak and only the trickster can play out without harm. (1989, 285)

These examples surely show the double edge of play. These examples are all too clearly born out of pain and difficulty, even though all of these kinds of play can be fun and not dependent on previous pain. They are, literally, child's play: playing a role, animating stereotypes, and saying or doing something acceptable only because it is done playfully. Against her own argument, Lugones is drawing attention to the importance of the loss of innocence, to the other edge of the double edge: to ways of dealing with the pain of pretence and of living "as if," to the way that, though role play and foolery can be can be done for fun, playfully, they are also done out of necessity. In *Feminisms and the Self* (Griffiths 1995), I draw attention to the implications for self-identity of black people "*acting* white," and girls in secondary schools trying to play the exacting *role* of being neither a slag nor a drag.

Lugones' examples can be put into a wider theoretical context. The ludic lightness of postmodernism has often been criticized for its distance from material realities faced by oppressed people. But just as often, postmodern theory has an interesting two-way relationship to feminist theory, drawing from it and in turn influencing it. I'm using Lugones' theory, because I find her so helpful. But I would note here that play in its various forms has been advocated by a number of feminist theorists working within some form of the postmodern. MacLure (1996), influenced by Derrida but drawing particularly on Donna Haraway (1991), also refers to the tricksters and jokers of transgressive practices of the self in her article about teachers making the transition to becoming researchers in the academy. From a feminist perspective, the focus on play seems to have arisen precisely out of the difficulties faced by dealing with difference. Further, the interest seems to focus on a kind of noninnocent, though ultimately moral, play. This lack of innocence is signalled by the use of words familiar in postmodern theory: words like trick, transgression, trespass, irony, and border crossing.

There are different possibilities of naughty playfulness. Here is one way of mapping them:

- Role play: Schizophrenic traveling between worlds. Playing the role, but knowing you are doing it. Surviving somehow, ducking and weaving. Flouting the rules. Trespassing beyond the boundaries, and then claiming the space.
- Playing with stereotypes: Activating stereotypes. Reclaiming them. Refusing them.
- Laughter: Irony. Playing the fool. Playing tricks. Laughter. Political jokes.
- Imagination: Playing one persona against another: Entertaining forbidden fantasies. Imaginative performances. Dreaming up and doing the unexpected.

However, I do not want to place the dead hand of category on what is, or ought to be—and indeed, must be—fluid, unfixed, imaginative, and creative. Instead it can be seen how these possibilities are realized in particular examples. The one I am choosing to use is Fatima Mernissi's wonderful evocation of harem life in Morocco in the 1940s, *Dreams of Trespass*.

Mernissi is a feminist, Islamic scholar who has written on democracy, the veil, and women rulers in Islamic history. Her narrative of childhood is vivid, affectionate, political, feminist—and full of lessons on naughtiness. Her mother gave her some of these with the help of her own mother, Grandmother Yasmina. Her mother had always rejected male superiority, as nonsense and totally anti-Muslim. "Allah made us all equal," she would say. (1994)

She was worried when her little girl just admired her cousin when he "staged his mutinies against the grownups," and let him do her rebelling for her. The little girl was told by her mother:

You have to learn to scream and protest, just the way you learned to walk and talk. Crying when you are insulted is like asking for more.

Mernissi goes on:

She was so worried that I would grow up obsequious that she consulted Grandmother Yasmina, known to be incomparable at staging confrontations. (1994, 9)

These confrontations were playful and political as well as dangerous. "What always saved Yasmina was the fact that she made Grandfather laugh," even though she asserted her wish to climb trees, go swimming, do acrobatics, and name the farm peacock Farouk after the Egyptian king who had unjustly divorced his wife. Yasmina explains:

The more masters one had, the more freedom and the more fun . . . Figuring out who has authority over you is the first step. That information is basic. But after that, you need to shuffle the cards, confuse the roles. That is the interesting part. Life is a game. Look at it that way, and you can laugh at the whole thing. (Mernissi 1994, 152–153)

Embroidery was another lesson in dreaming and getting freedom. The traditional women in the harem—led by the most senior woman Grandmother Mani—believed that all embroidery should be of the tedious traditional kind. They disapproved of modern designs which, explains Mernissi, were "pure fun, meant for personal enjoyment." (1994, 209) But she makes clear the traditionalists were right to see danger in the modern designs, which were symbolic of more than personal enjoyment. It was not by chance that the modernists used the freedom of "unexpected designs and strange color combinations" to stitch birds with wings spread in full flight. The less powerful of the modernist women had to hide when embroidering their birds. But, as her favorite among them, Aunt Habiba, tells her:

The main thing for the powerless is to have a dream. . . . Your Grandmother Yasmina's dream was that she was a special creature, and no one has ever been able to make her believe otherwise. . . . Your mother has wings inside, too, and your father flies with her whenever he can. (Mernissi 1994, 215)

It seems that play and the possibilities of play can be born out of the ambiguities and double vision of injustice. This is a difficult balancing act, carried out on the edges of dominant worlds, but one which leads to authenticity when it is achieved. This can never be a fixed achievement. It depends too much on the movement of creative energy and lively imagination. Authenticity is continually created, achieved, lost and reachieved, through playing precariously on the edge. As Donna Haraway says:

Irony is about contradictions that do not resolve into larger wholes, even dialectically, about the tension of holding incompatible things together because both or all are necessary and true. Irony is about humor and serious play. . . . All I am really asking for is permanent passion and irony, where passion is as important as irony. (2000, 171–172)

Note

1. This appeared in Griffiths (1995, 23).

Bibliography

Benhabib, Seyla. "Feminism and Postmodernism: An Uneasy Alliance." In *Feminist Contentions: A Philosophical Exchange*, edited by Seyla Benhabib, Judith Butler, Drucilla Cornell, and Nancy Fraser. London: Routledge, 1995.
Boden, Margaret A. *The Creative Mind: Myths and Mechanisms*. London: Routledge, 2004.
Butler, Judith. "Contingent Foundations: Feminism and the Question of 'Postmodernism.'" In *Feminist Contentions: A Philosophical Exchange*, edited by Seyla Benhabib, Judith Butler, Drucilla Cornell, and Nancy Fraser. London: Routledge, 1995.
Daly, Mary. *Gyn/Ecology: The Metaethics of Radical Feminism*. London: The Women's Press, 1979.
———. *Pure Lust: Elemental Feminist Philosophy*. London: The Women's Press, 1984.
Flax, Jane. *Disputed Subjects: Essays on Psychoanalysis, Politics, and Philosophy*. London: Routledge, 1993.
Gilroy, Paul. *The Black Atlantic*. London: Verso: 1993.
Griffiths, Morwenna. *Feminisms and the Self: The Web of Identity*. London: Routledge, 1995.
———. *Educational Research for Social Justice: Getting off the Fence*. Buckingham: Open University Press, 1998.

———. *Action for Social Justice in Education: Fairly Different.* Buckingham: Open University Press, 2003.

Haraway, Donna J. *Simians, Cyborgs and Women: The Reinvention of Nature.* London: Free Association Books, 1991.

———. *How Like a Leaf: An Interview with Thyrza Nichols Goodeve.* London: Routledge, 2000.

Harstock, Nancy. "Foucault on Power: A Theory for Women?" In *Feminism/Postmodernism*, edited by Linda J. Nicholson, New York and London: Routledge, 1990.

Heidegger, Martin. *Being and Time*, translated by John Macquarrie and Edward Robinson. Oxford: Basil Blackwell, 1962.

Hekman, Susan J. *Gender and Knowledge: Elements of a Postmodern Feminism.* Cambridge: Polity, 1990.

Hoffman, Eva. *Lost in Translation: A Life in a New Language.* London: Minerva, 1991.

Lloyd, Moya. *Beyond Identity Politics: Feminism, Power and Politics.* London: Sage, 2005.

Lugones, María. "Playfulness, 'World'-traveling and Loving Perception." In *Women, Knowledge and Reality*, edited by Ann Garry and Marilyn Pearsall. Boston: Unwin Hyman, 1989.

MacLure, Maggie. "Telling Transitions: Boundary Work in Narratives of Becoming an Action Researcher." *British Educational Research Journal* 22, no. 3 (1996):273–286.

Mernissi, Fatima. *Dreams of Trespass: Tales of a Harem Girlhood.* Reading: MA: Addison-Wesley Inc., 1994.

Nichols, Grace. *The Fat Black Woman's Poems.* London: Virago, 1984.

———. *Lazy Thoughts of a Lazy Woman.* London: Virago, 1989.

Nussbaum, Martha, and Jonathan Glover. *Women Culture and Development: A Study of Human Capabilities.* New York: Oxford University Press, 1995.

Stanley, Liz, and Sue Wise. "Method, Methodology and Epistemology in Feminist Research Processes." In *Feminist Praxis*, edited by Liz Stanley. London: Routledge, 1990.

Steedman, Carolyn. *Landscape for a Good Woman: A Story of Two Lives.* London: Virago, 1986.

Taylor, Charles. *The Ethics of Authenticity.* Cambridge: Harvard University Press, 1991.

Walkerdine, Valerie. *Schoolgirl Fictions.* London: Verso, 1990.

Young, Iris Marion. *Inclusion and Democracy.* Oxford: Oxford University Press, 2000.

~

CHAPTER NINE

Locating Traitorous Identities: Toward a View of Privilege-Cognizant White Character

Alison Bailey[1]

I address the problem of how to locate "traitorous" subjects, or those who belong to dominant groups yet resist the usual assumption and practices of those groups. I argue that Sandra Harding's description of traitors as insiders, who "become marginal" is misleading. Crafting a distinction between "privilege-cognizant" and "privilege-evasive" white scripts, I offer an alternative account of race traitors as privilege-cognizant white who refuse to animate expected whitely scripts, and who are unfaithful to worldviews whites are expected to hold.

> I had begun to feel pretty irregularly white. Klan folks had a word for it: *race traitor*. Driving in and out of counties with heavy Klan activity, I kept my eye on the rear-view mirror, and any time a truck with a confederate flag passed me, the hair on the back of my neck would rise. . . . I was in daily, intimate exposure to the cruel, killing effects of racism, which my Black friends spoke of in the same way that they commented on the weather, an equally constant factor in their lives. . . . I began to feel more uneasy around other whites and more at ease around people of color. . . . Maybe whiteness was more about consciousness than color. That scared me, too, the possibility of being caught between the worlds of race, white people kicking me out, people of color not letting me in. (Mab Segrest 1994, 80)

Recent scholarship in multicultural, postcolonial, and global feminism has motivated a reanalysis of both feminist and mainstream philosophical texts, methodologies, concepts, and frameworks. One project springing from these new approaches is a literature critical of white identities. At present, white identity is constituted by and benefits from injustice. Transformative work demands that whites explore how to rearticulate our identities in ways that do not depend on the subordination of people of color.

This chapter addresses a simple but troublesome puzzle: the problem of how to describe and understand the location of those who belong to dominant groups yet resist the usual assumptions and orientations of those groups. The discussion begins against the background of three archetypes of knowers: the disembodied spectator, the outsider within, and the traitor. It sets out Sandra Harding's (1991) account of traitorous identities. Then, it takes issue with her portrayal of traitors as insiders, who as a result of a shift in the way they understand the world, "become marginal." I argue that Harding's description is misleading and that it fails to capture her intended meaning. The chapter offers an alternative characterization of traitors that is less prone to misinterpretation. Crafting a distinction between "privilege-cognizant" and "privilege-evasive" white scripts, I characterize race traitors as privilege-cognizant whites who refuse to animate the scripts white are expected to perform and who are unfaithful to worldviews whites are expected to hold. Finally, the chapter develops the notion of traitorous scripts and explains how animating them helps to cultivate a traitorous character. Using Aristotle's view of character formation (1980) and María Lugones' (1987) concept of "world"-traveling, I briefly sketch what it might mean to have a traitorous character.

Disembodied Spectators, Outsiders Within, and Traitors

Feminist epistemologists have long been attentive to the relationship between knowing subjects' locations and their understandings of the world. Dissatisfaction with Enlightenment accounts of knowing subjects as faceless, disembodied spectators who hover over the Cartesian landscape has led feminist theorists to consider knowers as embodied subjects situated in politically identifiable social locations or contexts. Attention to knowers as socially situated creates a new angle of vision that allows us to consider the alternative epistemic resources these situated subjects offer. Patricia Hill Collins (1990) and Sandra Harding (1991), whose writings represent the variety of feminist standpoint theory I have in mind here, prefer this approach, because it is attentive to the social and political structures, symbolic systems, and discourse that grant privilege to some groups at the expense of others.

If the archetypal knower in Cartesian epistemic dramas is the disembodied spectator, then the starring role in feminist standpoint theory is played by the outsider within. Collins' description of black female domestics offers a clear illustration of this second archetype (Collins 1986, s14–s15; 1990, 11–13). As outsiders within, black women working as domestics have an unclouded view of the contradictions between the actions and ideologies of white families. This unique angle of vision is rooted in the contradictory location of the domestic, who is at once a worker, "privy to the most intimate secrets of white society," and a black woman exploited by and excluded from privileges granted by white patriarchal rule. Her "Blackness makes her a perpetual outsider," but her work of caring for white women "allows her an insider's view of some of the contradictions between white women thinking that they are running their lives and the actual source of power in white patriarchal households." (Collins 1990, 11–12)

Outsiders within are thought to have an advantageous epistemic viewpoint that offers a more complete account of the world than insider or outsider perspectives alone. Their contradictory location gives rise to what W. E. B. DuBois refers to as a "double-consciousness," a sense of being able to see themselves through their own eyes and through the eyes of others (DuBois 1994, 2). Extending Collins' analysis, Harding argues that women scientists, African-American women sociologists, or lesbian literary critics doing intellectual work in the predominantly white, heterosexual male academy also have "identities [that] appear to defy logic, for 'who we are' is in at least two places at once: outside and within, margin and center." (Harding 1991, 275) As strangers to the social order of the academy, they bring a unique combination of nearness and remoteness to their subject matter that helps to maximize objectivity (Harding 1991, 124).

Because insiders have few incentives or opportunities to cultivate a bifurcated consciousness, their identities are understood as obstacles to producing reliable accounts of the world. For example, class privilege makes it a challenge for those with money to understand why moving out of poverty is so difficult; the privilege afforded to white people by racism makes it hard for whites to grasp its pervasiveness. Similarly, heterosexuals are rarely in a position to analyze either heterosexual privilege or institutional and personal homophobia.[2]

For all of the social benefits afforded to insiders, some members of these dominant groups resist the assumptions most of their fellow insiders take for granted. Feminist standpoint theory has been less attentive to such subject positions than to disembodied spectators and outsiders within. However, in the final chapters of *Whose Science? Whose Knowledge?* (1991), Harding makes a compelling case for expanding the insights of standpoint theory to consider how traitorous identities might serve as sites for liberatory knowledge. Reaching deeper into the logic of standpoint theory she explains:

> One can begin to detect other identities for knowers . . . standing in the shadows behind the ones [identities] on which feminist and other liberatory thought has focused, identities that are struggling to emerge as respected and legitimate producers of illuminating analyses. From the perspective of the fiercely fought struggles to claim legitimacy for the marginalized identities, these identities appear to be monstrous: male feminists; whites against racism . . . heterosexuals against heterosexism; economically overadvantaged people against class exploitation. (1991, 274)

Harding's discovery suggests that insiders are not, by virtue of their social location, immune to understanding the viewpoints and experiences of marginalized groups. Antiracist whites do criticize white privilege, and feminist men do resist gender roles that reinforce women's oppression. So, "People who do not have marginalized identities can nevertheless learn from and learn to use the knowledge generated from the perspective of outsiders within." (Harding 1991, 277) Those who do so are said to have "traitorous identities" and to occupy "traitorous social locations." (288–296)

Harding observes a significant epistemic difference between how insiders who are "critically reflective" of their privilege, and insiders who are oblivious to privilege, understand the world. Traitors do not experience the world in the same way outsiders within experience it, but outsider-within political analyses do inform their policies. Outsider-within standpoints provide tools for members of dominant groups who may be unable to articulate or clarify the occluded nature of their privilege and its relation to the oppression experienced by outsiders. By learning about lives on the margins, members of dominant groups come to discover the nature of oppression, the extent of their privileges, and the relations between them. Making visible the nature of privilege enables members of dominant groups to generate liberatory knowledge. Being white, male, wealthy, or heterosexual presents a challenge in generating this knowledge, but is not an insurmountable obstacle.

Knowledge emerging from outsider-within locations, then, is valuable on two counts. First, it calls attention to the experiences of marginalized groups overlooked by earlier epistemological projects. Second, those who occupy the center can learn from and learn to use the knowledge generated by the analyses of outsiders within to understand their relationships with marginalized person from the standpoint of those persons' lives (Collins 1986, s29; Harding 1991, 277). Harding describes insiders who adopt a critically reflective resistance toward privilege as "becoming marginal." But I think this phrase leads to a misunderstanding about what it means to be a traitor.

In What Sense Do Traitors "Become Marginal"?

Describing subject identities in spatial terms initially offers a useful way of seeing social structures and imagining the power relations between knowers. In the margin-center cartography of feminist standpoint theory, traitors are described as people who "choose to become marginalized." (Harding 1991, 289, 295) But this description is misleading for several reasons. The problem with describing traitors as becoming marginal is more clearly understood if we keep a historical example in mind.

In 1954, Anna and Carl Braden purchased a home in a white section of Louisville, Kentucky, for the purpose of deeding it to Charlotte and Andrew Wade, a black couple. Andrew Wade, a politically conscious member of the Progressive party and a World War II veteran, was furious that, even with his service record, he could not purchase the home he wanted. The Bradens, a progressive couple who opposed segregation, agreed to buy the house and deed it to the Wades. Their choice to break with the unspoken practice marginalized them in a way that other white families, who followed expected house-selling practices, were not. After the transaction, Louisville's segregationists publicly denounced the Bradens as "traitors to [the] race." They argued that the Bradens ought to have known better than to transgress the unspoken rule that the races ought to live in separate communities (Braden 1958, 82). Within hours of the title transfer, the Bradens received threatening phone calls and bomb threats. Months later they were charged with attempting to overthrow the government of the Commonwealth of Kentucky. In what sense, then, could the Bradens be said to have chosen to become marginal? In her memoir, Anne Braden explains how, in the events that followed the house purchase, "some of the protections that go with white skin in our society fell from Carl and me. To an extent, at least, we were thrown into the world of abuse where Negroes always live." (1958, 7)

Braden's choice of words here suggests that the couple's subject position changed in some sense, but it also presents two problems. First, at a glance, to describe the Bradens as having become marginal makes it sound as if the Bradens actually came to occupy outsider-within subject positions like those occupied by the Wades. Deeding the house to the Wades did cause the Bradens to lose privilege in their community, so it might be said that they became marginal in the sense that they were ostracized from the white community because of their actions. But being cast out does not amount to the same thing as being situated as an outsider within. Given the wrath of segregationist whites, the Bradens' subject position might be said to have shifted in relation to white citizens who saw them as race traitors. However, because they were white in the eyes of those who did not know them, they did not completely lose their privilege. In spite of their actions, the Bradens continued to bear a socially privileged racial identity; the Wades never had this privilege. Whites who engage in traitorous challenges to segregation may undergo some shift in their subject position in the sense that they may be ostracized from certain communities, but they do not exchange their status as insiders for outsider-within status.

Harding anticipates this confusion and clarifies her position using the example of privilege-cognizant heterosexuals.

> Some people whose sexual identity was not "marginal" (in the sense that they were heterosexual) have "become marginal"—not by giving up their heterosexuality but by giving up the spontaneous consciousness created by their heterosexual experience in a heterosexist world. These people do not think "as lesbians," for they are not lesbian. But they do think as heterosexual persons who have learned from lesbian analyses. (1991, 289)

Although the Bradens did not live as black families in segregated Louisville lived, they could understand, even if incompletely, what it might be like to live in Louisville as the Wades lived in it. It is precisely this understanding that Harding thinks the narratives and analyses generated by persons of color can foster.

Thus, Harding's intended meaning here is that it is possible for people like the Bradens to learn about the world of segregated Louisville as the Wades experienced it without actually coming to inhabit that world as do those who are marginal. Describing the Bradens as "becoming marginal" best describes a shift in their way of seeing, understanding, and moving through the world. Part of the reason for this confusion is that the words "margin" and "center" are usually used in standpoint theory to describe subject locations, and here they are being used to describe an epistemic shift. "Becoming marginal" refers to the shift from a perspective to a standpoint. The first is the product of an unreflective account of one's subject location; the second, as the word "antiracist" indicates, is a political position achieved through collective struggle (Harding 1991, 123–27; Jaggar 1983, 317).

Harding's intended meaning of "becoming marginal" should now be clearer. However, even if we understand "becoming marginal" to refer to an epistemic shift, I would argue that this phrase does not really capture the meaning of the traitorous standpoint Harding finds so compelling. Describing traitors as "becoming marginal" encourages blurring or conflating of the location of the outsiders within and the location of traitors. The description makes it sound as if traitors have a foot in each world and are caught equally between them, and this picture does not foreground white privilege. If, for the moment, we retain the language of standpoint theory, it is more accurate to describe the Bradens' actions as destabilizing the center. Race traitors are subjects who occupy the center but whose way of seeing (at least by insider standards) is *off-center*. That is, traitors destabilize their insider status by challenging and resisting the usual assumptions held by most white people (such as the belief that white privilege is earned, inevitable, or natural). Descriptions of traitors as decentering, subverting, or destabilizing the center arguably work better than "becoming marginal" because they do not encourage this conflation of the outsider within and the traitor. Decentering the center makes it clear that traitors and outsiders within have a common political interest in challenging white privilege, but that they do so from different social locations. Understanding traitors as destabilizers tidies up earlier misunderstandings, but I still think standpoint theory's margin-center cartography tends to restrict Harding's description of these subjects. If this language encourages misperceptions about traitors, then we need to consider alternative descriptions of these disloyal subjects.

Privilege-Cognizant and Privilege-Evasive White Scripts

Perhaps a clearer, more descriptive picture of traitors, one that focuses on their decentering projects, will emerge if we think of traitors as privileged subjects who animate privilege-cognizant white scripts. The distinction Harding observes between insiders who are critical of their position and insiders who are not is more accurately expressed as a distinction between "privilege-cognizant" and "privilege-evasive" white scripts (Frankenberg 1993, 137–191). Understanding traitors along these lines requires spelling out what is meant by a racial script and how privilege-cognizant and privilege-evasive white scripts differ.

Like sexism, racism is a social-political system of domination that comes with expected performances, attitudes, and behaviors, which reinforce and reinscribe unjust hierarchies. Feminists have long paid attention to the ways gender roles encourage habits and nurture systems that value men's ideas, activities, and achievements over those of women. The existence of sexism and racism as systems requires everyone's daily collaboration.

To understand the nature of this collaboration, it is helpful to think of the attitudes and behaviors expected of one's particular racial group as performances that follow historically preestablished scripts. Scripts differ with a subject's location within systems of domination. What it means to be a man or woman is not exclusively defined by one's physical characteristics. Similarly, what it means to be black, white, Comanche, Korean, or Latina is defined not only by a person's physical appearance (so-called racial markers such as skin color, hair, facial features, body shape), but also by that person's performance—by the script that individual animates. When the concept of racial scripts is applied locally, what it means to be a white woman in Louisville or an African-American man in Chicago, includes a person's gestures, language, attitudes, concept of personal space, gut reactions to certain phenomena, and body awareness. Attention to race as performative, or scripted, reveals the less visible, structural regulatory function of racial scripts that exclusive attention to appearance overlooks.

Marilyn Frye's (1992) discussion of "whitely" behavior and "whiteliness" offers a conceptual distinction that is instrumental in understanding the performative dimensions of race and the distinction between privilege-evasive and privilege-cognizant scripts. Frye recognizes the need for a terminology that captures the contingency between phenotype (racial appearance) and the value of whiteness. Paralleling the distinction feminists make between *maleness*, something persons are born with by virtue of their biological sex, and *masculinity*, something socially connected to maleness but largely the result of social training, Frye argues for an analogous pair of terms in racial discourse and coins "whitely" and "whiteliness" as the racial equivalents of maleness and masculinity, respectively. As Frye explains: "Being white skinned (like being male) is a matter of physical traits presumed to be physically determined: being whitely (like being masculine) I conceive as a deeply ingrained way of being in the world." (1992, 150–151) The connection between "acting white" and "looking white" is contingent, so it is possible for persons who are not classified as white to perform in whitely ways and for persons who are white not to perform in whitely ways. Racial scripts are internalized at an early age to the point where they are embedded almost to invisibility in our language, bodily reactions, feelings, behaviors, and judgments. Whitely scripts are, no doubt, mediated by a person's economic class, ethnicity, sexuality, gender, religion, and geographical location, but privilege is granted on the basis of whitely performances nevertheless (Davion 1995, 135–139). A few examples can highlight some facets of whitely, or privilege-evasive scripts.

Lillian Smith, a white woman growing up in Jim Crow Georgia, offers one illustration of a whitely script. She was taught to "[act] out a special private production of a little script that is written on the lives of most Southern children before they know words." (1949, 21)

> I do not remember how or when, but. . . . I knew that I was better than a Negro, that all black folks have their place and must be kept in it, that sex has its place and must be kept in it, that a terrifying disaster would befall the South if ever I treated a Negro as my social equal and as terrifying a disaster would befall my family if I ever were to have a baby outside of marriage. . . . I had learned that white southerners are hospitable, courteous, tactful people who treat those of their own group with consideration and who carefully segregate from all the richness of life "for their own good and welfare" thirteen million people whose skin is colored a little differently from my own. (18)

Smith describes this script as a "dance that cripples the human spirit." It was a dance she repeated until the movements "were made for the rest of [her] life without thinking." (1949, 91) What I find remarkable about Smith's "little script" is the clarity with which she connects racial segregation and the control of white women's sexuality.

Anne Braden recounts a similar script growing up in Alabama and Mississippi in the 1930s. Braden's description is especially attentive to the spatial dimensions of racial scripts.

> Most of these things, it is true, were never said in words. They were impressed on the mind of the white child of the South's privileged class. . . .
> It was a chant of . . . we sit in the downstairs of the theater, Negroes sit upstairs in the balcony—you drank from this fountain, Negroes use that fountain—we eat in the dining room, Negroes eat in the kitchen—colored town, our streets—white schools, colored schools—be careful—don't go near colored town after dark—you sit on the front of the bus, they sit in the back—your place, their place—your world, their world. (1958, 21)

Braden also acknowledges an interesting linguistic facet of whitely scripts.

> Sometimes the commandments became quite explicit. For example, I could not have been more than four or five years old when one day I happened to say something to my mother about a "colored lady." "You never call colored people ladies [her mother replied]. . . . You say colored woman and white lady—never a colored lady." (1958, 21)

Attentiveness to maintaining the boundaries of one's racial location, then, is a strong dimension of all racial scripts.

Racial scripts are not regulated only by attitudes and an awareness of people's appropriate place; scripts also have a strong corporeal element that emerges in gestures and reactions to persons who we think of as being unlike ourselves. We are all, on some level, attentive to the race of persons with whom we interact, and this shapes our encounters. Even privilege-cognizant whites who are consciously committed to combating racism may react with aversion and avoidance toward people of color. African Americans receiving these avoidance behaviors feel noticed—marked. In his essay "Just Walk on By: A Black Man Ponders His Power to Alter Public Space," Brent Staples (1986) offers the following account of a white woman who passes him on the street at night.

> I often witness the "hunch posture," from women after dark on the warrenlike streets of Brooklyn, where I live. They seem to set their faces on neutral and, with their purse straps strung across their chests bandoleer style, they forge ahead as though bracing themselves against being tackled. I understand, of course, that . . . Women are particularly vulnerable to street violence, and young black males are drastically overrepresented among the perpetrators of violence. Yet these truths are no solace against the kind of alienation that comes of being ever the suspect, against being set apart, a fearsome entity with whom pedestrians avoid making eye contact. (54)

The majority of whitely scripts include being nervous around people of color, avoiding eye contact with them, or adopting closed, uncomfortable postures in their presence. The repeated animation of these scripts, however, reinscribes a racial order in which white lives, culture, and experiences are valued at the expense of the lives of persons of color, whose bodies are fearsome to whites and who are cast as deviant, dirty, criminal, ugly, or degenerate.

These accounts of privilege-evasive scripts provide a contrast to my account of privilege-cognizant scripts; they also help to explain why privilege-cognizant scripts count as traitorous. What all racial scripts have in common is that in a white-centered culture, everyone is more or less expected to follow scripts that sustain white privilege. The whitely scripts described by Smith, Staples, and Braden are privilege-evasive: They do not challenge whites to think about privilege, and their reenactment reproduces white privilege. If scripts sustaining white privilege are required by members of all racial groups, then members of both privileged and oppressed groups can refuse to cooperate. What holds racism in place, metaphorically speaking, is not only that African Americans have sat in the back of the bus for so long, but also that whites have avoided the task of critically examining and giving up their seats in front. By refusing to examine privilege, whites uncritically resign themselves to whitely scripts—to having their identities shaped in ways they may not have chosen (Harding 1991, 294).

Recognizing that whites can use the analyses of outsiders within to forge traitorous scripts means we can learn to think and act not out of the "spontaneous consciousness" of the socially scripted locations that history has written for us, but out of the traitorous (privilege-cognizant) scripts we choose with the assistance of critical social theories generated by emancipatory movements (Harding 1991, 295). A key feature of privilege-cognizant standpoints is the choice to develop a critically reflective consciousness. As one participant in Ruth Frankenberg's study of white women observes "Coming from the white privileged class . . . means you don't have to look at anything else. You are never forced to until you choose to, because your life is so unaffected by anything like racism." (1993, 161) Traitors *choose* to try to understand the price at which privileges are gained; they are critical of the unearned privileges granted to them by white patriarchal cultures, and they take responsibility for them.

Choosing to take responsibility for my interactions requires that I take responsibility for my "racial social location, by learning how I am connected to other whites and persons of color; by learning what the consequences of my beliefs and behaviors as a European American woman will be." (Harding 1991, 283) An integral moment in understanding my relation to people differently situated from me comes in learning to see how I am seen by outsiders. It requires a variation on DuBois' double consciousness.

Unlike whites who unreflectively animate whitely scripts, the traitor's task is to find ways to develop alternative scripts capable of disrupting the constant reinscription of whitely scripts. Privilege-cognizant whites actively examine their "seats in front" and find ways to be disloyal to systems that assign these seats. Some obvious examples include choosing to stop racist jokes, paying attention to body language and conversation patterns, and cultivating an awareness of how stereotypes shape perceptions of people of color. Telling, and permitting others to tell, racist jokes reinscribes images that are harmful. The traitor knows when it is appropriate to stop this reinscription. Similarly, the white woman who clutches her bags or steers her children away from African-American youth, or the white man who acts uncomfortable or nervous in the presence of people of color, sends signals to those around him that members of these groups are to be feared. Whites who interrupt, ostracize, or dismiss the contributions of students of color in the classroom reproduce their invisibility by sending the message that these students' contributions are unimportant. If traitors can rearticulate white scripts in ways that do not reinscribe these subordinating gestures, then we can begin to imagine ways of being, as Adrienne Rich (1979) says, "disloyal to civilization."

The language of racial scripts presents an account of traitors that avoids the misunderstandings generated by standpoint theory's margin-center cartography. It also offers a dynamic account of traitors that is consistent with the epistemic framework of standpoint theory's margin-center cartography. It also offers a dynamic account of traitors that is consistent with the epistemic framework of standpoint theory. This distinction between privilege-cognizant and privilege-evasive scripts is another way of articulating the distinction standpoint theorists make between a standpoint and a perspective. Privilege-evasive white scripts might be said to have unreflective perspectives on race. For example, most liberal discourse on racism illustrates a form of linguistic privilege-evasiveness characteristic of the whitely scripts. Phrases such as "I don't see color, I just see people," or "We all belong to the same race—the human race" erase color, which also amounts to a failure to recognize whiteness (Frankenberg 1993, 149). Privilege-cognizant scripts rely on antiracist standpoints because they come about through collective resistance to naturalized patterns of behavior and social actions that reproduce white privilege. Animating a privilege-cognizant script requires more than occasionally interrupting racist jokes, listening to people of color, or selling black families real estate in white neighborhoods. An occasional traitorous act does not a traitor make. Truly animating a privilege-cognizant white script requires that traitors cultivate a character from which traitorous practices will flow.

Cultivating a Traitorous Character

When traitors refuse to act out of the spontaneous whitely consciousness that history has bestowed on them, they shift more than just their way of seeing and understanding the world. To be a race traitor is to have a particular kind of character that predisposes a person to animate privilege-cognizant scripts. The shift from privilege-evasive to privilege-cognizant white scripts, then, can be understood as a shift in character. It is this change in character that causes whites to move "off-center," to reposition themselves with regard to privilege. This final section briefly explores what it might mean to cultivate a traitorous character and demonstrates why developing a traitorous character must include being a "world"-traveler.

The idea that animating privilege-cognizant scripts helps to cultivate a traitorous character, and that traitorous characters are more likely to animate these scripts is, at root, Aristotelian: Becoming traitorous is a process similar to the acquisition of moral virtue (Aristotle 1980). For Aristotle, virtues arise through habit, not nature. Virtue is a disposition to choose according to a rule; namely, the rule by which a truly virtuous person possessed of moral insight would choose. All things that come to us by nature we first acquire potentially; it is only later that we exhibit the activity. We become virtuous by doing virtuous deeds. Although states of character arise from activity, Aristotle makes a distinction between two sorts of activities and their ends. There are activities such as shipbuilding, in which the product of one's activity (the ship) is an end distinct from the process of shipbuilding; and, there are activities such as getting in shape where the product (a healthy and fit body) is part of the activity of working out and not a distinct end. The activity of virtue resembles the workout example. Just as a person does not become fit by doing a series of situps and then declaring, "There, I am fit!" so a person does not become virtuous by doing a series of good deeds and then declaring, "Finally, I am virtuous!" Virtue and fitness arise in the process of continually working out or doing good deeds. We become virtuous when we have the practical wisdom, for example, to act courageously to the right degree, for the right reasons, and under the right circumstances.

When Harding describes standpoints as achievements, I think she means "achievement" in the sense in which having a virtuous character is an achievement (1991, 127). Achieving a traitorous standpoint, like cultivating virtue, is a process. When a person has the practical wisdom to know which lines in whitely scripts to change, when to change them, and when to leave them alone, then they can be said to possess the practical wisdom necessary for a traitorous character.[3] Having a traitorous character is not the same thing as possessing a particular trait. Just as there is no recipe for attaining a virtuous character, there is no one formula for becoming a race traitor. It is a mistake to think that becoming traitorous is tantamount to completely overcoming racism. There will be times when our traitorous practical wisdom will be a bit off and we will fall back into privilege-evasive scripts, often without being aware that we are doing so. An account of traitorous character recognizes this instability. Developing a traitorous character requires a political strategy. It is not enough, as Harding says, to repeat what African-American thinkers say, and never to take responsibility for my own analyses of the world that I, a European American, can see through the lens of their insights. A "functioning anti-racist—one who can pass the 'competency test' as an anti-racist—must be an actively thinking anti-racist, not just a white robot programmed to repeat what Blacks say." (Harding 1991, 290–291)

Developing a traitorous character requires lots of legwork. Learning about the lives of those on the margins means understanding the material conditions that give rise to outsider-within analyses; and to gain such an understanding, traitors must be "world"-travelers. In her now-classic essay, "Playfulness, 'World'-Traveling, and Loving Perception," (1987) María Lugones offers an account of identity in which subjects are shifting and multiplicitous. Recognizing identities as plural takes place through a process she calls "world"-traveling.[4] Lugones believes that women's failure to love one another stems from a failure to identify with women who inhabit worlds they do not share; it is a failure to see oneself in other women who are different. Lugones' work addresses this failure, which she attributes to seeing others, who occupy worlds outside the ones in which we feel comfortable, with "arrogant eyes." When white women perceive Asian women with "arrogant eyes," or when African-American women view Jewish women with arrogant perception, they fail to interact and identify with one another lovingly. Because arrogance blocks coalition building, "world"-traveling must be done with loving perception.

The notions of "world," "world"-traveling, and "loving perception" help Lugones to explain why she is perceived as serious in Anglo, or white, worlds where she is not at ease, and as "playful" in Latina worlds where she is at home. The failure of white women to love women of color is implicit in whitely scripts in which Anglo women "ignore us, ostracize us, render us invisible, stereotype us, leave us completely alone, interpret us as crazy. All of this *while we are in their midst*." (Lugones 1987, 7)

The privilege-evasive scripts animated by white women are easily explained in the logic of world-travel. The failure of whites to see race privilege is, in part, a function of a failure to world-travel. In the United States, people of color world-travel out of necessity, but white privilege ensures that most whites need to world-travel only voluntarily. When Anglo women refuse to travel to worlds where they are ill at ease, they are animating privilege-evasive scripts. Most whites are at ease in white worlds where we are fluent speakers, where we know and can safely animate whitely scripts, where people of color are out of our line of vision, and where our racial identity is not as risk. When I restrict my movement to worlds in which I am comfortable, privilege is difficult to see, and whitely scripts are never challenged. Loving perception requires that white women world-travel as a way of becoming aware of the privilege-evasive scripts we have learned.

World-travel, then, is an indispensable strategy for cultivating a traitorous character. Traitors must get out of those locations and texts in which they feel at home. World-travel forces us to put or privileged identities at risk by traveling to worlds where we often feel ill at ease or off-center. Like virtuousness, traitorousness requires developing new habits, and one crucial habit might be to resist the temptation to retreat back to those worlds where we feel at ease—whole. In the process of traveling, our identities fall apart, our privilege-evasive scripts no longer work, and the luxury of retreating to a safe space is temporarily removed. Travel makes privilege-evasive scripts visible, and we get a glimpse of how we are seen through the eyes of those whom we have been taught to perceive arrogantly.

Mab Segrest's story is a moving illustration of how world-travel is integral to coalition building across boundaries of race, gender, class, and sexual orientation. As a white lesbian doing civil rights work in North Carolina, Segrest explains how "with Reverend Lee and Christina in my first months at Statesville, I crossed and recrossed more racial boundaries than I had ever managed in the eighteen years I had lived in my similar Alabama hometown. With them, I had access to the Black community, and I saw white people through their eyes." (1994, 17) Learning to see ourselves as others see us is a necessary starting point for learning to undo privilege-evasive scripts. Whites like Segrest, who, with "loving perception," travel to the worlds inhabited by African-American civil rights activists in the South, put their identities at risk and, in so doing, realize the difficulties surrounding the process of unlearning privilege-evasive scripts.

The approach I have outlined here is not a radical break from Harding's original insight. What I have tried to do is to rearticulate her insights in a language that avoids some of the confusion I think the margin-center cartography of feminist standpoint theory encourages. I have also tried to explore what it might be like to cultivate a traitorous character in a way that focuses on traitorous performances, rather than on traitorous identities and locations. The idea that traitorousness requires developing a traitorous character that makes one more likely to animate a privilege-cognizant script is very much in the spirit of Harding's work. Although Harding's descriptions of traitors as "becoming marginal" through a process of "reinventing oneself as other" limits her descriptions of traitors, I think that she is after an active account of traitorousness as more than just a political identity. Recall that "reinventing ourselves as other" refers to a shift in one's way of seeing, and Lugones' sense of world-travel certainly does this. Harding hints at this when she says "intellectual and political *activity* are required in using another's insights to generate one's own analyses." (1991, 290) Harding's description of traitorousness as political activity is closer to the performative notion I have in mind, and I think it is one with which she would agree.

Notes

1. This chapter is the product of many conversations I had during a National Endowment for the Humanities summer seminar on feminist epistemologies, June–July 1996, in Eugene, Oregon. I would like to thank Drue Barker, Lisa Heldke, Sarah Hoagland, Amber Katherine, Shelly Park, and Nancy Tuana for their thoughts on this topic during our time together.

2. As standpoint theory for uses on institutional systems, practices, and discourses that unequally distribute power, the word *privilege* is used to refer to systematically conferred advantages individuals enjoy by virtue of their membership in dominant groups with access to resources and institutional power that are beyond the common advantages of marginalized citizens (Bailey 1998).

3. Traitorous acts committed just for the sake of traitorousness can be dangerous. History and literature are filled with cases of well-meaning whites whose good intentions put the lives, jobs, or achievements of friends and acquaintances of color in jeopardy. See, for example, the fictional case of Bigger Thomas in Richard Wright's novel *Native Son* (1940).

4. For those unfamiliar with Lugones' work, "worlds" are neither utopias nor constructions of whole societies. They may be small parts of a society (e.g., a barrio in Chicago, Chinatown, a lesbian bar, a women's studies class, or a farmworkers' community). The shift from having one attribute, say playfulness, in a world where one is at ease, to having another attribute, say seriousness, in another world is what Lugones calls "travel" (Lugones 1987).

Bibliography

Aristotle. *Nichomachean Ethics*, translated by W. D. Ross. New York: Oxford University Press, 1980.

Bailey, Alison. "Privilege: Expanding on Marilyn Frye's 'Oppression.'" *Journal of Social Philosophy* 29, no. 3 (1998): 104–119.

Braden, Anne. *The Wall Between*. New York: Monthly Review Press, 1958.

Collins, Patricia Hill. "Learning from the Outsider Within: The Sociological Significance of Black Feminist Thought." *Social Problems* 33, no. 6 (1986): s14–s32.

———. *Black Feminist Thought: Knowledge, Consciousness and the Politics of Empowerment*. New York: Routledge, 1990.

Davion, Victoria. "Reflections on the Meaning of White." In *Overcoming Racism and Sexism*, edited by Linda Bell and David Blumenfeld. Lanham, MD: Rowman and Littlefield, 1995.

DuBois, W. E. B. *The Souls of Black Folk*. Mineola, NY: Dover, 1994 (1903).

Frankenberg, Ruth. *White Women, Race Matters: The Social Construction of Whiteness*. Minneapolis: University of Minnesota Press, 1993.

Frye, Marilyn. "White Woman Feminist." In *Willful Virgin: Essays in Feminist Theory*. Freedom, CA: Crossing Press, 1992.

Harding, Sandra. *Whose Science? Whose Knowledge? Thinking from Women's Lives.* Ithaca: Cornell University Press, 1991.

Jaggar, Alison. *Feminist Politics and Human Nature.* Totowa, NJ: Rowman and Allanheld, 1983.

Lugones, María. "Playfulness, 'World'-Traveling, and Loving Perception." *Hypatia* 2, no. 2 (1987): 3–21.

Rich, Adrienne. "Disloyal to Civilization: Feminism, Racism, and Gynophobia." In *On Lies, Secrets, and Silence.* New York: W. W. Norton, 1979.

Segrest, Mab. *Memoir of a Race Traitor.* Boston: South End Press, 1994.

Smith, Lillian. *Killers of the Dream.* New York. W. W. Norton, 1949.

Staples, Brent. "Just Walk on By: A Black Man Ponders His Power to Alter Public Space." *Ms.* 15, no. 3 (1986): 54, 86.

Wright, Richard. *Native Son.* New York: Harper and Brothers, 1940.

CHAPTER TEN

~

Mobility-Unlimitation-Acceleration: General Insights and Feminist Intentions

Birge Krondorfer

It is high time to realize that the aimed-at control of mankind over everything existing increasingly manifests itself as destruction; it is high time to realize that the dematerialization of the world, its transformation into images, representations, and signs has grown into an incomparable imaginary obsession which has a tendency to annul every difference between reality and fiction and, thereby, to create an incessant vertigo, it is high time to realize that especially the theoretical strategies for coping with the problems of life have become deadly machines that do not leave anything untouched. The growing scandal, however, lies in the fact that processes like these are not brought about by evil enemies, but by humans of good will. (Kamper 1987)

Contrary to what the media constantly want to make us believe, today's enemy is not "fundamentalism" but the cynic—even a particular form of "deconstruction" participates in universal cynicism by suggesting a "provisional morality": "In theory (in the academic practice of writing), you can deconstruct as much as you want to and what you want, but in everyday life, you have to join in the currently dominating social game." (Zizek 1993)

Presuppositions

This chapter will not be academic in the conventional sense of the term, nor will it be dedicated to specific goals of research. Rather, I would like to combine a particular attitude with the formation of a theory. By that, I do not mean to decorate an arbitrary opinion (a *Meinung* which, according to Hegel, can only ever state something that is already mine or that belongs to me)[1] with the results of some research. Working in a feminist tradition, I will rather link the concrete level of experience and knowledge with the abstract level of theoria (the female spectator) and academic discourses embedded within it. I would like to do this so that I may offer a supplement to the trend sketched as follows:

> Western feminist theorizing has evaporated into the thin air of academic philosophical discourse. Academic front gardens are being tended and extended. The results that get announced are very often banal, linguistically inflated everyday experiences. Since these female theoreticians steer clear of feminist-political practice they can only put off the demise of their "theory" by a means a "reign of discourse"—which seems to be the adequate term for the current state of postmodernist or neofeminist theoretical discussions. Abstaining from practice, on the one hand, leads to abstaining from theory, on the other. An everyday consciousness evacuated in the sense just explained is helpless in the face of the "trim" effected media message. (Editorial 1993, 6)

Contrary to this trend, I will speak here of a kind of knowledge that starts to think about the connection among contents, structures, and emotions; one that strives to conceive the split between knowledge and action—a split that is nowadays taken into account by the reflexively cushioned consciousness of cynical subjects—as an adjustment to a bad whole/general, or as an infringement on feminist movements and their modalities of thinking. This kind of knowledge would be a philosophy of practice and (the production of) theory considered from a feminist point of view, but also with feminist intentions, intentions that enormously complicate the point of view in every respect. This is because the "supposed" intention is not transparent for everybody and every woman. The intention is to "plunge into . . . that self-analytical process of mankind where both blockades and search operations can be detected in the collective formation of symptoms, and the object of knowledge confronts the cognizing subject with the necessity to approach [the object] as a riddle. A riddle which, on the one hand, s/he has to solve; a riddle which, on the other hand, he is already a part of." (Weiland 1990, 27)

The reason is this:

> By doing so, we should start a process of self-reflection that would necessarily have to work off the substrate of culture based on a "history of fascination."

"History of fascination" means the following: to read, all through history, that which both attracts and repels us as unsettled conflicts that still interfere with our decisions and preferences today. To aim at a generic analysis that takes its departure from the "history of fascination" as a collective formation of symptoms would not be a bad task for philosophy. Still, this task would require more than just "philosophizing." (1990, 27)

A merely hierarchized announcement usurps the genesis of the "coming-to-oneself" of female subjects—a genesis that turns itself against an arbitrariness disguised as liberality. This arbitrariness often mistakes itself for the potential of emancipation. This potential of emancipation, however, remains an abstract "liberation" because it misses the chance to find out about and reflect upon the common basis of the need for knowledge and to "translate" this common basis into politicized fields. To put it differently: What is crucial is the question of a political embodiment of theory construction and the ones working in this field, an embodiment mediated with all the other realms of practice.

If the history of mankind "can be described as a progressive differentiation of social bodies," (Heintel/Macho 1987, 303) women have not found or invented their bodies yet. It seems as if the temptation to become absorbed into the male-dominated symbolic order of the social fabric is as strong as rendering subjectivity (oriented towards consumption or production) absolute in an economically or technically supported (or demanded) sense—a process that confuses singularity with (common or single-minded) stubbornness. Since the systematic crossing and intertwinedness of sociality and corporeality, of thinking and organization, has not—throughout history—engendered a female "principle of design/creation" and terrain yet, it is easier to engage in decisive practices of initiation and (sacrificial) rituals than to rely upon the intertwined forlornness of female "a-topias."

This is not only to be understood as a reproach or imperative for current feminist research and teaching, because the concern with the organizational history of cultures of thinking and acting is hardly present in current discourses. The reasonable statement that the organization of thinkers determines the organization of thought is as simple as it is unknown and unacknowledged/unrecognized by most people.

The organization of theoreticians . . . does not remain an external element of thought, but determines the possibility of its development. Of course, this not only presents a dilemma but also at the same time a chance not to be missed: new thoughts also make possible new forms of associating people. (Macho 1984, 173)

This, however, would require a link between both meanings of the very concept of "association." The feminist labor of thinking would primarily have to aim for the reflection of the social fabric as a social formation endowed with a certain "truth," but without denying its historically and contemporarily, its individually and collectively presupposed inclusiveness.

Holdings

Mobility is usually regarded as an achievement of civilization within affluent societies as exemplified in the sector of tourism, in business, and in management, but also in the postmodernist discourse about aestheticized nomadism. A different view is suggested by the perspective of forced mobilization, as embodied by refugees fleeing the poverty outside of the so-called civil societies or by the flexibilized work force on the inside. Here, however, I want to reflect upon that side of the concept that brings the technical and economic aspect/mode of mobility into focus. For that purpose, I want to invoke the concept of mobilization. Above all, this term indicates the martial side of the mobile. Here are some notes about this aspect:

—The gait of the modern process of civilization presupposes violence. Disciplinary power is one of its inherent features (see Foucault 1977 and Girard 1992). The anth(d)ropocentric difference that was always supposed to be resolved technically, seems to have found a "relational substance" in the triad of "atom, bit and gene." In this triad, the "mediation of substance and subject" has become manifest. The "technological formation" appears as the dominant "self-interpretation" of man in which he can regain himself as real (see Hülsmann 1988). A critique of the metaphysics of understanding, of instrumental reason, and of the naive faith in the progress of technology cannot obscure the fact that world-society was formed Eurocentrically within/through the realm of that very metaphysics. This attempt of coping with difference, the defeat of the strangeness/foreignness (of nature) teams up with one side of the character of production (Heintel). The very old distinction between technology and art (*poiesis*) is, on the one hand, related to production as a methodly governed making-of-products and, on the other hand, to the production of a trace by the emergence-through-birth towards the open. (Political action must also be considered as a metaphorical taking up of the basic gesture of "born-ness," of coming-into-the-world and bringing-into-the-world [see Arendt 1989].) Our process of civilization "speeds up the escape of technology from 'the open.' Technology does not really 'produce' products in the proper sense of the word but is rather, according to its mode of production, a motherless forcing (or forcing-into-being) of things that function in a certain way. From the point of view of the usage of resources, technical technology and a dismantling consumption, from a kinetic point of view, it is an aggressive mobilization, from the point of view of bringing-into-the-world, it is a production of monsters by monsters." (Sloterdijk 1989, 156)

—In the modern age, self-conceived human being as the project of a kinetic utopia—cannot be grasped without the aspect of motion. The subject and his/her automobile belong to each other just like the mind/ soul and body do. Paul Virilio (1989) has described this state of affairs as the history of the "metempsychosis (transmigration of souls) of the passenger." The mutation of transportation ropes the body into dromoscopic devices and into three possible formations of movement: the homosexual couple of the duel, the heterosexual couple of marriage, the transsexual couple of the journey. Comfortably immobile, we sit in missiles where standstill and speed become one—as an effect of a history that starts out with the fact that "man is the passenger of woman" and the "wifey is the medium of man in order to be born." The "burden-woman"—a first "means of transportation"—makes possible the "hunter-man," the "warrior with free, released time (for fighting)," and the robbery of the bride. Today, it makes possible the assessorship with anonymous strangers that vanish as quickly as they arrive. (1989, 29–45).

> Swept along and captured by the violence of the trip, we can only affirm this acceleration which means a loss of the immediate. Through its violence, speed becomes both destiny and purpose . . . departure and separation from the living in favor of insubstantial quickness. (Virilio 1989, 34)
>
> The passenger who is freighted in an automobile box, who desires a metallic body and is desired by this body as well, re-enacts the original coupling. The materialist Occident has shifted its metempsychosis, as it were, into existing bodies through this revolution of transport; regardless of the transitions represented by birth and death, the motion industry fuels these transfers and we "function" from here to there, from this to that, locked into the periods of speed and walled into the energy of traveling, we are continuously being put together and pulled apart by the rhythms of technology. (p. 44)

—Now that the subject is dead and, therefore, its structure is more alive than ever (and rears its ugly male head under female "circumstances" and vice versa), there is a lot of euphemistic talk about the self—as in: self-consciousness, self-preservation, catching-up-with-the-self, passing-by-the-self—with the effect that one easily forgets that one cannot escape one's own objectification.

> The current situation of women is determined by their integration/exploitation in a world-wide system of production and reproduction that can be called a computer science of oppression. Housing, the workplace, public spaces, even the body itself—can all be scattered and tied together in almost an infinity of ways which has far-reaching consequences for women and others. The consequences are very different for different people and make it hard to imagine international oppositional groupings or their survival. (Angerer 1993, 740, quoting Donna Haraway)

Is this universally connected imaginary mobility a global prison? The body in the missile, the missile in the head? Anthropologically, weapons are media of distancing and an escape from the strange/foreign—an escape that is lowered into them. A virtual limitlessness which suggests mobile communication is equivalent to an identity based on the prohibition of bodily contact.

> Developments in the realm of "virtual reality"—which is exclusively based on digital technology—are effects of the fact that bodily contact belongs to a condemned order. . . . In the hierarchy of senses, touch is said to be blind. . . . Since touch does not abstract, it is annihilated, with eyes wide open. . . . "Virtual reality" seems to open up "worlds" never seen before. They are also supposed to be "solid-enough-to-touch." The signal which is electronically commanded by pressing a key realizes what is excluded from the sense of touch . . . the annihilation of the trace of sensing . . . by way of the perfect mediatization of bodily contact. . . . The wound that is feared in the case of bodily contact ultimately refers to an entanglement by the female . . . (which is) a reversal of birth that has always been considered as the beginning of the end of "immunity." . . . The woman as "illness" or "epidemic" that can only produce a transient life is the presupposition and the effect of the prohibition of bodily contact. (Treusch-Dieter 1993, 94)

The capacity of the formation and binding of "social uteri" is infringed upon, if not to say, destroyed. Orders of affiliation are shattered, restorative fantasies of descent emerge. Emigration (outside) and immigration (inside) find their complement here that is supposed to be left behind by the mobile limitlessness of a fantasmatic communication.

Insofar as politics in the classical sense has meant the art of belonging together in the towns and huge empires of the agricultural age, the "death of God" means that the bell tolls for politics. The spatial concepts of the middle world-age characterized by cultivating the ground cannot be applied to the new synchronous world-space that is increasingly emerging. The players in this new game of the industrial age do not define themselves in terms of a "home country" or soil, but in terms of access to railway stations, terminals, and possibilities of connections. For them, the world is a interconnected hyper-sphere. . . . (This) form of a large world continues the well-known megalo-pathetic stress in the shape of extended circles—but today people in the streets are supposed to worry in a way which once was appropriate for foreign ministers. That the politicians in charge are only rarely up for the challenges of the new situation—almost never with respect to intellect, occasionally with respect to morals, after a fashion with respect to pragmatics—all this contributes to the feeling of unease vis-à-vis the political class. (Sloterdijk 1993, 54)

Economy makes sure that the new situation of the big world also affects the stomach . . . distribution, packaging, burning, digestion unite huge populations across enormous distances into hybrid communities of metabolism. . . . The traditional and difficult synchronicity of forms of the should with forms of the world are not enough for an existence in the global world. The megalomania of long ago becomes today's holomania. . . . The old cosmopolitanism changes into a cosmo-pathetic nomadism—the earth becomes an arena for the members of the hyper-civilization in which the reformatting of the soul according to the demands of the synchronous world has to be practiced. (pp. 52–53)

The prosthesis of cosmopolitanism, information technology, and television, for instance, or the sublime replacement of sensitivity/introspection, as exemplified by the meditation industry and the psycho-boom, gives the false impression of an open-minded self-consciousness. Inside and outside—as categories of a genealogical system (a principle of ordering)—have lost their validity as a result of global economic and technological transformation processes. On the one hand, these categories are situated and restored by economic walls; on the other hand, the limit between inside and outside is transferred into the subjects themselves.

[The subjects] themselves are now supposed to take exclusive responsibility for the demarcation of their inner, private and their outer, public existence. The whole world—as the new outside—is opened up for the single subject—as the inside of acts of reflection, relations towards one-self, its drives and maxims—but it is also placed upon it as a burden. Cosmopolitanism and sensitivity/introspection: the modern subject is supposed to meet both demands: above all, what it has gained is the knowledge of the time limit of its own life—without the perspective of justice or a heavenly compensation for biographical asymmetries. (Macho 1991, 101)

—In postmodern times, identity—which (according to Hegel) is always constituted by identity and nonidentity—has to face a continuous am-bivalence between the so-called self/one's own and the so-called other/foreign if it does not want to offer itself to a cynically cushioned con-sciousness of fatalism nor to a warped (which means recoding) innate statute of values. A fundamental problem of human existence that is al-ways defined by coercion and liberty, necessity and self-invention is the problem of need (and its concept). This problem is increasingly being torn between maximization and impoverishment. Whereas appetite seeks momentary satisfaction, the notion of need means to sensibly place the tension between the present and a goal that is to be obtained in a durable context. Thought of as identity, this tension is both a pre-supposition and an effect of labor that nowadays has supposedly van-ished and that, paradoxically, has to be artificially created. Yet, the par-ticular individual is unable to derive a concrete functionality from an abstract and general formula in which she or he is mediated with all the others. Concreteness, however, does not matter to the contemporary (Western European) social synthesis of commodity exchange. This is because the fundamental character of post/modern universalization is unlimitation (*Entgrenzung*) and acceleration:

What is universalized is some abstract entity (a certain image of man) within which contents multiply in a way that makes the generalization of these contents impossible. The issue of human needs can illustrate this: As Hegel has analyzed, commodity exchange, by which the needs of bourgeois society are socially mediated, is totally detached from the level of concreteness. Abstraction applies to both the objects of needs and the needs themselves. What the object of need means from a social point of view, and what distinguishes this object of need in its social meaning from other objects, cannot be a concrete purpose anymore. Within social relations, use value does not matter anymore. What is rel-evant is the abstract exchange value. Conversely, it does not matter so-cially which concrete purpose and which concrete need an individual attaches to a certain object, as long as he attaches some purpose to the object. In fact, individuals in bourgeois society relate to each other in such a way that the concreteness of contents does not matter anymore, and this fact releases the enormous economic power of this society . . . "indeterminate multiplication and specification of needs, means, pleasures, which . . . have no limit," Hegel says. (Berger 1993, 240)

General imperatives do not have counterparts in social space that could legitimate them and make them practical. Real possibilities of a valid generalization of contents fail because the abstract whole/general allows just any content. This is the flip side of a plurality that suggestively validates itself as liberty after having been evacuated in terms of democracy.

—The production of more and more of the same (by the same) in order to improve and even save the world has reached its limits. The signature of general meaning and concrete being—and vice versa—has curdled into an economic calculation that seems to guarantee the general context in the same way as the true self-determination of individuals imagines itself in the acquisition of commodity design. The necessity of events is argued for by the force of circumstances and economic "reason," such that the future is only decipherable under a disastrous omen for many people. Against this, fundamental questions concerning the genealogy of our thinking, our assessments, our modes of production, our identifications, and our relations to nature must be asked. The central point of departure for this questioning is the "model of the modern age," which has universally come out on top as the Western model of production and consumption. The predominance of economy in the modern age determines all decision processes with respect to conflicts, contradictions, and shortcomings that are supposed to be overcome by an increasing dose of economy, whether or not these conflicts, contradictions, and shortcomings are even situated within the field of economy. The modern form of economy is not based on the principle of supply—like it used to be in premodern societies—but on the principle of production. The production of the labor market, together with the necessary "letting go" of individuals, could only be affected by disciplinary processes. These processes persist until the succession of the living—according to the principle of exchange as a means to overcome strangeness/foreignness—facilitates their subsistence in the paralyzed mobility of a progressing teleology of constantly increasing income. Since modern economy could only be so expansive in a triumvirate with technology and science—and in connection with specific forms of organization—the axioms and categories of this specific formation have to be shattered. The economic system in connection with technological science has become the epitome of modern rationality, which—through the utilization/exploration of nature, the body, and the soul—can be considered as closed off. The content of this project was the cold, male, calculating gaze that subjected all areas of human life to a calculating, mathematical understanding that had to function according to criteria of efficiency, success, and achievement. Consistency, measurability, generality, order, abstractness, production, growth, and positivity.

—Globalization, or the incorporation of all humans and spaces into the currently existing economic system, also incorporates time (or times, because the economy also occupies the future).

> It is one of the fundamental conditions of our system that time is money and that time is only considered as fulfilled if it is spent "productively"— i.e., in the sense of production. The acceleration and "productive condensation" of time prevents any accompanying reflection and, ultimately, thought in general. One has to take note of the fact that the currently existing economic system optimally protects itself from any collective self-reflection . . . especially by those concerned—through universalization . . . and acceleration of time; its internal process constantly decrees a ban on thought. (Heintel 1993, 33)
>
> It is the maxim of dispossessed time to produce more and more in shorter periods of time. "Saving time" is the motto, calculated in currencies. Still, there is less and less of it—of time, and of subjective temporality. The colonization of space has shifted to the colonization of time. Someone-else's-time, which labels itself as generality, ties the desubjectified subjects to a negative dialectics: The more mature we feel, the more dependent we are; the more independent, the more aligned; the more liberated, the more connected. Is the strategy of delay the only remaining variety within the apparatuses that program us?
>
> Is the acceleration of time a secularization of our ancient desires to become immortal? Is the strived-for simultaneity the complement of a mystical instantaneous eternity? Our modern age started out with the motto to "productively" overcome death. The more it has contributed towards this end, the closer we have collectively approached death. (Heintel 1990, 2)

Borders are transgressed with great ease; eternity has become easy to produce. Yet, that also means that we belong to a comprehensive, immanent system such that differentiations can only ever take place within that very system.

Whoever eats the same, drinks the same, travels to the same places, goes to the same theaters, reads the same in a newspaper etc. cannot believe to differ substantially from others in the long run: consumption, the tremendously differentiated range of items for sale—all this can be seen as an attempt to change things; . . . [These are], however, just external capacities of delay. . . . Dominant technologies of culture are being developed. They are supposed to meet every demand, . . . everybody uses the same technology in everyday life, everybody drives in a car. The era/calendar is correct (and "tunes" people) everywhere to the world. We are all subjected to the same order. We are synchronized in our media of understanding, of communication, and of transport; and it becomes more and more difficult to bring alternatives to bear. . . . This synchronization has become a necessary condition of a transnational understanding and of a general coping with everyday life; but how is the particular still possible within this synchronization? (Heintel 1993, 54)

Prospects

The position of theory vis-à-vis the system is up for scrutiny today. Is the formation of knowledge as a regulative idea finally outmoded? At the same time, the reflection of science as one of many models and its organization are on the agenda. So far, however, not a single form of organization has ever licensed difference. This "absolute immanentism" (Heintel 1993, 54) of universities, media, technology, economy, and politics—combined with the fact that we have all become "inmates of the system" (p. 54)—means a "loss of the outside" and hence, a loss of the capacity to act and create/arrange. How is a "transcendence of the system" (p. 54) possible? Can a practice of visions still be constituted? Can a concrete whole/general be constituted that does not miscalculate either in fundamentalisms or in arbitrariness (which would be the dynamic force of the abstract whole/general) and in which the individual "makes" sense in her/his difference? This is noticeable in the so-called free play of forces—which releases people from the responsibility to produce history/histories. But this play of forces can hardly be accepted as "true." There is the consciousness of the capacity to intervene, but this capacity is itself not so much an issue of individual abilities of insight—because this insight is obstructed by a self-propelled history authorized by us and by the corresponding subjective helplessness. Rather, what is at stake are "alternative forms of organization of a new collective concentration . . . and a new consciousness of organization." (Berger and Pellert 1993, 11) The latter might not so much be—as one would expect—on a narrowing, on the exclusion and the elimination of the other, but on a limitation of needs (in)to a measure "without a name." (Aristotle, quoted in Berger 1993, 248) This is not possible by falling back on categories of nature nor by an anticipation of the history of progress. The wound of the problem is the fact that so far all concepts have presupposed a whole/general, which must remain abstract regarding the uncoupling of the general from the particular in our culture. With respect to the thus unsurmounted difference between the concrete and the abstract, the answer was based on the superiority of partial realities (technology, economy, media, science) as paradigms of Western civilization. The superiority of partial realities has found "solutions" for all other realities by excluding all that does not fit into their scheme. What we really need is an outside within the inside, a difference within the undifferentiated, and to say it again: a transcendence of the system, an "ethics of the particular" which would be—emphatically speaking—a leaving-open of the whole/general that always has to be put in concrete terms in each specific case. However, the hope for accomplished social bodies cannot really offer any perspective if it is not complemented by the experience of borders and a contact with the "different." The reconciling dialectics of individual attributes and social tributes remain an ahistorical murmur beyond all accumulated enlightenment—even more so as long as insights into the process of degradation are obstructed by a limitless dynamics of feasibility.

> In the long term, the consciousness of affiliation can only be maintained as a consciousness of limits. . . . We have to climb over the fence or at least, look over the fence in order to know and learn to understand what is happening with the enclosure. (Macho 1987, 430)

Women have long been degraded as "particulars." They mark the (gender) difference within the dialectics of incorporation and exclusion, and therefore they are also a basis of the symbolic order. At the same time and to some extent, they slip away from it. Who else would be more appropriate to act as a consciousness of the limits than you?

If the history of mankind can be described as a progressive differentiation of social bodies, women have not found or invented their bodies yet. Since the systematic crossing and intertwinedness of sociality and corporeality, of thinking and organization, has not—throughout history—engendered a female "principle of design/creation" and terrain yet, it is so far (or once again?) easier to engage in decisive practices of initiation and (sacrificial) rituals than to rely upon the intertwined forlornness of female "a-topias." Against this suppression of suppression, a reflection of disparities is of high priority. Not as a positivist mediation, not as the postulate of a highest good or of the identity of substance and subject, not as a phantasmagoria of individual thinkers—but as the license of an a-topical place with which we are somehow already familiar and which—by setting off for extremes—holds up something that is not guaranteed (and cannot even be promised).

> The strategy of delay, the stalling game, is the only remaining variety within the apparatuses that program us. We can no longer be revolutionaries, only saboteurs. . . . We are counter-revolutionary because hesitation is the only strategy we have at our disposal as regards the dangers that are threatening us. Hesitation is the only possibility to stick by liberty and resist stupidity. (Flusser 1993, 16)

We have to allow ourselves a pause for reflection in order to deal with fundamental questions. A presupposition of this would be an attitude of the particular with respect to times of creation/arrangement and spaces of education—against a vacuous diversity—but of distance.

Note

1. In German, *Meinung* means "opinion," and *mein* means "mine."

Bibliography

Angerer, Marie-Luise (1993). "'The Pleasure of the Interface:' Beziehungsgeflechte in einer telematischen Kultur" in: *Zeitschrift für Philosophie und Sozialwissenschaften*, Hamburg: Argument, 737–748.
Arendt, Hannah (1989). *Vita Activa oder Vom tätigen Leben*. Munich: Piper.
Berger, Wilhelm (1993). "Begrenzung und Entgrenzung: Menschliche Bedürfnisse als ethisches Problem," in: Wilhelm Berger/Ada Pellert (eds), *Der verlorene Glanz der Ökonomie: Kritik und Orientierung*, Vienna: Falter, 237–248.
Berger, Wilhelm/Pellert, Ada (1993). "Introduction", in: Berger/Pellert (eds.), *Der verlorene Glanz*, 9–13.
Editorial (1993) in: Feminis-muß, *Sozialwissenschaftliche Forschung & Praxis für Frauen e.V.* Issue 35, Cologne: beiträge zur feministischen theorie und praxis, 5–8.
Flusser, Vilém (1993). *Nachgeschichte: Eine korrigierte Geschichtsschreibung.* Bensheim/Düsseldorf: Bollmannbibliothek.
Foucault, Michel (1977). *Überwachen und Strafen*. Frankfurt/Main: Suhrkamp.
Girard, René (1992). *Das Heilige und die Gewalt*. Frankfurt/Main: Fischer.
Heintel, Peter (1990). "Thesen zur Gründung des 'Vereins zur Verzögerung der Zeit,'" typoscripte.

———. (1993). "Alternative Modellbildung in der Ökonomie," in: Wilhelm Berger/Ada Pellert (eds), *Der verlorene Glanz der Ökonomie: Kritik und Orientierung*, Vienna: Falter, 17–72.

Heintel, Peter/Macho,Thomas H. (1987). "Der soziale Körper: Kynismus und Organisation," in: Peter Sloterdijk, '*Kritik der zynischen Vernunft*,' Frankfurt/Main: edition suhrkamp, 290–323.

Hülsmann, Heinz (1988). *Subjektivität und Technologie*. Klagenfurt: KTB.

Kamper, Dietmar. (1987). *Die unvollendete Vernunft: Moderne versus Postmoderne*. Frankfurt/Main: Suhrkamp.

Macho, Thomas (1984). "Gedankenorganisation", in: Gerd B. Achenbach (ed), *Philosophische Praxis*, Cologne: Jürgen Dinter, 161–176.

———. (1987). *Todesmetaphern*. Frankfurt/Main: Suhrkamp.

———. (1991). "Drinnen und Draußen: Reflexionen zur Ordnung der Räume," in: Birge Krondorfer/Wolfgang Müller-Funk (eds), *Die Kunst zu existieren: Lebensstil und Politik*, Tuebingen: konkursbuch, 93–103.

Sloterdijk, Peter (1989). *Eurotaoismus: Zur Kritik der politischen Kinetik*. Frankfurt/Main: edition suhrkamp.

———. (1993). *Im selben Boot: Versuch über die Hyperpolitik*, Frankfurt/Main: Suhrkamp.

Treusch-Dieter, Gerburg (1993). "Lückenhafte Anmerkungen zu Müttern und Amazonen mit einem unausgedachten Schluß," in: Rudolf Maresch (ed), *Zukunft oder Ende*, Munich: Klaus Boer, 89–99.

Virilio, Paul (1989). *Der negative Horizont: Bewegung/Geschwindigkeit/Beschleunigung*. Munich: Carl Hanser.

Weiland, René (1990). "Verkörperungsdenken," in: René Weiland/Wolfgang Pircher (eds.), *Mythen der Rationalität. Denken mit Klaus Heinrich*, Vienna: Turia&Kant, 15–29.

Zizek, Slavoj (1993). *Grimassen des Realen. Jacques Lacan oder die Monströsität des Aktes*. Colgne: Kiepenheuer & Witsch.

~

CHAPTER ELEVEN

Place, Movement, and Identity: Rethinking Empowerment

Marjorie C. Miller

The goal of "empowerment" is a significant part of feminist rhetoric, but it is a concept in need of further clarification. I will argue first, that empowerment is related to identity; second, that identity is entangled in metaphors of "place;" and third, that the metaphor of "movement" towards empowerment is one that distorts because it begins from "place" in ways that limit identity. Finally, I will develop an analysis of identity and empowerment that, I will argue, can help to answer questions about who we are and where we want movement to take us. My argument involves two distinct dimensions: First, I want to distinguish a feminist goal of empowerment from an abstract notion of power, often rooted in "power over." Second, I want to offer a conception of identity that disentangles it from the static and fixed dimensionality of "place." The point, I take it, is to understand identity in ways that are sufficiently fluid and multidimensional to take account of the complexity of our "situations" and that provide directions for empowerment that are not merely replays of the movements of power. The questions raised involve issues in feminist philosophy from both metaphysics and politics. I argue that we have to tackle both to effectively understand empowerment.

Empowerment, the acknowledged goal of feminist movement, is etymologically related to power. It entails the bestowing of power or authority. But as a slogan it says little about what sort of power, to be used by whom and in what manner, and exercised under what circumstances. Empowering enables, permits, authorizes—but empowerment means different things to people within and between nations as well as across continents. Conventionally, empowerment refers to at least varying measures of participation, to cognitive attainments, and to attitudes. The identity of the individual or group to be empowered is too often taken for granted. I shall argue that empowerment, as a slogan and as a goal, entails that a holder of power, an individual or group, be named and identified. Empowerment entails identification—both self-identification and recognition of identity on the part of [the] others who are to grant/accept/defer to the power or authority to be exercised. Clarifying identity—who am I and who are the we struggling for power—is crucial to the matter of empowerment.

I should like to explore this question, but I should like first to detour into another matter that will take us back to the questions of identity: the matter of feminist movement.

As is the case for many of our readers, I have been a participant in the Civil Rights Movement, the Women's Movement, the Antiwar Movement, as well as considering myself, at times, in "the Movement"—a label for those identifying with an amorphous collection of leftist groups working for change. One of the reasons for the change from specifically named movements to the general term "the Movement" was that none of the labels for oppressed groups has appeared to be adequate over time (a claim I shall talk more about in a moment); and one of the reasons for the loss of the Movement's momentum is that it was amorphous, and goals and strategies and solidarities were not clear. It is not clear where we want to go, and, above all, it is not clear who "we" are.

I want to begin with a discussion of movement—but to begin with movement one must define "place." Movement occurs from here to there, from then to now, and from now to then. It occurs over time and space, from site to site, across all sorts of borders. Places, times, sites are located by borders: borders that separate, borders that divide, borders that identify.[1] This border separates people of color from the white race in the United States; that border separates men from women; another border separates lower- and working-class people from the upper classes; borders separate people of different nations and regions, and still other borders separate "we ordinary persons" from "the others." We are the ones located here; we gain strength by acting in solidarity with our comrades—those who share our space: our neighborhood, our nationhood, our race, our gender, our class. And we show our strength through movement: We march, we are on the march, and we are expanding our space, changing our place, attacking the borders, redefining our relation to the others.

The movements I have named, and others besides, have figured the changes they are working for in the marches that have been their symbols.

We who share identification show solidarity by marching—by taking to the streets and showing our numbers, our determination, and, above all, our determination to *move*. But, there is a contradictory "rootedness" to our identification with those who share our place. We praise movement, we name ourselves a Movement, we pride ourselves on the power of our Movement to resist, but we sing:

> Just like the tree that's planted in the garden, we shall not be moved! We shall not, we shall not be moved; we shall not, we shall not be moved, just like the tree that's planted in the garden, we shall not be moved![2]

Of course, the literal meaning of this contradiction has to do with the determination of subordinated groups not to give up ground, to give way to the agendas and the priorities and the demands of the dominant groups. Resistance is also resistance to the movement imposed by others. But, for so long as subordinated groups insist on keeping the ground that is our identity, as long as we insist that we will not be moved, we cannot fully participate in movement. The source of this contradiction is in the relationship between the metaphor of place (as it is implied by the conception of movement), and our understanding of identity. Let me see if I can explain this by detouring a bit into the recent history of liberation movements in the United States.[3] (Of course there are many others, both before my story begins and outside its narrative thread. I just want to attend to some particular developments in the second half of the twentieth century and into the twenty-first, the times most relevant for the argument I want to make.)

Women in the United States who had worked in both the civil rights movement and the antiwar movement became aware of the deep gender inequalities and oppressions that functioned in both and had been directly addressed by neither. Women gained the awareness that critical and oppositional consciousness, that solidarity among women, were required for women to move out of our subordinate location and into fully responsible and empowered positions in the social order. And women began to realize that solidarity was forged out of identity: We needed to identify ourselves as women, raise our consciousness together, and recognize that our common location required and empowered concerted action.[4]

African Americans also were increasingly aware of the power of identification: Identity and common location were crucial in building the critical consciousness that aided empowerment. By the 1970s it was clear that blacks needed to take back control of their own movement in order to use the common site of oppression as a source of strength. Consciousness raising is part, though not the whole, of movement to resist oppression. Resistance began to be identified with black power, with the need to speak first with one another, then to use that speech to define their identity and to use it as a source of power.[5]

Then came the book *But Some of Us Are Brave*—whose subtitle is *All the Women Are White, All the Men Are Black: Black Women's Studies*.[6] The title refers to the peculiar separation of *the women's movement* and *the black power movement*. It refers to the American tendency to talk about "women and blacks." Clearly there is something wrong here. It was evident that among blacks, half are women; among women, many are black; among black people and white people some are upper class and some are lower class—and class and race exploitation exist between genders and within genders. It was evident that something profound was wrong with the sorting that separated the women's movement from the black civil rights movement, and both from the anticolonialist, anti-imperialist, antiwar movement. Those who had identified themselves as "In the Movement," wanting to be counted as part of the generic opposition to oppression in all forms, began to confront the fact that there were multiple oppressions *within* the Movement: that identity categories were not univocal. Further, as subgroups began to recognize the value of solidarity in identification, it became increasingly clear that earlier movements had ignored or marginalized the concerns of people of color who are not black; of Asian-Americans; of Latinos and Latinas; of Native Americans. As identity movements began to consolidate, as people who suffered oppression began to come to consciousness, to identify with those who suffered as *the same*, and to develop voice together, it began to be further evident that groupings already identified ignored or marginalized gays, lesbians, and transgendered, those who were differently abled, or those who were no longer young.

To marginalize is to put outside the center, to put on the edges. Like movement, it is a spatial metaphor rooted in a notion of place. Each identity group identifies by finding its *place*; locating *its* place as the center—at least for strategic purposes. And the move from margins to center (in the words of bell hooks[7]) allows those whose identity is now centered to become the subjects of experience, rather than the objects—the *others*—of those who had been the *one*. From the margins one sees things one would not otherwise see; from the center one can speak things that otherwise would have been silenced; one can make the world move.

So one direction of movement is movement toward the center. But I think we need to think a bit more about what such movement *means*. It means that there is a taken-for-granted assumption that leaders/important-people/the-ones-we-are-talking-about/those-who-are-actors (that is, active rather than passive)/the-people-whose-concerns-set-the-agenda-for-action/those-whose-acheivements-measure-success/those-whose-characteristics are typical—all these are white, upper-middle class men. Not me! Not those like *me*. It means my concerns are *women's* concerns—special, set apart, not *human* concerns, not real or basic *political* concerns like those with which *mankind* or *all men* are concerned. (The use of the label "special interest group" in the United States is one meant to apply to those working for women's rights, or the rights of African Americans, or the rights of Hispanics, or Asian Americans, or the disabled, or those who are gay, lesbian, or transsexual. Or those who work "on the clock" for a living. "Special interest groups" are contrasted with ordinary politics, those addressing the interests of mankind.) Such terms, *mankind*, or *all men*, were thought to be universal, because white *men* represented the universe, while *women* (and all *others*) were exceptional. To be at the center means that *women's* concerns *are* human concerns, and that responding to them is a basic task of political action—not a secondary goal, or a concern that is relevant to only a portion of human beings.

But when women gathered to plan political strategy, it turned out that the language of planning and the agenda of problems often reflected the class and race and other kinds of centering dominant in the society. Within women's groups, what it is *to be a woman* too often means to be a white, upper-middle class, heterosexual, sighted, and hearing, Christian, Euro-American woman. So for non-white women, or deaf women, or Jewish women, or lesbian women to feel that *our* agendas are not *special*, that that our agendas are political in the primary sense, that these genuinely political concerns represent human concerns and not mere, dismissible "special interests," political only in a marginalized sense, it becomes necessary for us to band together to raise our own consciousness, to identify ourselves in terms of our own location in the social world, and to move *that* location to the center. But within white and within nonwhite groupings of women, within deaf and hearing, lesbian and hetero groupings, once again other categories of identity come into play—and are often more significant in the oppression women suffer than their gender categories: categories of class, of race, of sexuality, religion, ethnicity, and ability and disability. These, too, involve identities that need to be centered.

Groups similarly located become more and more narrow in their denotations as further categories are added to the descriptions of those "in the same place." More and more groups are identified as identity groups. Not every identity can be at the center. It seems that movement to the center is one that must push some to the margins. Movement to the center becomes a race in which various categories, often embodied in the same individual, begin to feel as if they are competing with each other. And the ability to work together with others who are recognized as being in the same location, to feel the location as a site of solidarity, is seriously undermined.

So another form of movement has emerged. It is the movement to de-center. This is the path taken particularly in the academy, and particularly by those who call themselves postmodern or poststructuralist. This path requires that we recognize that the subject is dead or at least that it is a fiction. Identity, it is argued, is not something given or fixed, and hence not something that can be the foundation of a location at *either* margin or center. Identity, in the words of Judith Butler, is *performed*—it is something one acts—and one performs one's gender or race or class roles on the basis of the language and gestures available.[8] One can *resist* the scripted performance and transgress the boundaries of the role—and so the play is changed. But performances are always in the context of other performances, and the moves are limited. Every role is a site of resistance, and we all play many roles. For some, then, there are no women and no men—no blacks and no whites. There is no such *thing* as women. There is no *here*, so there is no *there* to move to. There are only roles that are played in relation to other roles. While the roles can be played subversively and the emphases can be varied, and the ensembles and the attention can be shifted, such a view denies the legitimacy of the identities that locate common oppression. But this seems, to me and to others,[9] to be an ultimately *apolitical* move. It diminishes the ability of those who find themselves, who feel themselves, who know themselves, in the same location to work *together* to change the location: to *move*.

Political change requires an understanding of power—an understanding that uses solidarity to pressure legislatures; to share in the expenses of political campaigns; to use common resources to take advantage of the existing legal apparatus; to generate new legal approaches; to use economic leverage to change corporate policies; to enlarge presence within the media, shaping the attitudes of the public, who will need to accept (if not to initiate) the changes that must be made; to communicate across boundaries to discover problems and sources of resources that might be attacked by existing or novel methods. The sort of subversive de-centering of the subject, which may indeed empower individuals, is hard put to generate the engagements in the apparatus of power that is crucial for public change.

Still, there may be other ways to understand the move to de-center. Ways that *do* respect the need for political movement. I would like to look at the possibility of decentering as meaning not so much the loss of the subject or of identity, but rather as entailing a changed conception of identity. I am arguing that we need to develop a conception of identity that does not give ontological priority to a given location in the determination of identity.

We need to recognize that identity (of either person—*myself*, or category—*women*) has multiple locations, which interact in complex orders to provide the meaning of our individual selves or the sites of political solidarity and action. Each of us is located in many orders. Each identity category is an order that includes many others. But the inclusion is neither hierarchical nor adequately captured in the geometric metaphors of circles and centers. It is situational, overlapping, and "thick."

Let me see if I can explain this by first explaining the hierarchical and circular views I want to reject. Hierarchy involves the encompassing of lower, more limited principles or sets by higher, more inclusive principles or sets. It is an ordering that implies a "highest" and "most inclusive." If there are multiple sets, it is clear that they are *parts*, and hence *lesser* than the whole, or the top, or the ruling principle. Overlapping or multiple sets can also be viewed on the metaphor of the circle—under this image a single center orders all the overlapping figures that can be drawn from it: circles with various radii. But the image of overlapping sets I want to invoke is neither of these. It has neither a single center nor an apex or highest point. It has no "least" and no "greatest," but has many "greater thans" and many "less thans," many circles but no center.

I think such a view can be developed in a feminist metaphysics—a metaphysics that is drawn from the experiences of connectedness and of relationship. Although the claim that feminist metaphysics demands a conception of self-in-relation has been repeated many times, it has not, I think, been adequately elaborated. Unfortunately, the full development of my view is more time consuming than we are permitted to indulge in here.[10] Let me just focus on the conception of orders of relatedness.[11]

Taking myself, Marjorie Miller, as an example: I am located in an order of women, but also in an order of white people. Neither order is more fundamentally, more foundationally what I *am*. The two orders overlap in some respects, not in others. Each overlaps with other orders in which I am located—and each locates other people who are not located in other orders in which I am. But again, none are primary, none more clearly what I am. In some contexts, it is my location in the orders of very big persons that is most salient to my identity; in other contexts it is the fact that I am a U.S. national, or that I am white, or that I am a woman, or a person over sixty years of age, or a parent, or a grandparent, or an academic, or an arthritic, that represents the integrity within which my traits and characteristics emerge. But it is not only the case that I am located in the order "women"—that women is a "larger" order than the order of "me." Rather, I am also the order in which women is located—in some contexts I am what determines "women." In other contexts, "women" is what determines me. In some contexts, white women are located in the order of women—in others, women are located in the order of whites. Neither is ontologically primary. Either is primary in a given situation.

I want to argue, therefore, that *situation* is a better term than location. The places from which movement begins and within which it grows are situations, not map coordinates or fixed identity coordinates. Identities are real and profoundly significant, but they are not two-dimensional (given by x and y axes)—they are thick and multiordinal, and we need always to recognize that the situation whose urgencies privilege one or another order may give way to new situations, in which other orders may emerge as primary. We begin from *identity situations*, not identity locations.

A simple change of figure can have implications for a different understanding of empowerment. Movement, especially as symbolized in marches, implying movement from *here* to *there*, is a problematic metaphor. It suggests that we define *here*. And the process of articulating the *here* seems to carry with it an inevitable and dangerous fragmentation. One that calls forth an equally dangerous refusal to credit the legitimate bases of solidarity. The term *situation* is, I think, a term that carries the implication of tangles: the characters, traits, possibilities, oppressions, and actions of those in a common situation clearly do not necessarily characterize the same individuals as they are enmeshed and realized in other situations. And situations, unlike locations, are not subject to the law of spatial noncontradiction: while one cannot be in more than one place at any given time, one can certainly find oneself in several "situations" at the same time. Situations are figured as not sharply bounded, not fixed, not given, but rather as complex, entailing subjective as well as objective factors, as emergent or senescent, and as involving possibilities and entailing specific limitations. One moves from a fixed location to another location. Situations, on the other hand, change, open, present new possibilities, reveal new limitations.

Since such characteristics typify situations, how might "empowerment" be figured with respect to situations? Rather than movements, symbolized by marches (a symbol carrying a history of military movement—as well as militant movement), rather than focusing on centering or de-centering, we might talk about "raising." I am thinking of the elasticity of rising dough—of the yeasty change that involves increased openness, increased "room," which does not involve a competition but rather increases the opportunities for further changing and shaping.

So we start from "thick," multiordinal identity situations to build coalitions and to raise momentum so we can *change*. Real coalitions are necessary to provide political resistance to real oppressions, and to create the changes necessary to produce liberated identities. But if, in emphasizing identity as entailing the thickness of our situations, we have agreed to de-center, where should movement take us? What, then, does change mean in the context of race, gender, and class politics?

It means that *no* struggle is the *only* struggle, no liberation is final, and no form of oppression can be addressed entirely by itself. No liberation is complete unless all are liberated. Empowerment involves a change of situations— and situations are material, embodied, praxical, engaged. But situations are not sharply bounded, "thin," unconnected to other situations. Situations are ramified; they are related to other situations. The change that is empowerment is change that modifies relations and hence changes situations. It means, I think, a rising—a leavening, a bubbling up. Not a climb up the ladder, but a discarding of the hierarchies and rigidities implicit in the ladder metaphor. It involves recognition of the plasticity and the thickness of identities, a new understanding of the ways in which identities interlock, being freed from old limitations, and the emergence of new possibilities.

One cannot entirely reject the metaphor of ladders when measuring particular changes: For example, we may ask if more women are employed at higher levels than we used to be. Are women reaching the top rungs of economic success, political leadership, and achieving agenda-setting positions? Such things can usefully be measured in hierarchical terms. But their very measurement conceals questions as to *which* women are climbing. And what opportunities are available to working-class women? And what is happening to disabled women, or those not yet in the workforce, or those who have retired from it. And what is happening to those who are not women? When we pay attention only to statistical ladders, we tend to substitute two-dimensional markers for the multidimensional situations whose changes need to be evaluated. We fail to see the ways in which the ladder conceals the composition of the masses struggling at the bottom.

The trick is to see "rising" more multidimensionally: not as progress up defined ladders, but as the yeast that allows the dough to spring back against the hands that knead it—the pressure that expands. It empowers through change in the structure of our identities and the possibilities inherent in the categories that locate us; change in the categories that we locate; change in our relations to one another. It speaks not of the liberation of some, nor of the perfection of a utopic future—but it speaks of more room, more space, more plasticity and elasticity in our situations. It speaks of melioration. Rising is the multiple ways in which empowerment opens spaces, and restructures boundaries, and makes new situations emerge. It does not deny who we are; it makes a rich sense of who we are possible.

Gender, the ontology of gender, is not a matter of deciding between essentialist, constructionist, linguistic, or other images of the nature, source, or characteristics of gender. Nor is it a matter of settling the sameness/difference question. Rather, on my account, gender itself, as a concept, a complex, is an order of or for relatedness. The complex of gender locates other concepts and other categories, but other concepts and other categories also locate *it*. I locate the feminine gender, as do you—as do the International Association of Women Philosophers and the Westchester Women's Shelter and the Huntington Women's Association. But *we* are also located (that is, we have some possibilities and lack others) because we are located in the category of gender. Our situation is amorphous and shifting. But it is ontologically categorizeable in terms of the contours of the order in which we are located as we undertake common action or face common concerns. Some have argued that what constitutes an "us" is our common interest. But I think any attempt to locate some dimension of our situation as primary will be overly unidimensional and both too narrow and too arbitrary. My position does not substitute an identity location for an interest actively pursued, but rather looks toward an ontological understanding of shifting identity situations not as ground, but as a sort of tropic yeast. It insists on the circularity of identity and interest, the inseparability of the being and acting that are reciprocally constituting. The recognition of this thick identity and of the reciprocity of being and acting is both empowering in itself, and a useful strategy for achieving the further empowerment of women.

Notes

1. See, for example, Zillah Eisenstein's discussion of borders: "Because we often fear that which we do not know, that which is strange to us, we take this fear and use it to smash difference, to try to annihilate it. This fear creates new ambivalent borders; we do not know which ones we want to cross or what we want to keep out. . . . [We] make the unimaginable manageable through an enforced closure. White vs. Black; man vs. Woman; west vs. the orient; hetero vs. homo; Christian vs. Muslim; Aryan vs. Jew—the fictive divisions are clear-cut and apparently soothing for many" Zillah Eisenstein, *Hatreds: Racialized and Sexualized Conflicts in the 21st century* (New York and London: Routledge, 1996), 23.

2. These are the words to a song sung by many in the various movements named earlier—by those marching, by those imprisoned, and by those at gatherings where movement is discussed.

3. Please note: This chapter was originally given at an international conference, for which the routine nature of the history given below was not as generally available as it would be for a strictly U.S. audience.

4. Of course, my version of the causes of the women's movement is entirely one-dimensional here. There are many other causes that ought to be acknowledged and that can be traced: causes continuous with feminist movement from Mary Woll-stonecraft through the suffragist and other feminist movements of the nineteenth and early twentieth centuries in Europe and America, and the later twentieth-century movements that followed Simone de Beauvoir's publication of *The Second Sex*. There are also causes having to do with women's involvement in other social welfare movements; changes in employment patterns before and especially during World War II, and many others. My story is only tracing one of the threads relevant here.

5. Cf. "We must first be able to dialogue with one another, to give one another that subject-to-subject recognition that is an act of resistance that is part of the de-colonizing, anti-racist process" bell hooks and Cornel West, *Breaking Bread* (Boston: South End Press, 1991), 5.

6. Gloria T. Hull, et al., eds., *But Some of Us Are Brave: Black Women's Studies* (Old Westbury, NY: Feminist Press, 1982).

7. bell hooks, *Feminist Theory: From Margin to Center* (Boston: South End Press, 1984).

8. Judith Butler, *Gender Trouble* (New York and London: Routledge, 1990).

9. See Nancy Fraser, *Unruly Practices* (Minneapolis: University of Minnesota Press, 1989), and the debate among Seyla Benhabib, Judith Butler, Nancy Fraser, and Drucilla Cornell in *Feminist Contentions*, Linda Nicholson, ed. (New York: Rout-ledge, 1995).

10. I have developed this view further in "Women, Identity and Philosophy," in *Is Feminist Philosophy Philosophy?* ed. Emanuela Bianchi (Evanston, IL: Northwestern University Press, 1999), 35–50.

11. I am drawing on categories taken, in part, from the metaphysics of Justus Buchler. See Buchler, *Metaphysics of Natural Complexes*, 2nd expanded edition, ed. Kathleen Wallace, Armen Marsoobian, and Robert Corrington (New York: State University of New York Press, 1990). See also Beth Singer, *Ordinal Naturalism* (Lewisburg: Bucknell University Press, 1983).

CHAPTER TWELVE

~

Theorizing Identities as Mutually Constitutive: A Critical Reading of Spelman, Aristotle, and Jewish Law

Marla Brettschneider[1]

The project of racing queer studies and queering race studies in a Jewish context must be seen as a part of a larger, and changing, historical context of feminist activism and thought.[2] Feminist theorizing of identity has changed since the beginning of the second wave of the women's movement. The origins of what we may call contemporary identity politics, since Karl Marx's focus on a liberatory politics based explicitly on class grounds, lay in identifying individual characteristics such as gender, race/ethnicity, ability, or sexual orientation that are singled out for analysis. The one identity aspect was often universalized and set at the center of visions for ending oppression. For Jewish feminists active in this period, universalizing one discrete aspect of identity proved limiting.[3] Activists eventually were able to articulate that the choice of being either a woman or a Jew for communal and political purposes was indeed a false choice.[4] We came to learn that oppression works through multiple mechanisms, and that identities cannot be seen in isolation from one another.

Discourse about multiple identities gave way to self-criticism including the recognition that identities were not simply many, but interconnected in an indefinite variety of ways. We could not just add critical race theory to feminist analysis, for example, because the way that one's life is gendered does not stand on its own as clearly distinguishable and then get added to the way that one's life is raced. Causes for celebration and resistance for Jewish women do not come in neat packages for them as women, and then other times in other neat packages for them as Jews. Many feminists, then, began to talk about the connection between identities or even the ways that oppressions "intersect."[5]

For others, however, intersectionality was not enough. Feminists began to theorize the ways in which identity signifiers are actually mutually constitutive. What they meant is that, for example, gender itself is a raced/classed/sexed/cultured category, as race is a gendered/classed/sexed/cultured category. Gender came to be seen as mutually constitutive of the construction of sexual orientation so that being male or female only made sense in the context of compulsory heterosexuality. The personal and social constructions of one's life as a Jewish lesbian feminist is a Jewishly and gendered sexing, a sexed and gendered Jewing, and simultaneously a sexed and Jewed gendering.

In large part, it has been the work of African-American, Latina, and other lesbians and feminists of color that has brought us to this point of analysis. In earlier works such as *Ain't I a Woman*, the anthologies *Home Girls*; *This Bridge Called My Back*; *Making Face, Making Soul*, and the most appropriately titled *All the Women Are White, All the Blacks Are Men, But Some of Us Are Brave*,[6] many women of color worked at describing and investigating the ways that race, class, culture, and sexuality all nuance and shift gender construction. There were certainly formally trained philosophers writing in these books. In hindsight, however, we can now see that there were both strengths and weaknesses involved in the appropriation of insights from these volumes into the works of formally trained feminist philosophers outside these marginalized communities. Further, despite the widespread activities of Jewish feminists, less attention has been paid to Jewish experiences and insights within these discussions of identities.

It is my intention in this chapter to address these strengths and weaknesses and to situate Jewish feminist queer thinking within the philosophical discussion of intersectionality and mutual construction. To do so, part one of this work takes up an early text by Elizabeth V. Spelman as a helpful, yet limited, example of philosophical writing on the mutual constitution of identities. Part two offers a critical reading of a specific Talmudic text as an alternative to Spelman's reliance on a hegemonic Western philosophical tradition. Through an analysis of works by Rebecca Alpert and Melanie Kaye/Kantrowitz, in part three, I discuss the ways that insights from both Western feminist and Talmudic traditions may be found at work in Jewish feminist queer discussions of identity politics.

Mutual Constitution Theory in Feminist Philosophy

It is probably all too obvious that those doing higher-level feminist philosophy have tended to be white women, or women not identifying in their written work with a nonwhite/Christian minority.[7] The second point of import here, addressed more specifically to conceptual content, is that although some have managed to include numerous aspects of identity politics into their analyses, in fact, some of the most insightful academic philosophical demonstrations of this view of multiple identity signifiers as mutually constitutive have used a two-tiered model.[8] Early work by Spelman, for example, demonstrated that gender and race mutually constitute each other.[9] As helpful as this scholarship is, however, it also has significant limitations. Such work has tended to slip from focusing on two identity signifiers into privileging one or two at the cost of others. In Spelman's case, despite her critique of such practices, she tends to privilege race as an identity category and this seems to follow from her reliance on standard canons of hegemonic Western civilization.

Spelman's Argument

In *Inessential Woman*, Spelman presents the following analysis of race and gender categories. According to Spelman, we often find ourselves and our political commentators asking about, for example, the status of women and Blacks in the military.[10] She reminds us that such a statement actually makes no sense, since some women in the military are Black and some of the Blacks are also women. Not only is this faulty language use, but given the racist biases in gender analysis and the sexist biases in race-based analysis, the category "women" is taken then to mean non-Black women, and the category "Black" is taken to mean Blacks who are not women. This structure leaves out an important group of human beings: Black women.

Spelman seeks to introduce the Black woman into (traditionally white) scholarly discourse and ultimately into the modes of political production. In order to make her point, she demonstrates that the additive method for understanding identity (adding one discrete identity signifier such as gender to another discrete identity signifier such as race, and so on) is insufficient for including Black women. The only way to end the exclusion of Black women is to understand identities such as race and gender not just as connected or as one added to the other, but to understand that the very category of gender is raced and the category of race is gendered.

Spelman's Method

Spelman begins her argument with a critique of race and gender in Plato, and hones the discussion further in a second chapter on Aristotle. There were certain distinctions that Aristotle made between human beings that set them into particular categories with respect to power. Not all people were considered citizens. In fact, children, women, slaves, and foreigners were expressly considered to exist by nature outside the bounds of possible citizenship. It is, however, the specific designations of women and slaves that mostly concern Spelman. Again, motivated by who is left out of theoretical treatises on the subject of "women and slaves in ancient Greece," including feminist ones,[11] Spelman reminds us that some females were slaves, as much as some slaves were female. Among nonslave Athenians, Aristotle distinguished between the men and the women. When referring to slaves, the distinction of gender is not made.[12] Spelman skillfully demonstrates, therefore, that when Aristotle referred to women (presumably the gendered category of females),[13] he was referring specifically and exclusively to nonslave females. Thus, for Aristotle, the very category of women exists only within a certain elite segment of the population.

It is at this point that Spelman's use of the hegemonic Greek text takes a problematic turn. She notes that the ancient Greek category of "slave" resembles a cross between our contemporary categories of race and class. She suggests that, for expository ease, this race/class category will have to be simplified. Driven by her own motivations within the context of contemporary political concerns, Spelman chooses to translate the ancient Greek notion of slave into the modern idiom of race.[14] The potential for a class-based analysis effectively drops out at this point.[15] We are left with a dual axis discussion of identity, based on gender and race.[16] Because of this particular interpretation, although Spelman eloquently shows that gender is raced, her argument that race is gendered functions slightly differently and brings her use of the Greek text into further difficulties.

As mentioned earlier, Spelman points out that Aristotle does not address gender distinctions among slaves. Allowing Aristotle's work here to function as a hegemonic text, Spelman, therefore, also does not make such a distinction.[17] Although she writes about this in Aristotle for critical purposes, she also does not distinguish between the maleness and femaleness of slaves.[18] Therefore, although she will ultimately argue that gender is raced and race is gendered, her explanations of the two are not parallel. Gender, on this account, is raced because one needed to be of a certain race to have a gender at all. Race is gendered, in this story, because the distinction of races is marked by those who have genders and those who do not. In short: Free Athenians have genders, slaves do not.

The issue of concern for those interested in theorizing identity is the way that Spelman's construction of the race of gender and the gender of race does not reflect the relations of power and identity in many of our lives, and therefore is limited in the ways it might be helpful in the work to overcome our oppressions as they operate in our lived lives (not only in our philosophical heritage). By setting up race and gender in the way that she does with the help of Aristotle, Spelman assumes that Athenian women stand above all slaves, whether male or female, in the social hierarchy. Spelman writes: "Since there are no natural rulers among slaves, a man who is a slave is not the natural ruler of a woman who is a slave (and surely not of a free woman)" and "whatever biological superiority male slaves have to female slaves, they are inferior to the wives of male citizens."[19] I could not say whether such a depiction is accurate. What is important is that Spelman then projects this set of relationships onto those she conceives of as among similar groups of our day. Thus, Spelman presumes that white women, in the contemporary political context, always stand above all African Americans.[20]

Critique

From within Spelman's theory one loses an ability to continue a critical gender analysis within a critical discussion about race. When Spelman relates Aristotle's view of slaves to the reality of African Americans, she also transfers what she understands as Aristotle's homogenizing characterization of slaves. As a result, in her argument, the fact of race trumps the fact of male and femaleness. If in Spelman's reading of Aristotle, slaves had no genders, then modern oppressed races have no genders. If modern oppressed races have no genders, then gender-based analysis cannot be applied. But, when critical gender analysis is not applied, maleness is the assumed norm. In effect, Spelman has thus erased the existence of African-American women and their concerns. Ironically, this is precisely the problem that inspired Spelman's inquiry to begin with.

There are, though, two additional problems. First, despite the obvious pervasiveness of racism, in the contemporary context, white women simply do not always have distinct power over Black men. Second, Spelman tends to essentialize the groups of Black men and white women in her characterization; thus, the structure of her argument causes her at times to lose sight of diversity among white women, and also among Black men and women. Bringing these two points together, we can say that within classes, for example, Black men often enjoy male privilege over all women in their own or lower classes, often enough including white women and also queer, non-Christian, and disabled women of various races, and that Spelman's unfortunate refusal to work within the reality of such renders this aspect of her argument absurd.

Although Spelman's account of Aristotle focuses on his two-tiered model of free/slave-male/female, at the moment Spelman chooses to translate the ancient Greek slavery from what she herself notes as a more complicated convergence of contemporary class and race, she limits the power of her own insights as well. However, it is my argument that Spelman's thesis on the mutual constitution of multiple identities is not inherently limited. My suggestion is that one reason she falls short of her own goals involves her particular methodological reliance on Aristotle, a preeminent Western canonical figure, in her critique of the dominant framework. Perhaps we will be better able to do the work Spelman sets out for us if we look for alternative ways of conceptualizing the issues from sources and traditions outside the Western canon. In light of this suggestion, I turn now to a discussion of countertexts.

There are certainly any number of texts that could be employed in order to help Spelman's analysis stay critical and multifaceted by applying a critique of a hegemonic text. What one ought to look for is a text capable of conceiving multiple categories as mutually constitutive that relies on an alternative epistemological framework to that relied on by hegemonic texts. We may look for answers to these questions in traditional, ancient Jewish texts.

Having said this, I realize that some familiar with feminist and queer studies might find this statement implausible. Due to the sexism practiced and institutionalized in so many Jewish communities, feminists often presume there is nothing left of worth in traditional Jewish thinking and texts. Similarly, due to religious—and explicitly biblical—invocations used to justify extreme homophobia, queers of all kinds may assume that Torah is inherently tainted with a heterosexist norm. What we also find, however, is that the epistemological framework manifest in certain ancient Jewish texts offers alternatives to current attempts at theorizing our multiple identities as mutually constitutive.

Jewish Texts as Countertexts

In this section, I develop a close reading of a Talmudic text.[21] Posing difficult dilemmas, the rabbis of ancient Israel puzzled through what Jewish tradition would prescribe in myriad specific circumstances. I engage a particular analysis of this text as an example of a countertext that can help perform the interrogatory function that Spelman's theory needs to stay critical. Before presenting the textual analysis, however, a few words on the use of these texts as countertexts are in order.

Political and Philosophical Potential of Countertexts

As feminist and queer scholars have argued, it is often helpful to turn to countertexts in order to see through myths of dominant cultural norms.[22] If we look at a nonhegemonic traditional text, we might be better able to explore the multiple layers of the ways in which identity categories are mutually constituted. Using Spelman's concern about lists of identities, and about how the additive approach blinds us to the reality of whole groups of people, we can look at a particular traditional Jewish text that resembles the Aristotelian model of listing "slaves and women" but with significant differences. I want to suggest that with the help of Spelman, an analysis of the countertext I will present holds more promise for those who are interested in theorizing the mutual constitution of multiple identities, and the ways in which they are complicated, than that of Spelman's use of the canonical Greeks only. Further, we find this methodology utilized in recent Jewish feminist lesbian and queer theorizings, however unselfconsciously.

Methodologically, it seems we would want to be able to say more about a text that qualifies in specific contexts as a countertext than that it is simply outside the canon.[23] A comparative analysis of the differences between Talmudic texts in the context of their use in Jewish history and Western political theory would take volumes. What I find most interesting in this set of countertexts for the subject of this chapter, however, is how they help us circumscribe the problems of modernist standpoint theory that could (and at times do) plague Jewish feminist queer work.

The main distinction important at this point between the method of thinking in the Aristotelian-based tradition and that found in rabbinic texts relates to how Aristotle's universalism relies on sameness to define identity concepts.[24] This is the foundational assumption in the problematic nature of essentialism. Jewish tradition has not worked this way, for the most part. It is not a universalist tradition, but rather particularist. As will be demonstrated, differences comprise the world of traditional Jewish understandings of identity. This suggests that what I present as "additional" categories to the two-tiered approach of Spelman are not merely multiplying, or adding, categories as is often found in the additive move, and critiqued by those wary of standpoint theory.[25] The Talmudic categories are not "added" to some essential and unchanging identity, as somehow external to one's "core" identity as a Jew.[26] The categories are internally constitutive of Jewishness itself; they explicitly make one the kind of Jew one is.

What I find interesting in the Talmudic text (later replicated in much Jewish feminist work) is the alternative system of complex hierarchies.[27] In the structure erected in this text, there is no single standpoint from which to take perspective. These texts are therefore both extremely problematic for their content vis-à-vis the history of Jewish communities while they also hold much promise for complex contemporary theorizing. Further, in using a countertext I do not wish to suggest that we can get outside of oppressive discourses simply by looking outside *dominant* oppressive discourses. What I am offering is the idea that other noncanonical modes of thinking—even if oppressive in their own context—might highlight aspects in the dominant mode in need of critique. They can provide a set of instances that disrupt the first set of oppressive categorizations.[28]

The following analysis of a countertext will also demonstrate the reciprocal benefit of utilizing a more multicultural analysis. Relying on canonical texts can often reinforce problematic modes of thinking. Looking to marginalized works may provide us with more alternative conceptualizations. But this is not all. Bringing together analytic discussions of concern in the dominant framework with those in marginalized communities can provide transformative insight into the problems faced by those within the marginalized framework as well.[29] This layer of countertextual analysis is imperative because not making the reciprocal move runs the risk of cultural essentialism by not acknowledging the interpretive struggles and historical power dynamics in the minority community. Without the reciprocal move in countertextual analysis, the critique potentially sets up the historically dominant powers within the minority culture as an unproblematized and representative norm. For Jewish feminist queers, this will simply not do. Finally, failing to engage in the reciprocal countertextual critique implicitly prioritizes justice work for those in the dominant community over those in the minority community.[30] As such, the following pages will point to the potential of both utilizing Jewish texts to revive Spelman's thesis as well as utilizing Spelman to challenge the power relationships in the Jewish text.

Talmudic Hierarchical Classifications for Saving a Life

Contemporary scholars and practitioners working in a Jewish framework will often turn to historically significant Jewish texts to understand the ancient logic of the rabbis in order to help solve contemporary problems. For example, we might imagine a dilemma for contemporary medical ethicists where in urgent cases, such as those of modern emergency rooms, the question of how to prioritize patients for triage is life-threateningly pressing. In examining the particular case of what a physician should do when faced with two patients of equal ill health at the same time, Jewish ethicists may turn to Talmudic sources for answers. In their search they are likely to come upon a text from the Babylonian Talmud Horayot 13b–14a, which addresses "matters concerning the saving of a life."

In this case the Rabbis reasoned through a maze of categories and came up with a specific answer. The rather shocking and very practical answer to this question of enormous gravity is that the male patient is treated first before a female patient, for it says in the Mishnah, "A man takes precedence over a woman in matters concerning the saving of life." Interestingly enough, the reasoning does not stop here in order to make sure that the writing can answer the problem completely. Gender categories are not the only significant categories in traditional Jewish culture. The text thus goes on to rank numerous groups of people in the order in which they should receive attention.

The next ranking runs according to the ancient Jewish caste system: One must treat a Cohen before a Levite, and a Levite before an Israelite. The Gemara also includes ten ranked subcategories of Cohens and some challenges to its chosen order. This system of categorization, which I have named caste based, actually works according to religious rights and responsibilities in ancient Israel. It is still in use today under certain circumstances and explains common Jewish surnames in the United States: Cohen, Cohn, Cahan, Kahane, Kane; Levi, Levy, Levitan, Levinson, Lewinsky; and Israel, Israeli, and so on. These names, or other familial identifications, tell where those individuals fall in the three thousand-year-old Jewish caste system. As a concrete example, I am of the Israelite caste.

This is not all. The next set of categorizations are what might best be understood today as national (i.e., who belongs to the nation). The Mishnah states that Cohens, Levites, and Israelites are all to be treated before bastards, "a bastard over a nathin,[31] a nathin over a proselyte, and a proselyte over an emancipated slave." The text does not mention slaves as a group at all. What is also interesting about this category of national membership since the modern period is that there are three subcategories of membership in the nation: biological, cultural, and geographic. Although presented in a simple hierarchy at this stage, the text in full through the Gemara interpretation keeps the relations between these three subcategories challenged within the text and thus may be seen as potentially fluid and shifting. Let us look at an example of this complex and morphing hierarchy.

What is presented, in terms of textual order, as the last category, scholars, actually turns out to override all the previous categories. This is the subversive category of the Talmud.[32] The Mishnah states clearly: "This order of precedence applies only when all these were in other respects equal. If the bastard, however, was a scholar and the High Priest an ignoramus, the learned bastard takes precedence over the ignorant High Priest." (The high priest refers to the Cohen caste, within which the Gemara makes sure to delineate many subcategories as well.) Mixing in political categories of hierarchical ordering, the Gemara also explains, "A scholar takes precedence over a king of Israel, for if a scholar dies there is none to replace him," and "A king takes precedence over a High Priest." There is a final category that crosses the political and religious: prophets, who are ranked below the political category of king. None of these classifications refer to those that affect women as a group as women, which we will see, such as marital status.

Spelman and the Confusion of the Talmudic Hierarchies

Given the multiplicity of categories and their nature, the Talmudic text can be quite interesting for contemporary political theorists working on identity issues and more promising than the twofold framework of Spelman's translated Aristotle. Due to the complexity of the Talmudic rankings, I will first attempt to clarify the conceptual incoherences and the nuances of the hierarchical orderings that often turn in on themselves. To do so I will utilize Spelman's methodology. First of all, a gender classification is in some ways distinct from the collection of castes among Cohens, Levites, and Israelites. These are, in turn, in certain aspects distinct from the national collection of bastards, nathins, converts, and emancipated slaves, which are to some degree distinct from the scholarly, political, and political/religious classifications. In this case the fact that slaves are not even mentioned is a silence waiting to be theorized.

The use of the term "Israelite" in this listing is particularly confusing for those who yearn for discrete and separable identity groupings, because it sometimes refers only to the priestly order (as when in the list of religious caste order), and other times it means all the rest of the people of Israel (as in the reference to a king of Israel), which would include those named under the gender, national, scholarly, political, and political-religious listings as well as Cohens, Levites, and Kings.[33] Also, historically there were instances when individuals moved in or out of the Levite cast, making that designation far more fluid than such placing in the list suggests. Further, in common understandings of Jewish law, once a person has become a Jew, there is to be no distinction, let alone discrimination, made between one who converted to become a Jew and one who is Jewish by virtue of being born to a Jewish mother. Here, on the matter of literal life and death, we find a substantial distinction. Otherwise, Israelites may have been converts, bastards, or nathins and could be among the group designated as emancipated slaves. Finally, aside from Cohens, Levites, and kings, all the other categories mentioned might be composed of both men and women.

Using Spelman to destabilize the Jewish text proves to be quite interesting. It forces a contemporary scholar to look at the multiplicity of categories and question their internal logic in ways not traditionally questioned. To explicate this for those less familiar with the mechanisms of this particular historical tradition, Jewish law is steeped in distinctions based on gender. In this case, the two top religious caste categories do not even include women. Laws for women apply to women only sometimes in the Israelite designation and usually in all the other categories designated; laws for men sometimes apply to all men and other times apply to men according to their membership in these other classes. The scholarly and religious-political references would usually refer to men, but there have on occasion been named women scholars and prophetesses. No woman was ever king. Although one might conclude that gender trumps all other distinctions, due to its appearance at the top of the original list, Spelman's analysis helps us see that such a conclusion is nonsensical. In ancient Israelite society, women could be converts, nathins, bastards, current or freed slaves. A la Spelman, saying "women and Israelites," or "women and converts" makes no sense and excludes those who fall into both categories. It also does not help us understand women and the caste system.

The Talmud and the Problem of a Two-Tiered Method
Due to the particularist tendency of Talmudic thinking, that there are many categories previously named does not mean that the categories of identity of interest to Spelman are simply multiplied. Instead we find a complex system of overlapping, shifting, and internally challenged hierarchies. This makes use of the additive method basically impossible. The following is a diagram that helps clarify this point.

Spelman's Aristotle   **Jewish Text**

Classifications

Race (slave/free status)   Gender
Gender (sex/gender status)   Religious Caste
                                     Nationality
                                     Learnedness
                                     Political

Groups Named

Free men/white men   Men
Nonslave women/white women   Women
Slave females/Black women   Cohen
Slave males/Black men   (Gemara has 10 ranked subcategories,
                                       with challenges)
                                     Levite
                                     Israelite A
                                       (religious caste)
                                     Israelite B
                                       (catch-all for others in the nation)
                                     Bastard
                                     Nathin
                                     Proselyte

196 ~ Marla Brettschneider

Spelman's Aristotle	Jewish Text
	Emancipated Slave
	Scholar
	King
	Prophet

Power Relationships

Free men	**FRAME** 1
|	Scholar
Nonslave women	|
| |	King
Slave females/Slave males	|
	Prophet

FRAME 2
Scholar
|
Cohen
   (as in four or in five below)

FRAME 3
Male
|
Female

FRAME 4
Cohen
|
Levite
|
Israelite A
|
Bastard
|
Nathin
|
Proselyte (challenged)
|
Emancipated Slave (challenged)

FRAME 5
Cohen
|
Levite
|
Israelite B
   (Kings, Cohens, Levites, Scholars,
   Prophets, Israelites, Bastards, Nathins,
   Proselytes, Emancipated Slaves—male
   and female except for Cohens, Kings
   and Levites)

Regarding the Jewish text, one must do the following (not necessarily lexically):

1. Put all these sets of relationships together
2. Figure out if including women into categories where they fit means that bastard males take precedence over bastard females
3. Rerank categories that include men and women
4. Open the possibility that women could stand above men in the case where a woman is a scholar
5. Include the groups not mentioned in even this long list but crucial to its implementation such as slaves and divorced women, wives of Cohens, Levites, Israelites, and Kings
6. Rerank according to how the unnamed groups change the hierarchy of the named
7. Figure out what to do in frame five where a Cohen and a Levite are both above Israelites and are Israelites themselves
8. Notice that it is impossible to perform steps one through seven

The diagram demonstrates conceptually the classifications, group names, and power relationships in the two examples, Spelman's Aristotle and this particular Talmudic text. What one finds is that the difference between Spelman's Aristotle and the Talmudic text is not simply that there are more classifications and groups named, but that the internal logic of the Talmudic text challenges its own named categories as discrete and separable entities and makes it impossible to develop a linear presentation of power relationships at all, let alone one that is stable or fixed.

Utilizing the countertext to help destabilize Spelman's Aristotelian categorizations, we can see that if this were the model that Spelman had relied on, she might not have translated the complicated racial/classed category of slave into the single contemporary signifier of race. It would not have helped her to do so. She would, therefore, also probably not have theorized race as a gendered category in the way that she does. Some particulars from this Jewish example are: certain castes have women, others do not; women in the families of the Cohen or Levite men led different lives in the social context than all other women; and women who were divorced, yet another category, were exempted from the possibility of marrying into the Cohen caste. Like life, the situation is more complicated than the easy slave/not-slave bifurcation, and importantly, the line of gender is not drawn on a dualistic model. In looking at the rabbinic text, we are forced to deal with multiple categories and myriad relationships that are often counterindicative. We would have to examine the whole complex of gender, caste, class, politics, learnedness, marital status, foreign origin, and so on, as it works in its own unique way through each constellation, as well as what similarities might run throughout, even as the categories and their relations themselves are questioned and shift. This model is probably more productive for contemporary thinkers seeking to theorize identities and power dynamics in the vast complex multiplicity of our lives.

The Talmudic Example and Jewish Lesbian Feminist Analyses

We must ask, therefore, how can we make use of this alternative mode, as found in traditional Jewish texts, for contemporary work in critical queer and race studies? In some ways, many Jewish feminists and queer (or queer-conscious) activists and thinkers have long been working out the answer to this question. Although the majority of queer and feminist Jewish intellectuals and organizers are not familiar with Talmudic or other ancient texts, we can find an interesting correlation between their epistemological assumptions. In addition, although many Jewish queers would not necessarily see themselves as consciously engaged in a contemporary application of ancient Jewish wisdoms, we might see them as such nevertheless.

There are two reasons for this that I think are important to highlight in the context of this chapter. First, there is a relationship between contemporary multicultural perspectives that look for, embrace, and honor particularities and the epistemological framework found in some rabbinic reasoning mentioned earlier. Second, the basic life experiences of feminist Jewish queers demands attention to their multiple identities—and concomitant power relations—beyond a dual grid. Even white and Ashkenazi Jewish lesbians who have not yet begun to problematize their racial/cultural location do, at least, engage in the tripartite complex hierarchies of sexuality, gender, and Jewishness. In many Jewish feminist and queer activist organizations and writings, we find sensitivity to the complexity of power dynamics operating on multiple layers that not only shade one another, but often change shape and turn in on each other depending on the context as well. Since this may be difficult to understand abstractly, I would like to present an analysis of two contemporary Jewish lesbian feminist activists and scholars. The first, Rebecca Alpert, is also a rabbi and therefore familiar with Talmudic texts (although I do not mean to imply that her book is a conscious application). The second, Melanie Kaye/Kantrowitz, is a secular Jew with less exposure to such texts. In looking at a central work by each woman, we can see more specifically how we may use Spelman's insights recast with a Talmudic legacy of multiple identities in theorizing Jewish issues in the complex nexus of race/ nationality, gender, sexuality, and class.

The Lesbian Legacy of "Bread on the Seder Plate"

Alpert is a Jewish lesbian feminist activist rabbi, and also a scholar in the secular academy. The goal of her book, *Like Bread on the Seder Plate*, is to "determine strategies" for Jewish lesbians to "participate [more] fully, as lesbians, in Jewish life."[34] Alpert does not seek inclusion of lesbians into Jewish communal life in an assimilationist mode (as in the universalist reliance on sameness). Instead, she seeks an inclusion of this previously ignored—and other times marginalized—group through means no less radical than the fundamental transformation of Judaism itself. Similar to the way that the Talmud both establishes authority even as it challenges it, at the outset of Alpert's vision we find that Jewish tradition is itself open and changing rather than essentially static. In order to make possible this deep change in Jewish history, Alpert primarily takes on the very traditional Jewish task of reinterpreting texts. There is, however, nothing essentially traditional in the aims of her methodology. Alpert offers lesbian-critical insights from readings of ancient religious texts, introduces new texts for consideration as part of a transformed canon, and develops suggestions for the creation of new sacred texts out of the lives of Jewish lesbians from the history of today and the future.

As the Talmudic example works with multiple, overlapping, and shifting categories to establish its newly authoritative perspective, Alpert deftly works a tripartite analysis of identities and their mutual constitution. She takes on gender, sexual orientation, and Jewish affiliation in a fluid weave. Within her tripartite analysis, Alpert is able to acknowledge and incorporate multiple aspects of difference though she privileges three categories. She is able to do so often enough without always treating the multiple aspects as discrete and separative. For example, Jewish diversity is not limited to factors of sexual orientation and gender (her two other privileged categories). Jews are one group in the privileged triplet, even as Jews are diverse according to historical context, race, geography, religious expression, nationality, and so on. Similarly, analysis of the category lesbian crosses Jewish and non-Jewish examinations as it is also related to gay male, bisexual, transgendered, transsexual, and queer categories. Her treatment of gender also draws on both Jewish and non-Jewish sources and complicates the very idea of gender through discussion of lesbian and other gender nonconformist interstices.

Alpert's project faces a number of challenges, however, when viewed through the lens of an attempt to race queer studies and queer race studies in a Jewish context. Most obviously, despite brief acknowledgement of other politically salient issues of identity such as race and class, Alpert's mode of exploration is not sufficiently open to race- and class-critical analyses. Having said this, there is actually another consideration that I would like to focus on more specifically: the delicate difficulty of privileging the conceptual category of lesbian over queer without incorporating the baggage of second-wave feminism's history of essentialism.

Although the reclamation of "queer" has become a hallmark of 1990s politics in the United States, it has not become so without contestation. Many lesbians in particular have resisted self- and movement labeling as queer due to the legacy of sexism within gay men's activist movements and within society at large. Sexist tendencies to eclipse the experiences, concerns, and contributions of women have found their place in coalitions among sexual minorities and in queer studies and activism. Lesbians, in particular those deeply situated in second-wave feminist movement, have often continued to demand distinct lesbian spaces, organizations, and modes of analysis. Although clearly situated within a broader spectrum of sexual minorities and queer ideology in particular, Alpert's project focuses on lesbians. In many ways the book itself demonstrates the need for such a prioritization.

However, as Spelman's work is designed to demonstrate, some aspects of second-wave feminism relied on various modes of essentialist thinking. Women were taken to be the subject of feminist political movement and too often even the feminist employment of the category of women reflected hegemonic patriarchal characterizations of who these "women" are. As has been much discussed, despite long-term activism among women from an array of minority communities, the closer one was to a white, middle-class, heterosexual, Christian, and able norm, the more likely one's voice was to be heard within feminist movement and in the U.S. media. Internalizing a narrow view of women, even as they often radicalized it, many second-wave feminists represented lesbians at an apex of the "feminist woman." The lesbian identity that emerged out of radical second-wave feminism was, as a political act, defined more through a feminist lens of her being "woman identified" than through a lens of sexuality and/or status as a sexual or gender outlaw.[35]

The consequence of this trend among feminists was that lesbians of this milieu more frequently aligned themselves with "women" than with gay men and bisexual, transgendered, or transsexual men and women. In fact, the nature of certain strains of feminist critique explicitly distanced lesbian identity and community from cultural forms developing in both gay men's communities (such as drag and male to female transvestitism) and other forms of queer women's culture (such as role playing, cross dressing, female to male trans-sexuality, or sadomasochism). This set of political alignments also set lesbian feminists against lesbians whose identity was forged prior to the advent or outside the centers of second-wave feminism. This meant that lesbian identities in rural areas and small cities, for example, without a college campus (specifically an elite or radical college campus) were marginalized as politically incorrect not only as feminists, but also as women and as lesbians. The same may be said for racial and class dichotomies: The radical feminist assertion of "feminism as the theory, lesbianism as the practice" emerged largely outside of working-class and poor lesbian worlds, as well as outside most lesbian communities of color.

Feminist movements presuming the priority of women *as* women left no room for women *as* anything else. Put more specifically, the notion of women as women assumed an essential identity of womanness that could be abstracted from other identity constructions and stand universally on its own. In fact, this essentialized universal womanness was of course a raced, classed, sexed, and cultured conception. Without attending to this fact, however, women from communities not assumed in the class/race/culture/gender/sexuality norm were seen as less purely *women*. Identifications imbricated with a cross-section of other communities were seen as tainted.

What we cannot overlook at this point is that these imbricating identities are ones that women would share with men as well as with other women and those gender identified beyond the binary. Just as Jews invested in Jewish patriarchy found identifying as feminists an act of mutiny, as it was assumed impossible to identify with women *and* Jews, some feminists found continued identification with class struggle and racial and religious communities an act of treason. In class, racial, and religious communities, women could not be women *as* women exclusively, they shared these politics with groups of men and transfolk. This bind within feminism was replicated within lesbian politics. Moreover, to the degree that lesbians were seen as hyperwomen (in a radical feminist sense), the elite pressure to define identities and align politically with women made coalition and joint identity construction with male and other sexual outlaws culturally and politically criminal.

I want to be clear here: I am not saying that these elements of exclusionary thinking are directly present in *Like Bread on the Seder Plate*. Alpert explicitly concludes the work with her "visions for the future." In this chapter Alpert points out that many of her concerns for a lesbian feminist Jewish agenda are shared with numerous other Jews: heterosexual feminists, gay men, heterosexual intermarried couples, bisexuals, transgendered people, single heterosexuals, those not traditionally observant, liberal Jews in general, progressive educators, "scholars of women's history, mysticism, and Mizrachi Jewish communities." This single mention of nonwhite/non-Ashkenazi Jews suggests, however, that they may be absent from the writer's/reader's conceptualizations about the other groups and may not even be interpreted to mean Mizrachi Jewish communities as all, but "scholars of." Further, Jewish lesbian feminists have made clear that tensions between lesbians and other sexual outlaws in the Jewish community, especially those involving "men," will not be adequately addressed until bisexual women take responsibility for certain aspects of relative privilege and until men make antisexist work central to their agendas. However, this does not exempt lesbians from taking responsibility as well. The history of essentialist thought at work not only in feminism, but also in lesbian feminism has affected some aspects of Jewish lesbian feminism. Gathering together in specific communities is necessary as we do the work of social justice. Attending to some of the problematic aspects that gathering has relied on historically is also, however, a necessary part of justice work. In this, lesbian feminists must also take seriously the potentially essentialist bases informing some of our choices to identify as lesbian, over and against identifying as queer.

The Issue *Is* Power

At this juncture I would like to undertake a brief review of one other work by a Jewish lesbian feminist that is more able to avoid the trap of essentialism. At the time Melanie Kaye/Kantrowitz was writing the essays for her book, *The Issue Is Power: Essays on Women, Jews, Violence and Resistance,* she was not yet using the term "queer;" her radical feminist identification as lesbian and dyke does not, however, exactly recall the historical problems of essentialism in feminist thought in the same way that Alpert's work does. Clearly advancing a lesbian-critical agenda, Kaye/Kantrowitz shows us that we need constantly to see the relationship between anti-Semitism, racism, classism, sexism, and homophobia if we are to build an inclusive, multicultural, and effective left in this "toxic wasteland" of our lives.[36] However, we must build these bridges with "our frail/sturdy human hearts outraged by injustice and committed to generosity."[37]

The Issue Is Power contains speeches from political events and essays of various lengths developed over a fifteen-year period. Kaye/Kantrowitz's message is delivered always in the cadence of a poet, with the urgency of an activist and the sensitivity, kindness, and self-criticism of a Brooklyn-born Jew re-created in the civil rights, women's, and lesbian liberation movements. From pieces on art and culture to politics, identity, and sexuality, Kaye/

Kantrowitz shows over and over that the issue, most certainly, is power and that we had better wise up, allow ourselves to feel it, talk to each other about it, and take action.

The book opens with a long essay on violence.[38] She opens the introduction: "First I learned about rape. I mean, I always knew, cannot remember learning. First I learned about the Holocaust. I mean, I always knew, cannot remember learning."[39] Kaye/Kantrowitz, who is antimilitaristic, takes the issue of violence very seriously and has decided that it is "a contradiction to be a Jew and a pacifist," that "pacifism is a luxury" because "victims resist every way they can . . . victims must fight back."[40]

But this is no diatribe through which Kaye/Kantrowitz might seduce you into any form of action and resistance if you are not careful. Her work on violence is far from a glorification, or a love affair such as Hollywood, the news media, or the nation-state have. Kaye/Kantrowitz, speaking with the insight of the oppressed, immediately asks: "What does it mean to be a *victim*? How does one/can one use violence to free oneself? And then how does one stop? When is one strong enough to stop?"[41] In this essay, Kaye/Kantrowitz is able to focus on violence against women and articulate what she has learned from resistance to such violence. But like any of the mutually constitutive categories of the Talmudic text, women do not stand alone in this piece as a separative category. What she knows about violence against women is made possible by what she has mutually come to know about anti-Semitic, class-based, racial violence, and militarism as well.

Many of the other essays treat more directly topics of Jewish identity and politics. Similar to what we saw in Alpert and in contrast to an essentialist view, Kaye/Kantrowitz benefits from a traditional legacy that values historical continuity as it presumes major disruptions and new developments within that historical trajectory. In these pieces she keeps in motion the movement to redevelop American Jewish identity. This emerging identity is Jewish and is placed in history; in her words, "to be a Jew is to tangle with history."[42] It is also well rooted in and relevant to our contemporary (U.S.)American experience, in the spirit of those with an unflinching commitment to morality and pride, both personal and collective. Kaye/Kantrowitz takes for her base a quote from Muriel Rukeyser, "To be a Jew in the twentieth century is to be offered a gift,"[43] and adds that "To be a Radical Jew in the Late 20th Century is . . . is . . . well, maybe we don't know yet exactly what it is." But in the face of the pain and loss particularly associated with assimilation, to be a radical Jew in the late twentieth century and still today begins with "the need to know the self, the people, the culture," to "figure out how to undo assimilation without being nostalgic or xenophobic," as we, as radical Jews, "tangle with Jewish identity and its relationship to Jewish culture, tradition and politics."[44]

In these essays, then, Kaye/Kantrowitz shares with us the delight and pain involved in her gradual process of "coming out as a Jew" and coming more wholly into her Jewishness. In the fashion of the Talmudic example discussed above, Kaye/Kantrowitz can celebrate a particular aspect of identity even as it *is* imbricated with other facets of human identity and therefore situated within complex and shifting sets of power dynamics. She writes that she (like how many Jews on the left?) "did not know what it meant to be a Jew, only what it meant to be a *mentsh*. [She] did not know that *mentsh* was a Jewish word in a Jewish language."[45] But having moved "along a mostly uncon-scious, gradual, zig-zag, and retrospectively inevitable path,"[46] she can now suggest that we must "reach out and in at the same time" in order to live our lives and do our work as radical Jews. Such work requires exploration and ex-perience within "Jewish space," as well as coalition work based on solidarity, rather than guilt.

On the issue of class and Jewish power, Kaye/Kantrowitz correctly points out, "The problem is not relative Jewish success. The problem is a severe class system that distributes success so unequally."[47] The author asks us to confront our relative success as a community in the United States in this historical period. She writes, "Used well, education, choice, even comfort can strengthen people, individually and collectively. . . . The question is what do we do with our education, our choice, privilege, skills, experience, passion for justice: our power." In holding the community responsible for its access and resources, Kaye/Kantrowitz does not mistake this communal situation for an assumption of wealth or access among particular Jews. Too often, work on Jewish success eclipses the reality of poor and working-class Jews, of the gendered and heterosexist aspects of Jewish wealth, and of the severe class injustice operative within the Jewish community.[48] As in the antiuniversalist tendency of the Talmudic tradition, Kaye/Kantrowitz is able to name communal responsibilities while simultaneously identifying particular intracommunal differentials. I wonder what would happen if, as Kaye/Kantrowitz suggests, we all (poor and privileged Jews) could be "proud of our collective strength, confident that we can use it right." I won-der what would happen if we as a community could make our *collective* strength more accessible for those within and without the Jewish commu-nity who need it most?[49] Yes, whether individually we are working class or middle class, as Jews we will likely be reminded that "someone will always call us pushy," but "Isn't it time to really push?"[50]

Kaye/Kantrowitz also brings the issue of class into a discussion of race, stating that "anti-Semitism—Jewhating—is not taken seriously because it hasn't kept Jews poor,"[51] but she writes unequivocally that "anti-Semitism protects christian wealth."[52] The author clarifies for us that, given the confluence of race and class, "Race relations in the U.S. are usually presented as a Black-white paradigm which disguises both the complexity of color and the brutality of class."[53] Her insights on this point make good use of the Talmudic example's capacity to work with mutually constitutive categories in a way that clarifies power dynamics rather than masking them. She adds that by framing the Jewish role in this situation in terms of "the Black-Jewish Question" we obscure both Christian hatred and white privilege embodied within the class system. Kaye/Kantrowitz brings many years of antiracism work—since her days as a seventeen-year-old in the civil rights movement to her position as executive director of the New York City-based Jews For Racial and Economic Justice—to these essays. She redefines race issues in the United States along a white/colored/black continuum and discusses how Jews in this country chose and then learned how to be white, and the cost—the cultural loss—of such a choice.

Multicultural Reciprocity and the Use of Countertexts

Getting inside a differing worldview as experienced by cultures outside the mainstream can help us as scholars to destabilize hegemonic paradigms of the dominant culture. Such cross-cultural study demonstrates the particular nature of dominant constructs that often appear all-encompassing to even critical contemporary theorists and as universal in cultural production. Here I employ an alternative paradigm to engage in critique of problematic power relations in the dominant mode in the service of justice for those who suffer within the dominant structures. But does this mean that the alternative paradigm is simply more just? Does this mean that although the dominant paradigm is torn asunder and its power dynamics exposed, the alternative mode remains in tact? As justice is sought for those in the dominant culture, is justice for those whose lives are constructed also within the alternative culture not a concern?

The countertext employed in this chapter enables the analysis of the mutual construction of identities necessary in the contemporary period in the West, aiding those such as Spelman in the project they set up for themselves/us. But what a strange countertext I have employed. Few if any contemporary Jewish medical ethicists would be able to utilize this text at face value given the intensely inegalitarian stance of the reasoning. Thus, the countertext itself is desperately in need of communal reinterpretation and ultimately reconstruction if it is to be helpful for Jews today. The project of contemporary Jewish feminist queers is to engage in that reinterpretation so that new insights will be developed.

If the analysis is not self-conscious of the power dynamics in the countertext, the method of countertext itself becomes imperialist. Contemporary movements for social justice often plumb minority cultures for how they help critique the dominant mode, without offering similar critiques of the minority example or work with those seeking justice within the minority groups. The most obvious examples due to their usurpation in popular culture come from native communities. Tidbits of native lifestyles are offered as alternatives and critiques of the individualistic and aggressive mechanisms of the colonizers' liberalism and capitalism. Rarely do those appropriating native imagery, art, or ritual attend to ways in which the materials appropriated have often been the markers of minority/marginalized subjugation within the alternative community. Scholarship relying on countertexts that does not come back to critique the power dynamics within the counterworld, aware of and in the service of the marginalized there, is seriously lacking.

The complicated and multilayered ranked categories found in the Talmudic texts can help us develop critical insight into the hierarchical categorizations found in hegemonic Western philosophy and keep activist and scholarly revisioning in that sphere more nuanced and liberatory. But it is also the contributions of philosophers such as Spelman, whose work concerns the dominant paradigms, that can supply those of us also working to transform power dynamics in the minority Jewish world with critical insight into Jewish texts and paradigms. Spelman's method enables those working with Jewish texts to identify the absurdity of Talmudic ranked categories in new ways. Suddenly one sees that there is an illogic to lists of genders, priestly rankings, birthright, and so on. These lists are sometimes overlapping, and other times mutually exclusive and on the surface do not make sense together. Spelman's insights compel us to look deeper into Jewish tradition and religious texts in order to understand what the lists are about, how they constitute a complex structural hierarchy, and how we may find newly reconstructed ways to use them. Scholars working within the Jewish framework can see Spelman's conception of the ways that multiple identities are mutually constituted comprises the terrain of hierarchical power within a particular cultural and historical framework. In this case those seeking justice will better understand this complex Jewish framework and be better able to do the work of *tikkun olam*, social justice, within the Jewish community as well.

Notes

1. Revised and reprinted with permission. "To Race, to Class, to Queer: Jewish Contributions to Feminist Theory," in *Jewish Locations: Traversing Racialized Landscapes*, eds. Bat-Ami Bar On and Lisa Tessman (Lanham, MD: Rowman and Littlefield, 2001).

2. Earlier attempts to work out the arguments of this piece were presented as papers at the 1998 Western Political Science Association Meeting (WPSA) session and the 1998 International Association of Women Philosophers (IAPh) Symposium and previously published in *Jewish Locations*. I would like to thank Lisa Disch for her thoughtful feedback and those at the WPSA session for the great discussion, Dawn Rose for introducing me to and helping with the Jewish texts in medical ethics, Wendy Lee-Lampshire and Uma Narayan for their thoughtful feedback on the IAPh version, and Lisa Tessman and Bat-Ami Bar On for being careful editors of the first printing.

3. For writings by non-Jewish activists and thinkers, see Gloria Anzaldua and Cherrie Moraga, eds., *This Bridge Called My Back: Writings of Radical Women of Color* (New York: Kitchen Table, Women of Color Press, 1982). The most widely circulated articulation of such a critique was published in 1977 as the "Black Feminist Statement" from the Combahee River Collective.

4. Judith Plaskow, *Standing Again at Sinai: Judaism from a Feminist Perspective* (New York: HarperCollins, 1991). We see the pain of these false choices again addressed by queers in the queer Jews issue of *Response* (Winter/Spring 1997): N67.

5. Such is the presumption of the academic journal *Race, Gender and Class*, for example. See also Gerda Lerner, *Why History Matters: Life and Thought* (New York and Oxford: Oxford University Press, 1997), on this discussion. For a specifically Jewish discussion, note that in the introduction of Christie Balka and Andy Rose, eds., *Twice Blessed: On Being Lesbian, Gay, and Jewish* (Boston: Beacon, 1989), the editors write, "Lesbian and gay Jewish experience is not monolithic. . . . Rather, it is influenced by the vicissitudes of religious identity, gender, age, class, geography, physical ability, and other factors." "Influenced" is the key word here. Balka and Rose take their primary categories of sexual orientation and Jewishness and "relate" them to additional categories. Attending to diversity among lesbian and gay Jews is important; in this instance they suggest that the way to understand multiple identity categories is to see that certain secondary factors affect (even a complex of) primary factors. They explain the situation of being "doubly other," whereby cultural aspects relating to sexual orientation marginalize Jewish lesbians and gay men from both Jewish and larger U.S. life.

6. Gloria Anzaldua, ed., *Making Face, Making Soul: Haciendo Caras; Creative and Critical Perspectives by Feminists of Color* (San Francisco: Aunt Lute, 1990). As an example of cross-discussion, see Norma Alarcon, "Theoretical Subject(s) of *This Bridge Called My Back* and Anglo-American Feminism," in Anzaldua, *Making Face, Making Soul*.

7. Judith Butler, for example, is Jewish and has a significant background in Jewish philosophy. She does not, however, problematize Jewish issues. Moreover, in her most popular written works she often relies on Christian cultural markers.

8. Notably, this is less the case for minority feminists. Angela Davis, *Women, Race, and Class* (New York: Random House, 1981), and Patricia Hill Collins, *Black Feminist Thought* (New York: Routledge, 1990) explicitly utilize a three-tiered model of race, gender, and class. Audre Lorde, *Sister Outsider: Essays and Speeches* (Trumansburg, NY: Crossing, 1984), is credited for working exquisitely with even more complicated sets of identity groupings, though she did not engage in the same kind of analytic frameworks as philosophers such as those discussed later in this chapter.

9. I will be referring specifically to Elizabeth V. Spelman, *Inessential Woman: Problems of Exclusion in Feminist Thought* (Boston: Beacon, 1988). Although she has published much since this work, I focus on this text because it helped many other philosophers and activists so significantly. Consequently, we were also affected by the problems in this work.

10. Spelman, *Inessential Woman*, 14, and the framework for chapter 5.

11. Spelman, *Inessential Women*, 48.

12. Spelman, *Inessential Woman*, 41. Though Spelman cites a passage from Aristotle in which he discusses a "community of slaves, male and female," she does so in order to demonstrate her central point regarding gender (i.e., the lack of "women" among slaves).

13. It is others such as Judith P. Butler (*Gender Trouble: Feminism and the Subversion of Identity* [New York: Routledge, 1990]), who will trouble the feminist reliance on gender as the socially constructed version of sex. Part of the point of this chapter is that, as helpful as works such as *Inessential Woman* are, their analyses break down when additional identity categories are taken seriously. Concomitantly, although demonstrating so is beyond the scope of this chapter, Butler's extremely important *Gender Trouble* does not hold up under the pressure from Spelman's race critical work.

14. Early in the text, Spelman refers to the Athenian distinctions as "class" distinctions. This begins to shift in the section of the chapter on Aristotle where Spelman utilizes her analysis to critique the racist bias of contemporary feminist philosophers; Spelman, *Inessential Woman*, 51. Although she is not clear as to why she must choose one contemporary equivalent to the category slave, she discusses the inadequacy of both modern usages of "race" and "class." She concludes that "'race,' is probably less misleading than 'class.'" (p. 200, 44 n). It is interesting to note, however, that when she first shifts to modern paradigms such as race within the text, she also names class, religion, sexual orientation, nationality, and servile status as other important factors of identity and refers to both class and race regarding slave status. (pp. 51–53) Fifty-four pages into the text, she is using the term "race" (in quotation marks) on its own.

15. Despite referring to class and race in the introduction to chapter five, Spelman explains before she begins her actual analysis in the chapter: "I shall not explicitly be examining class and classism, though at a number of points I suggest ways in which considerations of class and classism affect the topic at hand. Many of the

questions I raise about comparisons between sexism and racism could also be raised about comparisons between sexism and classism or classism and racism." See Spelman, *Inessential Woman*, 116. Her topic at hand is gender and race. It is likely true that there are many comparisons to be made with class, however this does not recognize that issues involving class need attention to their own specificity.

16. Such a two-tiered model is schematized most clearly in Spelman's charting natures vis-à-vis biological/psychological descriptions of male/female-slave/free. See Spelman, *Inessential Woman*, 46.

17. Thanks to Uma Narayan for helping me articulate this point.

18. In discussing Aristotle's conception of a "well-ordered political community," Spelman writes: "When a people are a slave people, it doesn't matter . . . whether they are male or female." See Spelman, *Inessential Woman*, 42. She also cites Angela Davis' account "of Black female slaves as 'genderless.'" (p. 201, 51 n)

19. Spelman, *Inessential Women*, 42–43.

20. Although Spelman will note in chapter five that her "point is not that Black men cannot in any way be sexist to white or Black women, for indeed they can," she also makes sweeping statements such as, "But this is a racist society, and generally, the self-esteem of white people is deeply influenced by their difference from and supposed superiority to Black people." See Spelman, *Inessential Woman*, 121. Even given the power of racism, to allow for this generalization in such stark terms we would have to consider white and Black people as undifferentiated entities with a single relationship of power, which is precisely the idea Spelman's book is intended to counter.

21. The term "Talmud" usually refers to the collection of teachings from the Babylonian rabbis consisting of the discussions and commentaries in the Mishnah and Gemara, codified between the ninth and early thirteenth centuries during the second exile in Babylon. The Mishnah is a compilation of laws and sayings by the early rabbis collected and arranged by Rabbi Jehuda ha-Nasi in the third century. The Gemara constitutes the development and discussion of the Mishnah by the Babylonian rabbis.

22. For the context of this chapter, Alicia Ostreiker's work on biblical texts demonstrates the power of looking to other texts that present fundamental challenges to the dominant narrative. See Alicia Ostreiker, "A House of Holies: The Song of Songs as Counter Text" (paper presented to Ma'yan's Jewish Feminist Research Group, New York, 1996).

23. I want to thank Lisa Disch and Jane Bennet for pushing me on this point.

24. See Lorde, *Sister Outsider*.

25. I am presenting a version in a Jewish framework of what Barbara Smith, "Notes for Yet Another Paper on Black Feminism, or Will the Real Enemy Please Stand Up," *Conditions* 5 (1979): 123–132, has referred to as a view of multiple oppressions that is not about "arithmetic," and to which Spelman herself refers in debunking the additive approach. See Spelman, *Inessential Woman*, 123.

26. Thus, one cannot even say that Jewishness is thickly bounded as one might find in an essentialist identitarian tradition. As the categories below assume, on can "become" Jewish as well. "Proselyte" names one who has converted to Judaism.

27. I want to thank William Connolly for helping me clarify and articulate this point for a context beyond Jewish scholarship into contemporary political theory.

28. Kathy Ferguson's contribution here is much appreciated.

29. This is Daniel Boyarin's methodological claim in his use of Talmudic texts for *Unheroic Conduct: The Rise of Heterosexuality and the Invention of the Jewish Man* (Berkeley: University of California Press, 1997). He asserts that his project has "two faces." In the introduction to the text, he writes that "Jewish culture demystifies European gender ideologies by reversing their terms, which is not, I hasten to emphasize, a liberatory process in itself but can be mobilized—strategically—for liberation." (xxi) He also aims at the goal of reconstructing a "rabbinic Judaism that will be quite different in some ways from the one we know and yet be and feel credibly grounded in the tradition of the Rabbis." (xxi)

30. This point could be supported by Uma Narayan's critique of gender essentialism, cultural essentialism, and cultural relativism in "Rethinking Cultures: A Feminist Critique of Cultural Essentialism and Cultural Relativism" (keynote address at the Annual Society of Women in Philosophy Eastern Division Spring Conference, Durham, University of New Hampshire, April 1998).

31. Nathins, who were descendants of the Gibeonites (from Joshua 9:27), are one of the peoples living in the land that the Israelites entered and claimed after the death of Moses. Although a conquered people, they were spared death, but were turned into a subnational caste. By King David's time, they were subject to most of the laws of Israel, but some special laws continued to apply to them.

32. The Talmud represents the rise to hegemonic power of the rabbis, a class of scholars, over the previous religious caste ordering. For an interesting example of new critical scholarship on the rise and consolidation of rabbinic power from a gender perspective, see Miriam B. Peskowitz, *Spinning Fantasies: Rabbis, Gender, and History* (Berkeley: University of California Press, 1997).

33. I much appreciate Tamar Kamionkowsky helping me to sort through this dimension of the maze.

34. Rebecca Alpert, *Like Bread on the Seder Plate: Jewish Lesbians and the Transformation of Tradition* (New York: Columbia University Press, 1987), 7.

35. Shane Phelan addresses a similar point in *Getting Specific: Postmodern Lesbian Politics* (Minneapolis: University of Minnesota Press, 1994), 21. In this work, as in Shane Phelan, *Identity Politics: Lesbian, Feminism and the Limits of Community* (Philadelphia: Temple University Press, 1989), Phelan delves deeply into aspects of exclusionary thinking at work within lesbian communities.

36. Melanie Kaye/Kantrowitz, *The Issue Is Power: Essays on Women, Jews, Violence and Resistance* (San Francisco: Aunt Lute, 1992), 127.

37. Kaye/Kantrowitz, *Issue Is Power*, 129.

38. In 1977, Kaye/Kantrowitz began writing a book on violence from her perspective as a woman and as a Jew. The three hundred pages of that manuscript have been edited and condensed into this essay.

39. Kaye/Kantrowitz, *Issue Is Power*, i.

40. Kaye/Kantrowitz, *Issue Is Power*, ii.

41. Ibid.

42. Kaye/Kantrowitz, *Issue Is Power*, 193.

43. Kaye/Kantrowitz, *Issue Is Power*, 92.

44. Kaye/Kantrowitz, *Issue Is Power*, 105.

45. Kaye/Kantrowitz, *Issue Is Power*, 97.

46. Ibid.

47. Kaye/Kantrowitz, *Issue Is Power*, 149.

48. For some work on these issues, see, for example, Felice Yeskel, "Beyond the Taboo: Talking about Class," in *The Narrow Bridge: Jewish Views on Multiculturalism*, ed. Marla Brettschneider (New Brunswick, NJ: Rutgers University Press, 1996); Balka and Rose, *Twice Blessed*; Dawn Rose, "Class as Problematic in Jewish Feminist Theology," *Race, Gender, and Class: American Jewish Perspectives* 6, no. 4 (1999) 125–135; and in the pages of *The Narrow Bridge*.

49. As one example, see Jeffrey Dekro, "Community Economic Development and the American Jewish Community," in *The Narrow Bridge*, ed. Marla Brettschneider.

50. Kaye/Kantrowitz, *Issue Is Power*, 149.

51. Kaye/Kantrowitz, *Issue Is Power*, 119.

52. Kaye/Kantrowitz, *Issue Is Power*, 121.

53. Kaye/Kantrowitz, *Issue Is Power*, 116.

~

CHAPTER THIRTEEN

Feminist Politics and Pluralism: Can We Do Feminist Political Theory without Theories of Gender?

Amy R. Baehr[1,2]

Philosophers writing in normative political theory have recently focused our attention on two competing understandings of the normative foundations of liberalism. According to those calling themselves political liberals, liberal political philosophy can and should proceed without the help of a particular conception of the person and of moral validity. It is argued that political philosophy should propose political principles that could be found acceptable to citizens holding a wide variety of doctrines concerning *what persons are, and what the proper ends of human and community life are*. On this view, the acceptability of political principles depends on the fact that they do not conflict with the fundamental values of dominant ethical traditions.[3]

Comprehensive liberals, on the other hand, argue that political philosophy cannot be done without the help of a determinate conception of the person and moral validity. According to this view, we cannot say much of interest about how we ought to live together without knowing *who we are and what the appropriate ends of human and community life are*. Indeed, the comprehensive liberal accuses the political liberal of tacitly assuming such conceptions.

Comprehensive liberals admit that their political doctrines, grounded as they are in particular and thus potentially controversial conceptions of the person and moral validity, may come into competition with common doctrines that citizens hold. But they believe that political philosophy cannot honestly avoid this result.[4]

Feminists have begun to consider the implications of this debate for feminist political philosophy.[5] A common claim is that feminists ought not to be political liberals because political liberalism buys its broad acceptability at the cost of diluting its commitment to substantive equality, a consequence that seriously challenges most feminist political projects.[6] While I am curious about these implications, I want to focus our attention on a somewhat different question this debate suggests for feminist political philosophy. As political liberals suggest that political philosophy can and should be done without foundation in a theory of the person and in moral theory, should feminists attempt to do feminist political philosophy without a foundational theory of gender? Or, on the other hand, as comprehensive liberals argue that political philosophy cannot be done without foundations, should feminist political philosophers found feminist political philosophy on a particular theory of gender? This question is similar to the question at issue between political and comprehensive liberals insofar as it asks about the relationship between the questions "Who are we?" and "How should we live together?"

This question is not merely academic. For, presumably, it would be politically efficacious to have a "big tent" feminism, that is, an account of feminist political claims that is palatable to feminists holding a diversity of views about gender—androgynists, difference essentialists, social constructionists, just to name a few. But is it possible (and desirable) to describe a feminist politics that is compatible with such diverse theories of gender? What would its normative foundation be?

Of course, these questions about normative foundations disappear when we simply abandon normative political philosophy altogether. It is suggested by some feminists that normative proposals habitually do not recognize that the conceptions of liberation they represent are always reactions to particular experiences of domination and subordination. As such they carry with them and are constrained by the experience of those particular forms of domination. Thus, far from offering a view of full liberation, they present partial and backward-looking conceptions of liberation that keep us from recognizing new forms of domination and imagining new forms of liberation.[7] This warning is surely warranted. But it does not require that we stop doing normative political philosophy altogether. On the contrary, it underscores the importance of such work while reminding us of its inevitable dangers. Rather than offering a comprehensive conception of human liberation, the warning requires that as feminists we see our work as contextual and pragmatic, responding to particular experiences of domination and subordination. On this view, normative political philosophy can accept the obligation to reflect on domination and human suffering, while recognizing that it operates within a particular horizon of political experience.[8]

Such situated reflection is the topic of this chapter. I begin by examining a number of prominent feminist political theories and discussing the central role played by gender theory in those theories. This first section is critical insofar as it shows that placing gender theory at the foundation of a theory of feminist politics gives that political theory a justificatory burden it cannot support in the context of feminist pluralism. In a second section, I argue for a particular version of feminist contractualism as an example of a feminist political conception that, while providing a normative foundation for feminist politics, is not committed to a determinate ontology of gender. This makes the conception more viable in the context of feminist pluralism.

Feminist Politics Grounded in Ontologies of Gender

Many feminists seem to hold that the validity of feminist political demands depends on the truth of particular claims about gender. For example, Elizabeth Cady Stanton writes,

> Here gentlemen, is our difficulty: When we plead our cause before the lawmakers and savants of the republic, they can not take in the idea that *men and women are alike*; . . . we ask for all that you have asked for yourselves in the progress of your development, since the *Mayflower* cast anchor beside Plymouth rock; and simply on the ground that the rights of every human being are the same and identical.[9]

Notice that Stanton's political claim that men and women ought to enjoy the same rights is shored up by her claim about the genders, namely that they are "alike."

A very different ontology of gender was offered by another type of early feminist. These feminists argued that, far from being the same, men and women are importantly *different* from one another. For example, a contemporary of Stanton, Jane Frohock writes, "It is woman's womanhood, her instinctive femininity, her highest morality that society now needs to counteract the excess of masculinity that is everywhere to be found in our unjust and unequal laws."[10]

Stanton and Frohock disagree about what men and women *are*; but note that they share a strategy. In each case a set of claims about what women (and men), qua women (and men), are is offered, from which a conception of gender justice is then derived. Presumably, if one were to determine that one of these theories of gender is incorrect, its corresponding normative claim would lose its warrant.

Difference of opinion concerning what women and men *qua* women and men are implies important differences in the content of feminist politics. Stanton's emphasis on sameness supported the extension of rights to women identical to those of men. Frohock's emphasis on difference supported some different rights, for example, protective labor law for women. We are familiar with these emphases on sameness and difference in their contemporary guise as the equality versus difference debate in feminist jurisprudence.[11] The disagreement between "sameness" and "difference" approaches has seemed quite impossible to resolve because, as Martha Minow has pointed out, feminist thinking is caught up in a "dilemma of difference." According to this dilemma, sameness approaches tend to ignore what seem to be obviously relevant differences between men and women. But difference approaches often end up stigmatizing those who differ from the norm and have the potential of legally entrenching the relations under which women have suffered.[12] That is, both approaches have potentially unhappy implications for women. Is it possible that this dilemma is the result of a particular feminist philosophical strategy, namely grounding feminist political claims in particular theories of gender? Though this question is not pursued directly below, what follows is motivated by the suspicion that a non–gender-theory-based conception of feminist politics, or at least one that makes extremely minimal ontological claims about gender, can help us to move beyond the unattractive choice between sameness and difference approaches. But before I develop that approach, consider how a connection drawn between politics and gender theory causes trouble in the work of two contemporary feminist political theorists.

Irigaray and Sexed Rights

An ontology of gender seems to be fundamental to Luce Irigaray's conception of politics. Indeed, Irigaray appears to draw political conclusions—statements about what the goals and strategies of the women's movement should be—from claims about the ontology of gender. In her reading of Freud, Irigaray shows that the stories our culture habitually tells about human psychological development portray women as existing only *in relation to*, and as *deviations from* a masculine norm. Girls are "inferior little men;" women's identity is limited to the role women play in men's "primal fantasy."[13] Because women are reduced to their relation to men, we can say that in patriarchy there really is only one sex, the masculine sex with *its* other. In the face of this masculine reduction of sexual difference to female difference from men, Irigaray insists that we acknowledge a substantive difference between men and women that is not reducible to this "dream of symmetry."[14]

Replacing the one [the masculine] by the two of sexual difference thus constitutes a decisive philosophical and political gesture, one which gives up a singular being in order to become a dual being. This is the necessary foundation
for a new ontology, a new ethics, and a new politics, in which the other is recognized as other and not as the same.[15]

Irigaray sees sexual difference situated in sexually distinct embodied experiences. She writes: "There is nothing that is generally valid for women and
men besides the economy of nature."[16] Thus while Western political philosophy has traditionally seen the extension of rights to women as a matter of
showing that women are relevantly similar to men, Irigaray claims:

People must have rights in civil society. These rights must necessarily be sex-
specific. I mean, even when one sex can identify itself subjectively with the
other, such identification is objectively impossible. Concretely this means that
a body has objectively sex-specific characteristics that stand in the way of a
subjective assimilation or identification [with the other sex]. Thus the discourse of equality remains an idealistic discourse so long as it abstracts from the
bodily reality.[17]

Among the sex-specific rights Irigaray lists are legal preferences for mothers' over fathers' rights; the right to abortion; the right to have "public signs,
as well as mass media programmes and publications . . . respect women's sexual identity. It would be a civil offense to depict women's bodies as stakes in
pornography or prostitution,"[18] and half of the media should be in the hands
of women.[19] Notice that a feminist politics inspired by Irigaray would not
want the state to be neutral on the meaning and value of sexual difference—
for attempts at neutrality will inevitably end up presupposing the male identity of the citizen.

Irigaray's substantive political proposals are worth considering.[20] Here,
however, we focus on a political question about Irigaray's philosophical
strategy: Are we to expect feminists, who presumably hold a diversity of
views about gender, to accept a political program that is presented as
grounded in a very particular theory of gender? One answer might be that
feminist politics *is dependent* upon a particular conception of gender—for
example Irigaray's or some other—so those who would be feminists must either accept it or rethink their politics. Another answer, that this chapter
explores, is that this strategy unduly burdens feminist politics. This answer
would be accompanied by the hope that one can articulate a conception of
feminist politics that does not depend for its validity on the truth of some
particular theory of gender.

But is this perhaps an unfair reading of Irigaray? A more careful reading might see in Irigaray's insistence on feminine difference not a claim about what women *are*, but merely a *strategic* assertion of difference meant to free women from the constraints of patriarchal accounts of women's identity.[21] If this is right, then Irigaray does not really mean that women are, actually, by nature, fundamentally different from men. She merely means that feminists should *think* of them this way now. Margaret Whitford writes: "This enables essentialism to be interpreted as a position rather than as an ontology, and Irigaray to be interpreted as a strategist . . . rather than as an obscurantist prophet of essential biological or psychic difference."[22]

If Irigaray is a strategic essentialist, then she offers only an account of what women are under patriarchy, more being epistemologically inaccessible. As we learned above, what women are under patriarchy is merely a "male fantasy," part of a "dream of symmetry," a rationalization of male dominance. The strategic essentialist argues that we should assert feminine difference nonetheless because doing so challenges the patriarchal construal of women's difference. It opens up the possibility that the other be recognized "as other and not as the same,"[23] not as a mere mirror image of masculine identity. Strategic essentialism *asserts* feminine difference so that it *makes a difference*.

If this is the correct reading of Irigaray's work, should we conclude that her political proposals do not rely on a determinate ontology of gender?[24] Yes and no. Epistemological skepticism is the foundation for her strategic essentialism. And while epistemological skepticism would seem to be agnostic about matters of ontology, it does cast serious doubt on many accounts of what women are. For example, if we cannot know what women really are, then simple feminist difference essentialisms should not be trusted. (Of course, a true skepticism would merely caution us against trusting any particular account but not venture to claim that an account is wrong.) Nor should androgynist feminists be trusted when they claim that women and men are essentially the same. So while Irigaray, the strategic essentialist, may indeed be agnostic about gender ontology in the sense that she does not put forward a determinate account, her view does imply that we should withhold trust from gender ontologies. Many feminists will find this withholding of trust to be in serious conflict with their own views about gender. Thus, because feminists can reject this skepticism without being unreasonable, a politics that is grounded in it will be less viable than one might hope.

Butler and the Radical Critique of Identity
At this juncture, perhaps we should turn to a theorist who explicitly seeks to develop a feminist politics that does not depend for its validity on an ontol-

ogy of gender, for example, Judith Butler. Butler writes, "It is no longer clear that feminist theory ought to try to settle the questions of primary identity in order to get on with the task of politics."[25] Butler seems to be saying that feminist politics ought not to rest on particular claims about what women are. Indeed, this idea has been her claim to fame, as she joined many feminists in the 1980s and 1990s to dismantle the myth of the universal woman as the subject of feminist politics. Some theorists reacted to this dismantling with alarm, asking, "How can we possibly do feminist politics without a conception of woman?" I join Butler, however, in asking how we could possibly have thought we could do it *with* such a conception. But I worry that Butler is not as committed to severing politics from the theory of gender as she would seem. Consider the continuation of the passage quoted above:

> It is no longer clear that feminist theory ought to try to settle the questions of primary identity in order to get on with the task of politics. Instead, we ought to ask, what political possibilities are the consequence of *a radical critique of the categories of identity*? What new shape of politics emerges when identity as a common ground no longer constrains the discourse on feminist politics?[26]

But what is this "radical critique of the categories of identity"? According to Butler, the radical critique tells us that identity is a "political construction." We must "unmask" the fact that gender is "a kind of persistent impersonation." Butler tells us that "'naturalness' is constituted through discursively constrained performative acts. . . . The practice by which gendering occurs, the embodying of norms, is a compulsory practice, a forcible production,"[27] and "Femininity is thus not the product of choice, but the forcible citation of a norm, one whose complex historicity is indissociable from relations of discipline, regulation, punishment."[28] Moreover, such regulation results in the creation of abject others. "This exclusionary matrix by which subjects are formed thus requires the simultaneous production of a domain of abject beings . . . those 'unlivable' and 'uninhabitable' zones of social life which are nevertheless densely populated."[29]

Butler suggests that a particular approach to politics flows from this account of gender (and identity). As I read her, this politics has at least three components. First, a Butlerian politics recommends careful attention to disrupting traditional gender categories and expectations ("denaturalization").[30] Second, it recommends a focus on the claims of the abject, those excluded others, especially perhaps those who progressive movements themselves create.[31] And third, Butler's account of gender and identity as performative suggests that significant transformation will occur via "resignification."[32] Examples Butler offers are the progressive appropriation of the term "queer" by the gay, lesbian, bisexual, and transgender movement. And in her work on hate speech, Butler suggests that a "politics of the performative" involves the transformation of meanings rather than their entrenchment in law.[33]

The point is not to put these intriguing claims about what gender is or about how progressive politics ought to proceed into question here. The point is merely that Butler *does* make claims about the fundamental nature of gender, and draws from them conclusions about the appropriate goals and practices of the women's movement (and the queer movement as well).[34] If this is right, Butler's view implies that we *do need* to have our gender ontology figured out before we do feminist politics. If we do not, we run the risk of proposing political programs that entrench oppressive identities and create a sphere of abject others. Ironically, then, while intending to sever politics from ontology, Butler actually ties the two together. But then Butler's feminist politics may not be capable of meeting with the acceptance of feminists holding a diversity of views about gender.[35] Just as I do not mean to disagree with Irigaray's substantive political proposals, my concern is not to criticize the politics that Butler's view of gender has inspired. I mean only to register a concern about the connection drawn between gender theory and politics.

But is Butler's work not antiessentialist and thus a rejection of particular ontologies of gender? That Butler's work is antiessentialist means that instead of offering an ontology (of gender or of anything else), she offers a *genealogy of ontology*:[36] an account of how we come to think things are the way we think they are. Indeed, as Butler uses the term, ontology seems to involve the fixing of identities, precisely what her work rejects.[37] She writes:

> Clearly this project does not propose to lay out within traditional philosophical terms an ontology of gender whereby the meaning of being a woman or a man is elucidated within the terms of phenomenology. The presumption here is that the "being" of gender is an effect, an object of a genealogical investigation that maps out the political parameters of its construction in the mode of ontology.[38]

This passage suggests that for Butler, to claim that gender is an effect is not to make an ontological claim. That is, it would seem that for Butler any and all ontologies are essentialist.[39] But surely this is an idiosyncratic use of the term "ontology." *Merriam-Webster*'s reports that ontology is "a particular theory about the nature of being or the kinds of existents." Butler tells us about the kind of being that gender is. She tells us that it is the result of "contingent acts" and not a natural substance. Indeed, Butler herself writes:

> That the gendered body is performative suggests that it has no ontological status apart from the various acts which constitute its reality.[40]

That it has no ontological status *apart* from the acts that constitute its reality means that its ontology, what it is, is determined by those acts. And while this writer is not unsympathetic to Butler's account of gender, it is still an account of gender. And such accounts make problematic foundations for feminist politics because of the disagreement they inevitably engender in the context of feminist pluralism. If it is possible to do feminist political theory without doing gender ontology at all, then that political theory might be interestingly viable.

One might defend Butler against the claim that she is proposing an ontology of gender by suggesting that her project is ultimately epistemological, not ontological. Veronica Vasterling suggests that Butler's claim (in her 1993 work) that the body is linguistically constructed should be interpreted as a claim about the limits of our knowledge, and not a claim about what bodies are.[41] Would it be plausible to read Butler's earlier work on gender (1989) in this way? Such a reading would say that Butler does not tell us that gender *really is* the effect of "the embodying of norms," but that is all we can know about it. Space is lacking here to pursue this question in sufficient depth. But briefly, even if Butler's claims about gender do only amount to claims about the limits of knowledge and not about what things are, they still imply a serious rejection of many accounts of gender common to a pluralistic culture like ours, and common even among feminists. Just to give one example, if Butler's view is that all we can *know* about what women are is that it is an effect of power, then her view is in serious conflict with the belief, held by many feminists, that science will gradually get behind our social practices and reveal the inaccuracy of sexist beliefs about women. If this is the case, Butler's epistemology might not provide a reliable foundation for a conception of feminist politics.

To summarize the discussion above about Irigaray and Butler: Even if both theorists are read as proposing accounts of the limits of our knowledge about gender, and not accounts of what gender is, their theories still have serious implications for feminist thinking about gender ontology. Most importantly, they enter the fray, seriously challenging common feminist accounts of what women are. The concern that motivates this chapter is that such controversy at the very foundation of feminist political theory might not serve it well.

An Overlapping Consensus of Feminist Doctrines?

It is possible that a conception of feminist politics (Butler's or Irigaray's or some other) could be found acceptable to feminists holding theories of gender that differ significantly from the one its original defender uses as a foundation.

This would imply that a conception of politics might stand even if its originally justifying conception of gender falls. Perhaps such a conception of feminist politics could find support in diverse feminist theories that are held in a
pluralistic feminist culture like ours. That is, perhaps a conception of feminist politics can be seen to be justified from a variety of feminist points of
view—though feminists holding those diverse points of view would disagree
about why the conception is justified because they disagree about the nature
of gender (or about other philosophically fundamental issues). For example,
it is possible that feminists holding a variety of incompatible views about
gender could agree on the political claim, made by Butler, that feminist politics ought to be vigilant about self-criticism, to be sure that it not create abject others. If there were such agreement, it might be because Butlerians
could support the claim for Butlerian reasons, while humanist feminists could
support it for humanist reasons, difference essentialists for difference essentialist reasons, ecofeminists for ecofeminist reasons, and so on. If this happened, there would be an overlapping consensus of feminist doctrines supporting a component of a conception of feminist politics.[42] This possibility is
interesting because it represents an account of the normative foundations of
feminist politics that does not make the truth of some particular ontology of
gender carry the justificatory burden.

Accepting overlapping consensus as the *sole* ground of feminist politics
has the happy consequence of not being associated with any difficult-to-
defend ontological claims.[43] But it has an unhappy consequence as well. It
makes feminist politics seem self-validating. It suggests that whatever we
feminists say is right is right. It holds us to no higher standard than our own
current convictions. The immanent critique of feminism offered by lesbians
and women of color in the past decades has shown us that any generation's
current convictions are hardly entirely trustworthy. Thus the overlapping
consensus approach seems to take justification too lightly, more lightly in
fact than I think most feminists themselves take it.

Indeed, surely most feminists do not think their political demands are
right merely because an overlapping consensus of feminist doctrines supports
them. It is more likely that they think their demands are right for some other
reason. If the foregoing readings of Irigaray and Butler are accurate, they
think they are right because they have discovered something about the nature of gender. But this brings us back to the beginning. Does the rightness
of feminist politics depend on the truth of some particular theory of gender?
Can we begin to answer the question "Why are feminist political claims
right?" without making use of a particular ontology of gender? The remainder of this chapter is dedicated to answering that question.

A Feminist Contractualist Alternative

A number of feminists have considered versions of contractualism as candidates for an explanation of the normative foundations of feminist politics.[44] Contractualism has long attracted thinkers who wish to reconcile political justice with pluralism of the sort that we find in the women's movement, and thus it would seem a logical place for us to look. But many feminists have criticized contractualism as incapable of anything but the affirmation of conventional values.[45] In the remainder of this chapter I propose a version of feminist contractualism. If it is successful, we will have reason to doubt that contractualism is so limited. I first explain the conception and the kind of normative grounding it provides for feminist political claims. Then I consider whether the feminist contractualism sketched really avoids assuming the truth of a particular ontology of gender, and thus whether it is compatible with feminist pluralism.

Feminist contractualisms will begin with the critical intuition that if there is a hypothetical contract justifying current social relations, it is a hypothetical contract between a select group of people (or between parties representing a select group of people), and not between all persons in society. This is because, as far as feminists are concerned, *existent social relations clearly benefit some over others for reasons that could not be found acceptable to those left worst off under them*, many of whom, of course, are women.[46] In other words, if contractualism is meant to explain the validity of current conventional social relations, then it is merely an exercise in rationalization. What feminist contractualisms affirm is the deeper normative claim that social relations are justified only if they are, in some sense, capable of acceptance by those who are subject to them, including those left least well off. But who are "those subject to them"?

Some feminist theorists have argued that theorists should not attempt to describe these folks, because any description will be subject to bias. Instead, we are advised to think of the parties to contractualist discourse as actual people and discourse as real discourse. For example, Marilyn Friedman writes in support of real discourse: "No universalization without representation!"[47] Seyla Benhabib writes: "The condition of ideal role-taking is not to be construed as a hypothetical thought process . . . but as an actual dialogue situation in which moral agents communicate with one another."[48] And even Virginia Held, normally quite opposed to contractualism, writes: "Actual dialogue between actual persons . . . [is] much more likely to be satisfactory" than imagined discourse.[49] This would mean that social relations are justified if they could be found acceptable to actual people deliberating. But these actual people are likely to have biases as bad or worse than the fictional inhabitants of a Hobbesian or Lockean state of nature. That is, their views about themselves and others, and about the appropriate arrangement of social relations are also likely to reflect relations of domination and subordination. Thus, insisting on real dialogue is no sure antidote to bias in contractualism. Real dialogue *might* be something like an antidote if we made "dialogue" mean something like cooperative discussion motivated solely by the desire to reach consensus.[50] Then dialogue might work to weed out bias. But *real people* are rarely, if ever, solely motivated by the desire to reach consensus. Thus we would no longer be talking about real discourse.

But the advocates of real discourse have an important point. Since the answer to the contractualist question—What conditions for our common life together are capable of acceptance by all?—depends on parties' senses of who they are and what their most important needs and interests are, and as these things vary from socio-historical context to context, an adequate contractualism will have to exhibit some flexibility.[51] Now, clearly we do not want a political conception to be flexible in the sense of uncritically shifting to fit the changing constellations of power in society—so that a racist society should have a racist conception of justice, a sexist society a sexist one. What the advocates of real discourse seem to be pointing toward is what I would like to call *right flexibility*.[52] When contractualism is flexible in the *wrong* way it favors some folks by tailoring principles of justice to reflect their needs and interests, to the detriment of others' enjoyment of the fruits of social cooperation. *Right flexibility* avoids such partial tailoring while still permitting principles of justice to fit specific contexts. By context I mean these three things: First, what it means to be an autonomous citizen—to live one's life as one sees fit and participate in the framing of the conditions under which one must live—varies from socio-historical context to context. That is, *who* citizens are is not static. Second, because *whose* autonomy it is varies, *what resources* citizens need to exercise this autonomy will also vary—these resources are what Rawls calls "primary goods."[53] And third, the precise ways in which these resources remain scarce varies. By permitting the flexibility necessary to reflect these specific conditions, a contractualism can help us to construct principles of justice that apply to specific socio-historical situations. The proposal I sketch below is an attempt to illustrate this right flexibility.

The Proposal

The feminist contractualism I have in mind begins with the idea of contractualist discourse between *parties described in ways informed by some of the insights of feminist scholars and activists*. In what follows, I explain which insights those are, what a discourse among parties so described would look like, and why this feminist description of parties, as an example of right flexibility, should be preferred.

There are many insights of feminist theorists and activists that could be fruitfully operationalized in a contractualist theory. Rather than attempting to be comprehensive, I focus here on the insights of what Eva Kittay calls feminist "dependency theorists."[54] Thus what I propose is part of a feminist account of justice, not the whole. Dependency theorists have developed a conception of the person according to which persons have, among other things, a fundamental interest in seeing that the needs of people who depend on them for basic care are met. This interest is neglected in conventional contractualist accounts, because those accounts presuppose that the needs of the dependent[55] will be met by "others," namely by "volunteer forces of those who accept an ethic of care,"[56] by "the invisible hands of women."[57]

What does contractualist discourse look like once we *privilege* the sense of self of these volunteer forces? Parties with an interest in seeing that the needs of dependent others be met could not be described as mutually disinterested utility maximizers. They would not be disinterested because they would see each other and themselves as potential dependents for whose well-being they are concerned, or as potential caregivers on whom they might depend.[58] But these parties are not purely selfless either. They would be concerned with their own autonomy—with living their lives as they see fit, and with being coauthors of the conditions under which they live.[59] Thus, deliberation would not revolve around how to secure the conditions for the exercise of the autonomy of independent parties, but rather how to make possible both autonomy and the fulfillment of dependency-related obligations. Parties would want the basic structure of society to ensure that their autonomy can be exercised in a way that is compatible with seeing that the needs of their dependents are cared for.[60] We should think of the parties as *desirous of personal and political autonomy compatible with dependency-related obligations.* As such they would insist that social arrangements make the interests in autonomy and care compatible. Thus they would endorse an explicit reference to dependency-related obligations in a principle of equality—requiring, for example, that *the determination of what goods count as basic, and the distribution of such basic goods, not favor nondependency workers over those engaged in dependency work.*

Consider just a few of the policy implications of this principle of equality. First, some will choose not to take on dependency obligations related to childbirth and childrearing.[61] Thus for women to enjoy autonomy, they must be able to choose to terminate pregnancies that they do not wish to carry to term. Second, the principle of equality articulated above seems to require that care work and wage work be made compatible. Possible methods for reconciliation include flex-time and part-time work at decent wages, adequate paternity and maternity leave, transitional vocational training for those moving from care work to wage work, and high quality, affordable professional dependent care. Third, the principle might require making care work sustainable without wage work. This would require public support for full- or part-time care work, including leisure time equity for care workers, which would imply the availability of high-quality, affordable professional dependent care available also to relieve full-time care workers. Fourth, the principle would seem to require an end to the devaluing of dependency work, such as we might find in a policy of comparable worth. And finally, it would seem to require policies intended to create effective equality of political voice for caregivers. This might involve quotas in decision-making bodies.[62]

In short, that social relations should assure the compatibility of autonomy and care is the overarching demand of justice that the dependency conception of the person implies. It is important to note that the dependency conception of the person, and the idea of justice to which it belongs, are not meant to represent the whole of a feminist conception of justice. They are developed here to illustrate how part of a theory of justice would look if it took seriously some of the considered convictions of feminists.

This model is rightly flexible in at least three ways. First, autonomy is not understood abstractly—indeed, it is not at all clear what autonomy is if it is not *somebody's* autonomy—but as the autonomy of concrete persons: persons potentially charged with dependency-related obligations. Second, though this point would need to be fleshed out, the feminist contractualism described lets the operative conception of autonomy determine what goods count as "primary goods," that is, what goods the principles of justice are to distribute. And third, note that this contractualism takes account of the specific ways in which the scarcity of primary goods is maintained—say by a culturewide systematic devaluing of work defined as "women's work"—and permits principles of justice to speak to this specific situation.

Justifying the Conception
But why should this conception of the person be privileged? Justification in contractualism is an extremely complex topic on which there is a large literature.[63] I will lay out here the path that, as I read him, Rawls has taken concerning the justification of his conception of justice. I use this path as a guide for explaining what sort of justification is available and appropriate to feminist contractualism.

Contractualist political theories depend crucially on the way they characterize parties to deliberation. The feminist contractualism I have described above is no exception. Rawls' early work was roundly criticized by writers desiring to know how his particular description of the parties was to be justified. Rawls' first answer was to argue in two directions.[64] On the one hand, Rawls deepened the philosophical argument for the description of the parties explaining that it was grounded in a Kantian conception of the self as autonomous. At the same time, Rawls argued that the conception is justified because it is "implicitly affirmed" in our political culture. He puts this criterion later this way: The conception is justified because it is one of the "deep-seated convictions and traditions of a modern democratic state."[65] These two justificatory strategies were shown by critics to work at cross-purposes. And Rawls later argues that his conception of parties does not depend after all on the truth of a Kantian conception of the person but is rather a "political" conception of the person that carries no such heavy philosophical burden.[66] Continuing the second strand of justification begun in 1980, Rawls argues in 1993 that his description of the parties fits into the "deep-seated convictions of a modern democratic state" precisely because, rather than modeling some very specific philosophical conception of the person with which many citizens may be reasonably expected to disagree, it models a very minimal sense of what it means to be a reasonable citizen, to live together with others with whom disagreement about fundamental matters is to be expected, but who desires nonetheless to live together with these others under conditions that are mutually acceptable. Rawls weakens his justification of the description of the parties one step further, prodded by criticisms of Jürgen Habermas, who himself desires a retreat to a stronger Kantian justification.[67] Rawls writes, "the overall criterion of reasonableness is general and wide reflective equilibrium."[68] General and wide reflective equilibrium is achieved when citizens severally consider candidate conceptions of justice, "and the force of various arguments for them," and come to "affirm the same public conception of political justice."[69] Earlier Rawls had put this criterion this way: The conception must "prove acceptable to citizens once it was properly presented and explained."[70] Meeting this criterion is, in one sense, an empirical matter. But in another sense it is not. Because it is not clear what it means that the conception has been presented "properly." Nor is there any way to be sure that citizens' acceptance or rejection of the conception followed upon due consideration. Despite these clear problems, Rawls conjectures that justice as fairness can meet the requirement. Some critics have applauded this retreat from Kantianism,[71] and others have lamented it.[72] I would like to explore what Rawls seems to have learned about justification in contractualism, and consider how a feminist contractualism might be justified against this background.

As I see it, Rawls' work taken as a whole suggests that a contractualism must show four things to justify itself.[73] But, as should become clear, *justification* is not to be thought to settle the matter once and for all. Instead, philosophical justification of a political conception should be thought of as a matter of showing plausibility, as a contribution to public discourse about justice.[74] In this sense, writing political philosophy is a political activity. The four things it must show are these: First, the conception of the person on which the feminist contractualism above depends must not commit citizens to a particular metaphysical conception of the self or of morality. This is important for political philosophy in general, but as the first part of this chapter makes clear, it is also important for any feminist political theory. Second, the feminist conception of justice, and the reasoning to it, must be shown to be part of the "deep-seated convictions of a modern democratic state." And third, it must be capable of achieving what Rawls calls "general and wide reflective equilibrium." This is closely connected to showing, fourth, that it models what it means for citizens to be reasonable. I discuss these criteria in order, showing that each is fulfilled well enough by the feminist contractualism, and thus that it is justified well enough.

The first criterion requires that the description of the parties not commit one to any particular doctrine concerning the person or morality. But why this? Could one simply not argue that the dependency conception of the person is true, or at least more true than, say, the Rawlsian conception? Would the truth of the conception—once established—not explain why it should be privileged? The answer is, no. For, even if we could determine that the dependency conception of the person is true (or more true than others), its being true would not sufficiently explain why it should be privileged in a normative theory. If it is true about people, then surely many other things are also true about people. To decide which description of persons should be normatively privileged, we need something more than, or other than, its truth. Also, basing a contractualist account of justice—or part of a contractualist account, as is given here—on a supposedly true conception of the person would mislead the reader into thinking that I plan to provide a stronger justification than I think one can provide. I mean my proposal to be contextual, to respond to particular experiences of disadvantage. And finally, if the conception were presented as true, it would demand the acknowledgment of citizens, violating the condition of pluralism argued for above. The conception of justice pursued here is capable of meeting with the agreement of citizens holding a wide variety of views about what persons are and what morality is, as well as about the nature of gender. As Rawls writes, the conception of the person in contractualism should not be thought of as true.

> When, in this way, we simulate being in the original position, our reasoning no more commits us to a particular metaphysical doctrine about the nature of the self than our acting a part in a play, say of Macbeth or Lady Macbeth, commits us to thinking that we are really a king or a queen.[75]

Feminist contractualism does not depend on the dependency conception of the person being, or being accepted as, true—citizens need not believe that all persons are, by their very nature, bound tightly in a social web such that they are concerned to see that their dependency-related obligations are met, and such that any denial of that would be alien to one's true self or false consciousness.[76] Meeting this requirement is important, but it still does not show that the dependency conception of the person is the one we should adopt. Criteria two and three bring us closer to showing that.

The second requirement is that the conception of justice, and the reasoning to it, be implicit in the traditions of the modern democratic state. Can feminist contractualism meet this requirement? While a conception of justice worked up for a particular people—which is how this proposal is meant—will not stand much of a chance if it is not presentable as consistent with that people's political traditions, our political traditions have been decidedly sexist. This means that the dependency conception of the person will not have played as central a role in our state's foundational thinking—political, judicial, philosophical—as will the conception of the person as independent. A feminist contractualism will thus not require that its conception of the person be drawn from the dead center of our political tradition. It will be satisfied to show continuity with important parts of our tradition. (Of course, what constitutes the center and the parts of a tradition is always a matter for reinterpretation, of the sort undertaken here.) While it is not seen as central, the dependency conception of the person is not alien to our tradition either. Thus the conception *can* be presented as "implicitly affirmed" in some of what are today understood as the foundations, and not just the periphery, of our political culture. For example, it is a longstanding although waning idea in our political culture that while men owe an obligation of military service to their country, women owe an obligation of care to their families. To make this obligation to care for families legally explicit, or simply to imply it legally,[77] is to acknowledge state—and thus common—interest in the well-being of dependents and in the ability of caretakers to fulfill their dependency-related obligations. Another example to consider is the longstanding traditional obligation that adult children have to care for their aging parents.[78] This obligation was transformed into a common obligation early in the last century, when economic realities made the fulfillment of that obligation extremely hard or impossible for many citizens. Beginning with the New Deal, in the United States it has been thought appropriate that the community—through the agency of the state—assure the well-being of aging parents. Thus the fulfillment of a particular familial obligation is again transformed into a general political obligation.[79] In addition to cases such as these, consider also that the dependency-conception of the person, and the conception of equality to which it belongs, are expressible with the conceptual vocabulary of autonomy, the preferred language of our political culture. This places the feminist contractualism developed in the company of other feminist political theories attempting to transform but not jettison the conception of autonomy at the root of our political culture. Feminist proposals that abandon the language of autonomy may be criticized as parentalistic,[80] but also because they do not present their ideas with the vocabulary of our political tradition and thus fail to make clear the interface between our current political realities and an envisioned better future. Thus, to conclude these remarks about the second requirement, while a feminist conception of justice need not fit neatly into the center of our political tradition—because that center has been sexist—it should, and can, be presented as implicit in important parts of our tradition.

I have shown that the feminist contractualism outlined above fulfills criteria one and two—it does not commit citizens to any divisive metaphysical doctrines, and it can be shown to be implied in the traditions of a modern democratic state. These criteria outline necessary but not sufficient conditions for a conception of justice being justified. The third criterion brings us a bit closer to a sufficient condition, but as should become clear in what follows, the language of sufficient conditions leads us to believe we will be getting a stronger justification than is possible or prudent. According to the third criterion, a contractualist theory must model citizen reasonableness. This is so that principles of justice are those that reasonable citizens would accept. But how do we get the conception of reasonableness? Recall that Rawls has abandoned a strong Kantian justification for his conception. Rawls looks for a conception that makes no metaphysical commitments (criterion one above), that can be found implicit in our political traditions (criterion two above), and that is in reflective equilibrium with a set of considered convictions about justice that he takes to be central. This is the best that a political philosopher can do. In our case we have included in our considered convictions about justice the claim that society should be organized in such a way that citizens' dependency-related obligations may be fulfilled without the systematic disadvantaging of those citizens who are socialized to, or naturally desire to, see to them. That is, we have augmented the conception of reasonableness so that citizens are reasonable when they recognize that citizens will come to differing answers to fundamental metaphysical questions, and yet they desire to live with these others under conditions that are mutually acceptable, and they desire to see that their dependency-related obligations are met in a way that is compatible with their enjoying personal and political autonomy. How can it be shown that this conception of reasonableness is the appropriate one rather than Rawls' or anyone else's for that matter? This brings us to the fourth criterion.

The fourth criterion requires that a conception of justice be capable of achieving what Rawls calls "general and wide reflective equilibrium,"[81] in other words, that it would "prove acceptable to citizens once it was properly presented and explained."[82] But how are we to know whether this criterion is ever met? Clearly the political philosopher has no choice but to speculate. While empirical data would not be entirely useless, they alone would not determine what conception would pass this test. This is because it is not clear what the test requires. What does it mean to present the conception "properly"? How would we know when citizens' acceptance or rejection of the conception followed upon due consideration? At this point, the political philosopher has no choice but to act as social critic, and suggest to the public what it might affirm, were it to engage in sustained and reflective discourse on the question. But surely the proposal made here suffers the same fate as Rawls', or anyone else's, at this point. Indeed, Rawls believes that his political conception, along with its conception of the person, will ultimately stand the test of "wide and general reflective equilibrium." But he admits that he is speculating. As long as we are speculating, let me say that I think that the dependency conception of the person is more likely to "prove acceptable to citizens once it was properly presented and explained." This chapter is an exploration of that conjecture and its implications.

The conjecture is based on some facts. The economy in the United States has changed fundamentally in the past thirty years so that single-earner families are nearly unheard of. According to recent estimates, merely seven percent of American families have a mother at home caring for children or elderly parents and a father doing wage work.[83] As has been well documented, this change has meant that women are now working both inside the home, doing the lion's share of housework and childcare, as well as outside the home.[84] The injustice of this arrangement consists not only in women's working disproportionately long hours, much of it unpaid, but also in the harm to women's equal opportunity in the job market caused by men's relative freedom from domestic burdens. Most importantly for our purposes here, however, is the fact that this economic change has created nothing short of a national consensus on the idea that the family is in crisis. Citizens on the left and the right are in fundamental agreement that the way we are now organizing our common life ignores our individual obligations to our dependents, or it seems to presume that someone else—the housewife—will be caring for the dependents. She, of course, no longer exists. Most citizens know this. It would seem to follow that we must organize our common life in a way that makes it a communal concern that all citizens be able to fulfill their dependency-oriented obligations. Under conditions of pluralism we will not come to agreement on how those obligations are to be fulfilled. But we can come to an agreement about the importance of their being fulfilled. In summary, one can construct a contractualist model informed by some of the insights of feminist scholars and activists that provides support for a particular principle of equality. According to this principle of equality, basic goods must reflect the needs of citizens with significant dependency-related obligations, and be distributed in a way that does not systematically disadvantage those with such obligations. This principle of equality is meant as *part* of a feminist contribution to a theory of justice.

Evaluating the Feminist Contractualism

Earlier in the chapter I showed that feminist political theories depending for their validity on the truth of a particular theory of gender pose a problem in the context of feminist pluralism. They make it necessary for feminists, who presumably hold a variety of views about gender, to agree to a particular conception of gender before they accept a conception of feminist politics. That section showed that both Luce Irigaray and Judith Butler make the validity of their political proposals depend on the truth of the claims they make about the nature of gender. This makes their political claims less viable than they might otherwise be. I suggested that feminist contractualism might turn out to be attractive because it provides a conception of feminist politics without an underlying theory of gender.

A critic might worry that the model sketched *seems to rely on* claims about the nature of gender. Drawing on the work of dependency theorists, it seems to suggest that women *qua women* are fundamentally interested in caring for dependents. If the feminist contractualism sketched above does this, then its normative claims presumably would stand or fall with the truth of certain claims about gender. And it might have to be rejected by feminists holding conflicting theories of gender.

But to sign on to the feminist contractualism sketched one need not believe anything very particular about what women really are. One might think that women are natural caretakers, or are socialized into being that way. One might think that gender difference is merely an effect of power, or that it is not. One need only affirm that society is unjust if it systematically disadvantages those who, regardless of how they got that way or whether they will stay that way or should or should not, experience themselves as having obligations to dependent others.

The feminist contractualism sketched above is, to use Christine Littleton's words, an "acceptance approach" to equality.

> [An] acceptance [approach] does not see differences as problematic per se, but rather focuses on the ways in which differences are permitted to justify inequality. It asserts that eliminating the unequal consequences of sex differences is more important than debating whether such differences are "real," or even trying to eliminate them altogether. . . . The focus of equality as acceptance, therefore, is not on the question of whether women are different, but rather on the question of how the social fact of gender asymmetry can be dealt with so as to create some symmetry in the lived-out experience of all members of the community. . . . The function of equality is to make gender differences, perceived or actual, costless relative to each other, so that anyone may follow a male, female or androgynous lifestyle according to their natural inclination or choice without being punished for following a female lifestyle or rewarded for following a male one.[85]

The conception does depend, in some quite minimal sense, on gender being an element of our social world. If the conception could not depend on this, it could not begin with the considered conviction that disadvantage linked to one's status as dependency worker is suspicious. This disadvantage is particularly suspicious because it is linked to women (as well as to race and class). Indeed, dependency worker status is, to a significant degree, a proxy for women. But these claims—that gender is an element of our social world (for good or ill, necessarily or contingently), and that women make up the majority of dependency workers—are minimal and, most importantly, not controversial.

An additional worry might be that the acceptance approach runs afoul of many feminist doctrines due to its apparent acceptance of traditional gender roles and its apparent reluctance to criticize them. Does not an acceptance approach say it is all right to be a traditional housewife, to live primarily for others? And does it not thus conflict with all those feminisms that see gender roles themselves as oppressive?[86] If it did, it would fail to offer a conception of feminist politics viable under conditions of feminist pluralism because it would depend for its validity on a theory of gender, namely, a theory that says traditional gender roles are not the result of oppression. But the acceptance approach does not take a stand on whether wanting to live a traditionally female life is the result of oppression. It merely insists that the disadvantages involved in living out a life gendered traditionally feminine be removed. The acceptance approach says that if traditional gendered lives are compatible with equality (as described above), then there is nothing wrong with them from a political point of view. This does not mean that feminists ought not to agitate to change them. Such agitation is an appropriate part of a culture like ours. But until they are changed, and if they never are for whatever reason, the acceptance approach says that women should not be penalized for it.

Conclusion

Is something important lost when feminist politics is severed in this way from theories of gender? Is it not appropriate that feminist politics be grounded in theories of gender since so much has been learned about the ways in which conventional politics has been grounded in misogynist conceptions of the person? Surely feminists should not stop doing gender theory! This work is crucial to countering misogyny and heterosexism in many realms. The suggestion made here is more modest: An account of feminist politics might be more viable if it can be presented without grounding in a particular theory of gender. Does this attempt at wide acceptability result in a watering down of the feminist commitment to thoroughgoing social critique? To radicalness? Perhaps. But it would seem that the feminist contractualism sketched here is quite hostile to traditional gender roles, if those depend on a significantly unequal distribution of social power.

Notes

1. © Blackwell Publishing, 2005, 9600 Garsington Road, Oxford OX4 2DQ, UK and 238 Main Street, Cambridge, MA 02142, USA. Printed with permission.

2. This chapter has been improved by comments from participants in a number of forums, including the International Association of Women Philosophers, the American Political Science Association, and the Society for Women in Philosophy. Thanks are due to them, and to three anonymous reviewers for the *Journal of Political Philosophy*.

3. For example, Larmore 1990 and Rawls 1993.

4. For example, Raz 1990 and Sandel 1982.

5. For example, Becker 1999; Exdell 1994; Lloyd 1994, 1998; Okin 1994; and Yuracko 2003. For an overview of contemporary feminist liberalisms, see Baehr 2002 and introduction in Baehr 2004 a and b.

6. For example, Okin 1994.

7. Brown 1995.

8. I echo Nancy Fraser's hope for a critical feminist theory "simultaneously situated and amenable to self-reflection . . . potentially radical and subject to warrants." (1997, 219) I endeavor to engage in "philosophy as defense," in which "Arguments are meant to serve as public justifications rather than as deductions from premises about human nature or rationality." (Laden 2003, 379)

9. Quoted in Cott 1987, 19.

10. Ibid.

11. For a helpful overview, see Goldstein 1993a.

12. Minow 1990, 47.

13. Irigaray 1989, 27, 33.

14. Irigaray 1989, 11.

15. Irigaray 1995, 19.

16. Irigaray 1990, 348.

17. Irigaray 1990, 339–40. Author's translation from an essay published in German translation.

18. Irigaray 1994, 76, 75.

19. Irigaray 1990, 343.

20. Some critics point to "a tension in Irigaray's work between the sexual difference model (which argues for two subjects, a male and a female one) and the critique of universalism (which opens the way to a greater plurality of subject-positions)," (Whitford 1994, 16) and endorse the latter, but not the former. For example, Gail Schwab writes that Irigaray's work can be read as the foundation "for the construction of an ethics of difference modeled on sexual difference, an ethics for the future of humanity in all of its diversity." (1998, 76) Others distinguish between Irigaray's specific political proposals and her more abstract claims about political change, again endorsing the latter but not the former. The latter include the idea that "women's full participation in public life will become possible only when the political realm is radically redefined so that . . . it remains inherently connected to the world of intimate bodily relations." (Stone 2002, 34) On this, see also Cheah and Grosz 1998.

21. Schor 1994, 10. Commentators arguing that Irigaray is using essentialism strategically (or in Margaret Whitford's case, "provisionally") include Schor 1994, Stone 2002, Whitford 1994, 28, and Xu 1995. According to Whitford, at times Irigaray herself appears to clearly repudiate essentialism (see Whitford 1991, 173). See also Schor 1994, 76, n. 28.

22. Whitford 1994, 16.

23. Irigaray 1995, 19.

24. I take no side on whether Irigaray is best read as an essentialist or a strategist.

25. Butler 1989, xi.

26. Ibid.

27. Butler 1993, x, 231.

28. Butler 1993, 232.

29. Butler 1993, 145.

30. Butler 1993, 240.

31. See Butler 1993, 112, 114, and 227. Butler recognizes the importance of "provisionally institut[ing] an identity and at the same time . . . open[ing] the category as a site of permanent political contest. That the term is questionable does not mean that we ought not to use it, but neither does the necessity to use it mean that we ought not perpetually to interrogate the exclusions by which it proceeds." (1993, 222)

32. Butler 1993, 240. An important question about Butler's politics concerns whether she can account for any difference between positive and negative resignification. On this, see Oliver 1999.

33. Butler 1997. Butler notes that using state power to address oppression can result in the entrenchment of the identity of the victim, rather than in her liberation. Importantly, Butler does not believe that resignification results from sovereign subjects taking meaning into their own hands and transforming it. The nature of language as volatile and the self as an effect of power foreclose this.

34. Butler 1993, 223ff.

35. I do not suggest that Butler intends her view to be so capable.

36. Butler 1989, 32–33.

37. Butler 1993, 148. Butler writes, "Discursive practice by which matter is rendered irreducible simultaneously ontologizes and fixes [a] gendered matrix in its place." (1993, 29) "Being" or "ontological weight is . . . always conferred" by a power regime. (34)

38. Butler 1989, 32.

39. Stella Sandford makes the same point: "Butler . . . makes no distinction between this 'metaphysics of substance' and the more general notion of an ontology." (1999, 20)

40. Butler 1989, 136.

41. Vasterling 1999, 22.

42. Overlapping consensus is described by John Rawls (1993). Rawls intends to develop an account of justice suitable for a democratic society divided along moral and religious lines. As Rawls uses the term, an overlapping consensus exists where a conception of justice "is a module, an essential constituent part, that in different ways fits into and can be supported by various reasonable comprehensive doctrines that endure in the society regulated by it." (1993, 144–145)

43. On Rawls' view, the fact that there is overlapping consensus on a particular political conception does not, by itself, justify that conception. But any conception that failed to be the subject of an overlapping consensus would not be suitable for a society in which there is serious disagreement about moral and religious matters.

44. For example Benhabib 1987; Hampton 1993; Lloyd 1998; Okin 1989, 1994; O'Neill 1989; and Thompson 1993.

45. Alison Jaggar writes: "Of course, the tacit acceptance of conventional or dominant values is an inevitable result of the skepticism about the human good that lies at the heart of liberal theory." (1983, 189) Other important feminist critics of contractualism include Held 1993, Nussbaum 2000, and Pateman 1988.

46. Women are disproportionately represented among the least well off in societies like ours. For documentation of this claim, see the substantial literature on women and poverty. One might begin with Diana Pearce's "The Feminization of Poverty" (1978). For an international context to the subject of interpersonal comparisons of well-being, with special focus on women, see Sen 1993. What makes a feminist a contractarianism feminist is the special attention paid to the connection between women and disadvantage.

47. Friedman 1993, 8.

48. Benhabib 1987, 93.

49. Held 1993, 41.

50. This is Jürgen Habermas' strategy (1990, 1995).

51. On this issue see also Nancy Fraser's discussion of the "politics of needs interpretation." (1989)

52. The idea of right flexibility has conceptual affinity with Rawls' idea of some things not being "political in the wrong way." (1993, 40)

53. Rawls 1982. On expanding the list of primary goods, see Johnston 1994.

54. Kittay 1998. See also see Baier 1987, Held 1993, and Thompson 1993.

55. To be dependent is to require significant aid, financial, physical, or psychological, from another person or persons to see that one's basic needs are met. Some forms of dependency are socially constructed. But other forms of dependency are not. In these forms the dependency does not cease when the social context changes. (I thank Wendy Lee-Lampshire for raising this issue.)

56. Baier 1987, 49.

57. Thompson 1993, 264. Dependency work is, in our society, gendered, but also raced and classed. The extent to which conventional conceptions of justice ignore the relevance of human dependency reflects the extent to which the voices of women, but also of the poor and racial and ethnic minorities, have been ignored.

58. Because parties see themselves as potentially dependent, they are concerned that caregivers be able to provide care. Is this sufficient to give contractualist voice to the legitimate interests of the dependent themselves? Martha Nussbaum is not convinced. See Nussbaum 2000. Jean Hampton argues that while contractualism is not suited to articulate fully the moral-political relationship between those who are substantially unequal, it can provide some guidance (1993).

59. There is an interesting literature on the value of autonomy as it relates to care. See for example Clement 1996, Held 1993, Meyers 1989, and Nedelsky 1989. For recent work on relational autonomy, of which my model is an example, see Mackenzie and Stoljar, *Relational Autonomy*, 2000.

60. See Janna Thompson's version of this point (1993, 269–71).

61. Dependency obligations are often unavoidable, for example when children or a partner become disabled, or parents age.

62. On this issue, see Phillips 1991.

63. See for example Ackerman (1994), Habermas (1995), Hampton (2004), Raz (1990), Sandel (1982), and Scheffler (1994).

64. Rawls 1980.

65. Rawls 1993, 300.

66. Rawls 1993.

67. Habermas 1995.

68. Rawls 1995, 141.

69. Rawls 1995, 141, n. 16.

70. Rawls 1980, 518.

71. Rorty 1991.

72. Ackerman 1994 and Habermas 1995.

73. Each of these conditions is controversial. There is an impressive literature suggesting that Rawls' own conception of the person does not satisfy them (for example Scheffler 1994, 13; Wenar 1995, 54). And critics have asked whether satisfaction of these criteria should even count as justification (Ackerman 1994; Scheffler 1994). I will not settle these issues here. I use these conditions to explain what sort of justification is available and appropriate to the feminist contractualism sketched.

74. On this see Laden 2003 and note 8 above.

75. Rawls 1993, 27.

76. Something like this is the social ontology implied in care ethics.

77. See Kerber 1998.

78. This obligation was, and continues to be, interpreted as an obligation that women owe their parents, or even their husbands' parents. Caring for elderly relatives adds burdens to women already working one shift outside the home, and another shift providing the majority of care for children and the majority of housework. For data on women's "second shift" work, see Spain and Bianchi 1996.

79. For an argument in support of seeing New Deal policies as part of the foundations of our political culture, see Ackerman 1991.

80. See for example Noddings 2002.

81. Rawls 1995, 141.

82. Rawls 1980, 518.

83. Spain and Bianchi 1996.

84. For more data, see Williams 2000, 234.

85. Littleton 1991, 37–38.

86. I thank Charlotte Witt for raising this concern.

Bibliography

Ackerman, Bruce. *We the People*. Cambridge, MA: Harvard University Press, 1991.

——. "Political Liberalisms." *Journal of Philosophy* 91 (1994): 364–386.

Antony, Louise, and Charlotte Witt, eds. *A Mind of One's Own.* Boulder, CO: West-view Press, 1993.

Baehr, Amy. Introduction in *Varieties of Feminist Liberalism,* edited by Amy Baehr. Lanham, MD: Rowman and Littlefield, 2004a.

——, ed. *Varieties of Feminist Liberalism.* Lanham, MD: Rowman and Littlefield, 2004b.

——. "Liberalism in Recent Feminist Political Philosophy and Philosophy of Law." *American Philosophical Association Newsletter on Philosophy of Law* 2, no. 1 (Fall 2002).

Baier, Annette. "The Need for More than Justice." In *Science, Morality and Feminist Theory,* edited by Marsha Hanen and Kai Nielsen. Calgary: University of Calgary Press, 1987.

Bartlett, Katharine T., and Rosanne Kennedy, eds. *Feminist Legal Theory.* Boulder, CO: Westview Press, 1991.

Becker, Mary. "Patriarchy and Inequality: Towards a Substantive Feminism." *University of Chicago Legal Forum* 21 (1999).

Benhabib, Seyla. "The Generalized and the Concrete Other." In *Feminism as Critique,* edited by Seyla Benhabib and Drucilla Cornell, 77–95. Minneapolis: University of Minnesota Press, 1987.

Benhabib, Seyla, and Drucilla Cornell. *Feminism as Critique.* Minneapolis: University of Minnesota Press, 1987.

Brown, Wendy. *States of Injury.* Princeton, NJ: Princeton University Press, 1995.

Burke, Carolyn, Naomi Schor, and Margaret Whitford, eds. *Engaging With Irigaray.* New York: Columbia University Press, 1994.

Butler, Judith. *Gender Trouble: Feminism and the Subversion of Identity.* New York: Routledge, 1989.

——. *Bodies That Matter: On the Discursive Limits of "Sex."* New York: Routledge, 1993.

——. *Excitable Speech: A Politics of the Performative.* New York: Routledge, 1997.

Cheah, Phen, and Elizabeth Grosz. "Of Being-Two: Introduction." *Diacritics* 28, no. 1, special issue on Irigaray and the political future of sexual difference (1998): 3–18.

Clement, Grace. *Care, Autonomy and Justice.* Boulder, CO: Westview, 1996.

Cott, Nancy. *The Grounding of Modern Feminism.* New Haven: Yale University Press, 1987.

Exdell, John B. "Feminism, Fundamentalism, and Liberal Legitimacy." *Canadian Journal of Philosophy* 24, (1994): 441–463.

Fraser, Nancy. *Unruly Practices.* Minneapolis: University of Minnesota Press, 1989.

——. *Justice Interruptus.* New York: Routledge, 1997.

Friedman, Marilyn. *What Are Friends For?* Ithaca: Cornell University Press, 1993.

Gerhard, Ute, Mechtild Jansen, Andrea Maihofer, Pia Schmid, and Irmgard Schultz, eds. *Differenz und Gleichheit.* Frankfurt am Main: Ulrike Helmer Verlag, 1990.

Goldstein, Leslie Friedman. "Can This Marriage Be Saved? Feminist Public Policy and Feminist Jurisprudence." In *Feminist Jurisprudence,* edited by Leslie Friedman Goldstein. Lanham, MD: Rowman and Littlefield, 1993a.

———, ed. *Feminist Jurisprudence*. Lanham, MD: Rowman and Littlefield, 1993b.

Habermas, Jürgen. *Moral Consciousness and Communicative Action*. Cambridge: MIT Press, 1990.

———. "Reconciliation Through the Public Use of Reason: Remarks on John Rawls' *Political Liberalism*." *Journal of Philosophy* 92 (1995): 109–131.

Hampton, Jean. "Feminist Contractarianism." In *A Mind of One's Own*, edited by Louise Antony and Charlotte Witt. Boulder, CO: Westview Press, 1993. Reprinted in *Varieties of Feminist Liberalism*, edited by Amy Baehr. Lanham, MD: Rowman and Littlefield, 2004.

Hanen, Marsha, and Kai Nielsen. *Science, Morality and Feminist Theory*. Calgary: University of Calgary Press, 1987.

Held, Virginia. *Feminist Morality*. Chicago: University of Chicago Press, 1993.

Irigaray, Luce. *The Speculum of the Other Woman*. Ithaca, NY: Cornell University Press, 1989.

———. "Über die Notwendigkeit geschlechtsdifferenzierter Rechte." In *Differenz und Gleichheit*, edited by Ute Gerhard, Mechtild Jansen, Andrea Maihofer, Pia Schmid, and Irmgard Schultz. Frankfurt am Main: Ulrike Helmer Verlag, 1990.

———. *Je, Tu, Nous. Toward a Culture of Difference*. New York: Routledge, 1993.

———. *Thinking the Difference. For a Peaceful Revolution*. New York: Routledge, 1994.

———. "The Question of the Other." *Yale French Studies* 87 (1995): 7–19.

Jaggar, Alison. *Feminist Politics and Human Nature*. Totowa, NJ: Rowman and Littlefield, 1983.

Johnston, David. *The Idea of a Liberal Theory*. Princeton, NJ: Princeton University Press, 1994.

Kerber, Linda. *No Constitutional Right to Be Ladies*. New York: Hill and Wang, 1998.

Kittay, Eva. *Love's Labor: Essays on Women, Equality, and Dependency*. New York: Routledge, 1998.

Laden, Anthony Simon. "The House That Jack Built: Thirty Years of Reading Rawls." *Ethics* 113 (2003): 367–390.

Larmore, Charles. "Political Liberalism." *Political Theory* 18 (1990): 339–360.

Littleton, Christine. "Reconstructing Sexual Equality." In *Feminist Legal Theory*, edited by Katharine T. Bartlett and Rosanne Kennedy. Boulder, CO: Westview Press, 1991.

Lloyd, S. A. "Family, Justice and Social Justice." *Pacific Philosophical Quarterly* 75 (1994): 353–371.

———. "Toward a Liberal Theory of Sexual Equality." *Journal of Contemporary Legal Issues* 9 (Spring 1998). Reprinted in *Varieties of Feminist Liberalism*, edited by Amy Baehr. Lanham, MD: Rowman and Littlefield, 2004.

Mackenzie, Catriona, and Natalie Stoljar, eds. *Relational Autonomy*. New York: Oxford University Press, 2000.

Meyers, Diana. *Self, Society and Personal Choice*. New York: Columbia University Press, 1989.

Minow, Martha. *Making All the Difference*. Ithaca, NY: Cornell University Press, 1990.

Nedelsky, Jennifer. "Reconceiving Autonomy." *Yale Journal of Law and Feminism* 1 (1989): 7–36.

Noddings, Nel. *Starting At Home: Caring and Social Policy*. Los Angeles: University of California Press, 2002.

Nussbaum, Martha. "The Future of Feminist Liberalism. *Proceedings of the American Philosophical Association* 74, no. 2 (2000). Reprinted in *Varieties of Feminist Liberalism*, edited by Amy Baehr. Lanham, MD: Rowman and Littlefield, 2004.

Okin, Susan. *Justice, Gender and the Family*. New York: Basic Books, 1989.

———. "Political Liberalism, Justice and Gender." *Ethics* 105 (1994): 23–43.

Oliver, Kelly. "What Is Transformative About the Performative? From Repetition to Working-Through." *Studies in Practical Philosophy* 1, no. 2 (1999): 144–166.

O'Neill, Onora. *Constructions of Reason*. New York: Cambridge University Press, 1989.

Pateman, Carol. *The Sexual Contract*. Stanford, CA: Stanford University Press, 1988.

Pearce, Diana. "The Feminization of Poverty." *Urban and Social Change Review* (1978): 28–36.

Phillips, Anne. *Engendering Democracy*. University Park: Pennsylvania State University Press, 1991.

Rawls, John. *A Theory of Justice*. Cambridge, MA: Harvard University Press, 1971.

———. "Kantian Constructivism in Moral Theory: The Dewey Lectures." *Journal of Philosophy* 77 (1980): 515–572.

———. "Social Unity and Primary Goods." In *Utilitarianism and Beyond*, edited by Amartya Sen and Bernard Williams. Cambridge: Cambridge University Press, 1982.

———. *Political Liberalism*. New York: Columbia University Press, 1993.

———. "Reply to Habermas." *Journal of Philosophy* 92 (1995): 132–180.

Raz, Joseph. "Facing Diversity: The Case of Epistemic Abstinence." *Philosophy and Public Affairs* 19 (1990): 3–46.

Rorty, Richard. "The Priority of Democracy to Philosophy." In *Objectivity, Relativism, and Truth: Philosophical Papers, #1*. Cambridge: Cambridge University Press, 1991.

Sandel, Michael. *Liberalism and the Limits of Justice*. Cambridge: Cambridge University Press, 1982.

Sandford, Stella. "Contingent Ontologies: Sex, Gender and 'Woman' in Simone de Beauvoir and Judith Butler." *Radical Philosophy* 97 (1999): 18–29.

Scheffler, Samuel. "The Appeal of Political Liberalism." *Ethics* 105 (1994): 4–22.

Schor, Naomi. "Previous Engagements: The Receptions of Irigaray." In *Engaging With Irigaray*, edited by Carolyn Burke, Naomi Schor, and Margaret Whitford, eds. New York: Columbia University Press, 1994.

Schwab, Gail. "Sexual Difference as Model: An Ethics for the Global Future." *Diacritics* 28, no. 1 (1998): 76–92.

Sen, Amartya. "Positional Objectivity." *Philosophy and Public Affairs* 2 (1993): 126–146.

Sen, Amartya, and Bernard Williams, eds. *Utilitarianism and Beyond*. Cambridge: Cambridge University Press, 1982.

Spain, D., and S. M. Bianchi. *Balancing Act: Motherhood, Marriage and Employment among American Women*. New York: Russell Sage Foundation, 1996.

Stone, Alison. "Sexing the State: Familial and Political Form in Irigaray and Hegel." *Radical Philosophy* 113 (May/June 2002).

Thompson, Janna. "What Do Women Want? Rewriting the Social Contract." *International Journal of Moral and Social Studies* 8, no. 3 (1993): 257–272.

Vasterling, Veronica. "Butler's Sophisticated Constructivism: A Critical Assessment." *Hypatia* 14, no. 3 (1999): 17–38.

Wenar, Lief. "Political Liberalism: An Internal Critique." *Ethics* 106 (1995): 32–62.

Whitford, Margaret. *Luce Irigaray: Philosophy in the Feminine*. New York: Routledge, 1991.

———. "Reading Irigaray in the Nineties." In *Engaging With Irigaray*, edited by Carolyn Burke, Naomi Schor, and Margaret Whitford, eds. New York: Columbia University Press, 1994.

Williams, Joan. *Unbending Gender: Why Family and Work Conflict and What to Do About It*. New York: Oxford University Press, 2000.

Xu, Ping. "Irigaray's Mimicry and the Problem of Essentialism." *Hypatia* 10, no. 4 (1995): 76–89.

Yuracko, Kimberly A. *Perfectionism and Contemporary Feminist Values*. Bloomington: Indiana University Press, 2003.

CHAPTER FOURTEEN

~

Arendt, Foucault, and Feminist Politics: A Critical Reappraisal

Dianna Taylor

I began thinking about the significance of the work of Hannah Arendt and Michel Foucault for contemporary politics generally, and feminist politics more specifically, about ten years ago when I was preparing to write my dissertation; indeed, that project was dedicated in large part to exploring the nature of and asserting that significance. I wrote the original version of this chapter, which addresses the significance of Arendt's and Foucault's work for contemporary feminist politics, shortly after completing my dissertation, and although I remain convinced of the importance of the work of these two thinkers (both continue to figure prominently within my scholarship), I returned to this text uncertain of its capacity for revision. Sociopolitical developments in the ensuing period, perhaps most importantly the events of September 11, 2001 and their effects, have both altered the sociopolitical landscape within the United States and redefined the country's position within the international community. Such broad political developments have in turn influenced my thinking about feminist politics, as well as shifted my attention to particular aspects of Arendt's and Foucault's work, which I believe can facilitate insight into, as well as analysis and negotiation of, the present.

Sociopolitical developments and my own uncertainty notwithstanding, I was surprised and interested to note important similarities between present conditions and those I had been writing about in the late 1990s and, therefore, the contemporary relevance of many of my earlier observations. My intention in this essay, then, is to reassert both the significance of a particular way of approaching feminist politics, and the value of Arendt's and Foucault's work in facilitating such an approach. I begin by providing an overview of the aspects of the sociopolitical context with which I was concerned in the late 1990s. Next, I outline what I perceive to be important similarities between that context and the present. Given these similarities, I argue that the way of approaching feminist politics that I originally conceived, supplemented by one additional criterion, remains relevant, and I proceed to illustrate how Arendt's and Foucault's work can contribute to such an approach. I conclude by reasserting the contemporary relevance of the kind of "politics without blueprints" that Arendt's and Foucault's work facilitates.

In the late 1990s, like many feminists I was concerned with how best to articulate a cohesive and effective politics that could account for difference in meaningful ways. This concern was not, however, unique to feminists. Inspired in part by increasing conservatism and inefficacy within the Democratic Party (and the social, political, and economic effects of both), a variety of left-leaning intellectuals and scholars at the time were engaged in debates about the future of progressive politics in the United States, and issues of cohesiveness and difference, as well as the relationship between the two, figured prominently within such discussions: The Left was perceived by both progressives themselves and also more generally as fragmented and ineffectual; hence, calls were being made from within for it to unify.

The "First Principles" series, introduced in April of 1997 by *The Nation*, provided a forum for progressives to engage the issue of unification. In launching the series, *The Nation*'s editors state that its purpose is "to begin a conversation about first principles in search for a definition of what it means to be a progressive in the twenty-first century. . . . It is our hope that at the end of the series . . . we will be able to fashion a short manifesto whose basic principles are capable of both inspiring thinkers and activists *and* uniting a majority of Americans."[1] As stated here, the purpose of the series is two-fold: to "begin a conversation" about the nature of progressive politics, and to achieve a unified progressive majority. Both objectives were important: Striving to create a progressive majority was politically strategic insofar as doing so had the potential to provide an alternative to increasingly center- or even right-leaning Democrats, as well as to counter the political right itself. As I pointed out in the original version of this chapter, however, the conversation the Left was attempting to generate, while serious, was not as imaginative as it could have been or needed to be.

This lack of imagination is apparent in the way in which the proposed conversation was framed. The mission statement of the "First Principles" series, crafted by *The Nation*'s editors, asserts that the Left had contributed to its own inefficacy "by failing to unite around economic issues of fairness."[2] This assertion implies that economic injustice must be the focal point of an effective progressive politics, which in turn means that the intended purpose and outcome of the proposed conversation are in fact defined in advance: To be a progressive in the twenty-first century is to be concerned first and foremost with economic injustice. Insofar as this is the case, both "unification," the process of discussion and deliberation through which a progressive majority will be formed, and "unity," that majority itself, are conceived in terms of agreement or consensus: Whoever does not agree with the idea that economic injustice is the linchpin for progressive politics will not be a full participant in discussion and deliberation and probably won't be part of the resulting "majority."

I originally identified two harmful effects of framing the conversation about the Left's viability in this way. First, it is exclusionary. Insofar as the proposed conversation does not foster the coming together of all progressive persons, it threatens to undermine its own stated objective of achieving a majority: Only persons who share or are at least willing to adhere to a pre-given set of beliefs are brought together and, therefore, no genuine discussion about what unity is and how to achieve it (i.e., what unification might look like) is possible. Second, The Nation's proposed majority is not merely exclusionary; it is achieved at the expense of progressive groups who are (also) concerned with other types of injustice and therefore possesses the potential to be oppressive to such groups. That is, if economic injustice is the focal point of progressive politics, then other concerns, including other types of injustice, will necessarily be treated as subordinate. The Left's emphasis on consensus exacerbates this subordination of certain group interests in the name of majoritarianism. As Susan Bickford argues, insofar as "the norm of common interest . . . is posited as neutral," it facilitates the assertion of more dominant viewpoints, and therefore makes it difficult for less powerful individuals to voice differences of opinion.[3] The concerns of marginalized groups, therefore, come to be seen as "particular, partial, or selfish."[4] As Bickford points out, "[An] orientation toward consensus can thus undermine the very purposes of democratic participation, for the benefits of thinking things through together are lessened when some voices are not heard."[5]

The marginalized voices within conversations about the status of progressive politics were predominantly feminist. While not disputing the value of an organized progressive movement, many feminists were nonetheless critical of forming such a movement in the ways outlined within the "First Principles" series. More specifically, they disagreed with the view, expressed implicitly as well as explicitly, that concerning itself with issues of gender, race, and sexuality had weakened the Left by depriving it of a clear focus. Whether intentionally or not, feminists argued, Left factions favoring unification on the basis of economic injustice and defining unification and unity in terms of consensus—which, following Judith Butler, I referred to as the "orthodox" Left—subsumed feminist concerns under the auspices of and subordinated them to a general progressive politics.[6] As I did in the original version of this chapter, then, I'll next provide both specific examples from the "First Principles" series that illustrate this subsumption and subordination, and feminist critiques of the orthodox Left's agenda that appeared in both "First Principles" and elsewhere.

One way in which the orthodox Left subsumed feminist concerns was through asserting its own perspective as not being a particular perspective at all, but rather as an objective universal. This rhetorical device is apparent in, for example, Ira Katznelson's contribution to the "First Principles" series. Katznelson argues that while a progressive politics needs to "support" equality and "tolerate" diversity, to be effective such a politics must be grounded in "the liberal tradition."[7] According to Katznelson, "The communitarianism now popular in parts of the Left" is problematic because it tends "toward exclusion and homogeneity," whereas liberalism is adequate to the task of adjudicating multiple justice claims within a pluralist context.[8] Katznelson's rationale for grounding liberalism in an "egalitarian and pluralist" notion of autonomy, however, does not convince.[9] His proposed solution bolsters existing liberal conceptions of multiculturalism that attach a rather innocuous notion of "cultural diversity" to abstract universal rights. That is, abstract universal rights are asserted and simply "extended"[10] to already marginalized groups, whose justice claims remain subordinate. Jeff Faux makes a similar argument in his essay, "A Progressive Compact." While he recognizes that "extending the benefits of an otherwise beneficent society to variously defined minorities who have been left behind by an affluent and bigoted majority . . . is a politics of permanent marginalization," Faux nonetheless believes that a notion of abstract universal rights can ultimately accommodate real notions of difference.[11] Relying upon the liberal schema of benefits and burdens,[12] he argues, "We need an explanation of how the world works that tells us that by virtue of being an American—not your race, your gender or your luck and talent in the marketplace—you have a set of rights and obligations."[13]

(The dynamic described earlier by Bickford is readily apparent within the context of both Katznelson's and Faux's arguments: Liberalism functions as the point of "common interest," the "neutral" perspective around which political organization takes place. As a result, on the one hand, alternative perspectives such as feminism appear as self-interested and particular. On the

other hand, however, insofar as they are not concerned primarily with economic injustice, such perspectives appear, more specifically, as apolitical, and
it is primarily upon this basis that they are subordinated).

I was able to identify two ways in which feminist perspectives were characterized as apolitical within the context of orthodox arguments. First,
within "First Principles," as well as in other texts, the orthodox Left both implicitly and explicitly invoked an opposition between "the political" and "the
cultural." Even though most orthodox arguments acknowledged the significance of feminism and the other new social movements,[14] insofar as these arguments view economic injustice as the primary focus of progressive politics,
they relegate issues of sexuality, race and ethnicity, and gender to the non-
political and therefore subordinate realm of culture. One of the most overt
statements of the opposition of the political and the cultural is apparent in
Faux's assertion that "the political claims of economic class are not morally
superior to the claims of those disadvantaged by race, gender, or sexual preference. But they have an inherently greater power to unify, and are therefore
a sounder foundation upon which to base a majority politics."[15]

Like those of Katznelson and Faux, contributions to "First Principles" by
the late Senator Paul Wellstone and Richard Rorty also assert the primacy of
economic concerns.[16] Even Barbara Ehrenreich, arguing that most Americans
are more open to economic reforms than to "cultural" ones, affirms the opposition of the economic/political and the cultural, and concurs with the idea
that economic injustice ought to function as the rallying point of progressive
politics.[17] Ellen Willis,[18] however, both challenges the notion of unity presented in the "First Principles" series and critiques the "political/cultural" opposition that is operative within orthodox arguments.[19] Drawing upon her experiences in the women's liberation movement, Willis argues, contra the
orthodox idea that unity demands consensus, that "it's not necessary to round
up popular support before anything can be done."[20] She contends, rather, that
support for a political movement can be stimulated by action—even action
undertaken by only a few individuals. Willis also makes the crucial point that
"class itself is a cultural as well as an economic issue," and she calls into question the characterization of feminist perspectives as partial by drawing attention to ways in which subsuming the cultural under the economic/political
both reflects and appeals to a "comfortable-white-male-perspective."[21] "Who
else," she asks, "would project their own straightened worldview onto 'the
American people' instead of simply speaking for themselves?"[22]

The second way in which feminist concerns were subordinated was
through their conflation with identity politics. Given that feminist perspectives had already been relegated to the realm of culture, it's not difficult to

see how they could be further reduced to a mere concern with identity and characterized as part of a collection of divisive groups, each vying to assert its "oppressed identity" as *the* source of oppression. According to Todd Gitlin, for example, the "cultural Left" amounts to a "weak unity based not so much on a universalist premise or ideal but rather on a common enemy—that notorious White Male."[23] The conflation of the new social movements and identity politics is facilitated, at least in part, by the fact that within orthodox arguments exactly what constitutes "identity politics" is frequently, as Bickford points out, "left implicit."[24] If, however, on the most basic level, identity politics can be understood as a politics that concerns itself with articulating a group identity and making claims for justice on the basis of that identity, then as Judith Butler argues, "*There is no reason to assume that* [the new] *social movements are reducible to their identitarian formations.*"[25]

Butler's point calls the logic of orthodox arguments into question. For if identity politics is indeed the major factor contributing to the erosion of the Left since the 1970s, and the new social movements are not merely identitarian, then subsuming these movements under a Left orthodoxy, while it functions to justify their subordination and defines "unification" precisely in terms of it, does not eradicate the problem of progressive political inefficacy. Both Butler and Ellen Willis argue that such subordination is at best unnecessary and at worst more damaging to the Left, because the new movements were at that time its most politically viable components. The two feminists further contend that an inclusive and therefore truly progressive politics is characterized by a contentious process of deliberation characterized by discussions that seek not only to rethink notions of unity, unification, and progressive politics but also, as Butler asserts, to "[sustain] conflict in politically productive ways."[26] The "groundless ground" of such a politics, according to Butler, is difference, conceived not in terms of "external differences between movements . . . but, rather, as the self-difference of movement itself, a constitutive rupture that makes movements possible on nonidentitarian grounds, that installs a certain mobilizing conflict."[27]

Thus while the orthodox Left and feminists—as well as the other new social movements—ostensibly had much in common, it is clear that the perspectives of these groups were in tension with one another. Whereas the orthodox Left believed it had developed a political approach that would produce a vital, unified progressive movement, feminists argued that the Left failed to realize that its proposed approach in fact threatened to recreate divisions similar to those that originally led women, people of color, and gays and lesbians to conclude that they would have to combat the injustices they faced within the context of their own movements. Ironically, when feminists voiced their concern that the Left might be redivided along old fault lines, progressive men responded much as they had when women attempted to make them aware of the existence of sexism within the New Left: They accused the feminists of being divisive, and claimed that once again the "cultural Left" was impeding the progressive political agenda.[28]

In returning to this chapter, I discerned important similarities between the political situation I describe as internal to the Left in the late 1990s and the current, broader sociopolitical context within the United States. As I have described it here, the orthodox Left was imposing its views about progressive politics, in the form of an objective universal, on the whole of the Left in the name of promoting unity. Alternative, feminist views about what constitutes unity and how to achieve it, as well as feminist critiques of the dominant perspective, were routinely dismissed, criticized, or subordinated in ways that were oppressive to persons relegated to the margins and that, insofar as they inhibited the development of a truly progressive politics, were harmful to the whole of the Left as well.

In retrospect, I believe the orthodox Left's actions can be seen as, albeit in at least some instances unintentionally, promoting both conformity with a preexisting standard or norm and obedience to a single, dominant vision of and for progressive politics. And it is these specific aspects of the situation within the Left during the late 1990s that resonate within the post-September 11, 2001 U.S. political context. As I argue elsewhere, and as many other analyses have shown,[29] since the September 11 attacks, the Bush administration has asserted its particular agenda in the form of an objective universal: Only one way of interpreting the attacks, and therefore only one way of responding to them, is considered valid, where validity is presented not in terms of what serves the administration's objectives, but rather as what is considered (from the administration's perspective) to promote national (or even global) interests. This attitude is apparent in incidents ranging from the President's proclamation, "You are either with us or you are with the terrorists," to the invasion of Iraq, to the wiretapping of U.S. citizens and collection of their financial records in the name of (inter)national "security." Thus, while the administration has ostensibly acted in the name of promoting (inter)national unity, dissenting viewpoints have not only been dismissed, they have been actively demonized, as when, for example, opposition to the war in Iraq is equated with contempt for U.S. soldiers and therefore portrayed as "unpatriotic" or "un-American." As with the Left, then, although ties among persons sharing the administration's perspectives may have been strengthened, divisions run deep within the country more generally. While the positions of the orthodox Left in the late

1990s and that of the Bush administration are by no means synonymous, insofar as both positions ultimately promote conformity and obedience, both have the potential to produce harmful effects. Such effects may be easier to recognize in the case of the Bush administration insofar as its attempts to impose its views have been more overt and its actions and their repercussions have been much more harmful, but this does not mean that the inadvertent effects of the Left's actions ought to be minimized or ignored.

As I see it, then, feminist critiques of the late 1990s orthodox Left agenda remain relevant today, not only within the context of progressive politics but also more generally. Progressives may have at least temporary bracketed some of their differences in order to come together in the face of right-wing dominance, but that does not mean that these differences no longer exist; it therefore seems prudent to begin thinking about how they might be productively negotiated before the next political crisis emerges (or at least before the next election takes place). Given the ongoing need to negotiate a complex political terrain, I believe the characteristics I originally identified as being important for feminist politics—agonism, creativity, and nonidentitarianism—remain relevant today. As Butler's critique of the orthodox Left illustrates, agonistic feminist politics does not view conflict as merely or necessarily divisive. Thinking about and developing conflict as something potentially productive and creative makes possible a politics that, as Bickford puts it, "takes conflict and differences seriously and yet allows for joint action."[30] I defined a creative politics as being inventive and focused on the world, as seeking to develop new ways of thinking as well as acting. A creative politics is thus not merely concerned with developing theories but is also "pragmatic" in the sense described by Iris Marion Young.[31] According to Young, politics is pragmatic insofar as it is concerned with "specific practical and political problems."[32] With respect to the issue of identity, a politics can be nonidentitarian in either a strong or a weak sense. In a strong sense, nonidentitarianism views identity as having no productive political potential and therefore rejects it. A weak nonidentitarian politics acknowledges that identity has been and can be useful (and is sometimes required) for political activity, but it does not consider identity as the foundation for political action. Rather, it perceives the political deployment of identity as ultimately limited and limiting, and therefore seeks to develop new ways of making claims for justice. Even feminists who criticize identity politics recognize the fact that within the current U.S. political system groups cannot help but make claims for justice on the basis of a recognizable identity.[33] This reality does not mean, however, that doing so is not politically problematic or that groups should not seek alternative political strategies. As Butler points out, insofar as identity categories are always normative and therefore exclusionary, if groups uncritically deploy identity they run the risk of rearticulating their own oppressed and devalued identities.[34]

Current sociopolitical conditions within the United States merit the addition of a fourth characteristic: the ability to facilitate the identification and analysis of, and resistance against pressure toward, conformity on the one hand and obedience to authority on the other. The significance of this ability is illustrated by the fact that the tendency toward such pressure exists not only on the Right, but also among progressives themselves. Since such pressure has intensified within the post-September 11, 2001 United States, and given that the Democratic party has thus far failed to mount a compelling alternative to the Bush administration's agenda, conversations about how to engage in a unified and efficacious progressive politics have become simultaneously more important and more difficult to enter into at all, let alone in ways both serious and imaginative. As I have shown here, feminists such as Bickford, Willis, and Butler point to the potentially harmful effects of both conformity and obedience in their critiques of the conflation of consensus and unity.

I believe that the kind of political approach described above is important not only because it may promote the practice of freedom in general, but also and more specifically because such an approach may contribute to feminist political endeavors which seek to articulate ways of engaging contemporary, practical issues that do not reinscribe the status quo of women's oppression. I originally argued that the work of Hannah Arendt and Michel Foucault can facilitate such articulation, given these thinkers' conceptualizations of agonism (Arendt), creativity (Foucault), identity (both), as well as their mutual commitment to "thinking differently." After briefly reviewing and reasserting my arguments to this effect, I'll show that the work of Foucault and Arendt is all the more relevant within the current sociopolitical context, given the need to resist conformity and obedience.

Agonism

Arendt does not conceive of agonism in classical terms. As Bonnie Honig argues, "The Arendtian agon [is not] essentially and necessarily a site of classical heroic individualism."[35] Rather, Arendt appropriates and reconceptualizes classical agonism by way of her notion of plurality. "Human plurality," she argues, "the basic condition of both action and speech, has the twofold character of equality and distinction."[36] Merely performing for others, as in the classical agon, may bring about recognition of "otherness," a realization that the performer is "not like everyone else," but it cannot express that individual's "unique distinctness."[37] For Arendt, agonism is a "practice of concerted action."[38] It is only through acting in concert with others that an individual may distinguish her or himself, that her or his unique potential may be "expressed," where expression entails the communication of oneself, and not merely of "something," of a "who" and not merely a "what."[39]

Difference and the conflict it engenders characterize Arendtian political activity. A consensus that asserts a particular viewpoint at the expense of all others is, by her account, inherently antipolitical. Thinking about conflict in Arendtian terms may be beneficial for feminist politics both internally and in coming together with other groups; so conceived, conflict does not prevent coming together with others, but insofar as it facilitates the expression of "unique distinctness," it does mediate against being dominated by them.

Creativity

Although I originally conceived of creativity in terms of "invention," I think it is more accurate to conceive of it in terms of "innovation." Foucault identifies innovation, which he defines as "seek[ing] out in our reflection those things that have never been thought or imagined," as one of the "moral values" to which he adheres and within which he "situates" his work.[40] Foucault explains that he considers himself a "moralist" in the sense that he "believe[s] . . . one of the meanings of human existence—the source of human freedom—is never to accept anything as definitive, untouchable, obvious, or immobile."[41] "No aspect of reality," Foucault argues, "should be allowed to become a definitive and inhuman law for us."[42]

In tying innovation to human freedom, Foucault indicates that he is concerned with concrete, emancipatory change. The two other values he identifies, refusal and curiosity, further illustrate this point. Refusal Foucault defines as not "accept[ing] as self-evident the things that are proposed to us;" curiosity entails, "the need to analyze and to know, since we can accomplish nothing without reflection and knowledge."[43] It seems clear that if persons are not to simply accept what is presented to them as natural and necessary but are rather to figure things out for themselves, they must actively and critically engage the world in which they live; hence Foucault's conceptualization of freedom in terms of practices. While, as Moya Lloyd points out, practicing freedom in the Foucauldian sense of refusing, being curious, and innovating does not "[guarantee] that dominant social structures will crumble," she argues that such practices can nonetheless have transformative effects insofar as they "impinge *critically* upon social consciousness . . . by utilizing existing practices" in ways that provoke new ways of thinking and acting.[44]

Feminists have always refused to accept what they have been told women must be and do, have always been critical thinkers, have always sought out ways of doing things differently in the name of promoting freedom—and they have done so regardless of whether their actions were widely supported (and frequently precisely because they were not). In these ways, then, Foucauldian practices of freedom are highly compatible with creative feminist politics.

Identity

Likewise, Foucault's and Arendt's views on identity are compatible with the weak nonidentitarian politics I have described. Neither thinker rejects identity outright, but neither do they posit shared identity as a foundation for politics. According to Foucault, identity is not simply given; rather, it is a product of one's relationships with oneself, others, and the world. Foucault sees the assertion of a positive identity as ethically and politically important for oppressed persons in the sense that such assertion is "liberatory."[45] Acts of liberation, according to Foucault, release persons from states of domination and, as such, enable them to negotiate relations of power; because Foucault sees power and freedom as mutually implicating one another, he argues that "power is exercised only over free subjects and only insofar as they are free."[46] Yet while liberation is necessary, it is not in and of itself sufficient; if we stop at liberation, from Foucault's perspective, not only do we cease to refuse, we don't exercise curiosity or innovation. Thus, while acts of liberation "have their place," Foucault believes that ultimately they are incapable "by themselves of defining all the practical forms of freedom."[47] It is not sufficient to assert an identity and then uncritically rely upon it for the purposes of political action; practicing and therefore furthering freedom involves critically engaging with one's own commitments and values.

That Arendt speaks of the "uniqueness" of a "who" that "expresses" itself seems to suggest that she grounds action in identity. Like Foucault, however, she makes clear that identity is produced by way of political engagement with others; the "who" is not a pregiven self. Identity cannot be a shared ground for political activity because it is not something people have in common. Produced by and through speech and action, it is specific to an individual. What is shared among persons is, rather, the capacity for expressing one's identity. Thus, positing shared identity as the basis for politics does not merely limit but in fact prohibits political action because it erases human plurality, and thereby renders speech and action (conditions for the possibility of political space) superfluous. "If men were not distinct . . .," Arendt writes, "signs and sounds to communicate immediate, identical needs and wants would be enough."[48]

Thinking Differently

Both Arendt and Foucault believe that the conditions of their presents call for "thinking differently." Arendt argues that the totalitarian regimes that developed out of the "political and spiritual chaos" following the First World War accomplished what thought itself—even "radical and adventurous thought" (specifically that of Kierkegaard, Marx, and Nietzsche)—never could: an irreparable break with history and tradition.[49] According to Arendt, "Totalitarian domination as an established fact, which in its unprecedentedness cannot be comprehended through the usual categories of political thought, and whose 'crimes' cannot be judged by traditional moral standards or punished within the legal framework of our civilization, has broken the continuity of Occidental history."[50] Given totalitarianism's destruction of the categories and standards persons have relied upon to make sense of the world—which Arendt refers to as "banisters"—persons must practice thinking differently.[51] Thinking differently is not concerned with "telling others what to think or which truths to hold;" neither is its objective to "retie the broken threads of tradition or invent some newfangled surrogates with which to fill the gap between past and future."[52] Nor, finally, is its objective to establish new banisters. Rather, thinking differently is an "exercise" through which persons learn how to make sense of the world without the aid banisters—to critically engage the world for themselves through experimental and innovative thought and action rather than relying upon "categories and formulas which are deeply ingrained in our mind, but whose basis of experience has long been forgotten and whose plausibility resides in their intellectual consistency rather than in their adequacy to actual events."[53]

Whereas Arendt believes that totalitarianism creates the need for thinking differently, from a Foucauldian perspective this need stems from the nature and function of modern power. Part of what Foucault illustrates in his work is that modern subjects constitute themselves by way of practices (which he refers to as "practices of the self") that are not distinct or separable from relations of power; rather, we constitute ourselves as subjects precisely in and through relations of power, in and through social norms. Insofar, then, as modern subjectivity is thus bound up with subjugation, there are not "good" norms that persons can choose to take up and "bad" norms that they can reject. I can't, for example, constitute myself only through feminist norms while avoiding harmful norms associated with femininity: The same norms through which I constitute myself as a subject both enable me as a feminist who can critique gender norms and constrain me as a "woman."

This situation is not cause for despair. To reiterate: I *do* constitute myself as a subject with the capacity for critique, for thinking differently "instead of legitimating what is already known"—with, in other words, the capacity to negotiate relations of power which, for Foucault, is the capacity to practice freedom.[54] Thus, Foucault can legitimately talk about the "movement by which the subject gives himself the right to question truth on its effects on power and question power on its discourses of truth," movement that he also refers to as "[an] act of voluntary insubordination."[55] As is the case for Arendt, then, thinking differently for Foucault takes the form of exercises— as Ladelle McWhorter puts it, we have to practice practicing.[56] Foucault tells us that we have come to see this practicing, this thinking differently, as something "preliminary"[57] and therefore insignificant; as his work shows, however, we have things quite backward. Insofar as thinking differently clearly possesses not only transformative but also emancipatory potential, it is valuable for contemporary feminist politics.

Against Conformity and Obedience: Antinormalization

Both Arendt and Foucault believe that harm stems from conformity and obedience to authority. Arendt believes that modern societies promote both of these problematic phenomena. Persons within such societies, she argues, are encouraged to adhere to pregiven meaning-making systems, in the form of moral, social, and political standards, categories, and rules. To the extent that adherence is achieved, modern societies become populated with complacent, uncritical, and unreflective individuals, a situation Arendt perceives as dangerous. When people fail to engage the world, to make sense of it for themselves, they are much more likely to uncritically accept what is presented to them as natural, necessary, or beneficial; they are easily manipulated, and therefore more susceptible to allowing or even participating in the execution of harmful acts.[58]

According to Arendt, the most serious problems associated with the cultivation of an unreflective, uncritical citizenry become apparent when persons are confronted with unprecedented phenomena that cannot be made sense of by way of existing concepts, standards, and rules. When so confronted, persons will still invoke their familiar meaning-making tools—they will rely upon their banisters—thus revealing "how inadequate these [have] become."[59] Even when this inadequacy is revealed, however, instead of critically reflecting on what is happening in the world and trying to make sense of things for themselves, because they are so accustomed to making sense by way of pregiven meaning-making systems, persons simply cast about for other such systems upon which to rely. Hence Arendt's assertion that the content of these systems is much less significant than their mere existence. Persons become habituated "not so much [to] the content of . . . rules" but rather to the practice of "holding fast to *whatever* the prescribed rules of conduct may be at a given time in society."[60]

> If somebody . . . should show up who, for whatever reasons and purposes, wishes to abolish the old "values" or virtues, he will find it easy enough provided he offers a new code, and he will need no force and no persuasion—no proof that the new values are better than the old ones—to establish it. The faster men hold to the old code, the more eager will they be to assimilate themselves to the new one; the ease with which such reversals can take place under certain circumstances suggests indeed that everybody is asleep when they occur. This century has offered us some experience in such matters.[61]

Arendt provides support for her claims through analyzing the actions of persons who cooperated with the Nazi regime not because they agreed with it, but because they believed doing so would enable them to surreptitiously provide assistance to persons in need. These cooperators, Arendt argues, were acting in accordance with what she refers to as the "argument of the lesser evil"—the idea that, when faced with two evils, persons have a "duty" to choose the lesser one as it would be "irresponsible to refuse to choose altogether."[62] According to the argument of the lesser evil, persons who participated in public life[63] so that they could, for example, provide forged documents for and therefore aid some Jews are above reproach because they at least tried to do something to help. But Arendt challenges this interpretation by arguing that "choosing" the lesser evil is not, in fact, properly a choice at all. "The argument of the lesser evil," she writes, "is one of the mechanisms built into the machinery of terror and crimes. Acceptance of lesser evils is consciously used in conditioning the government officials as well as the population at large to the acceptance of evil as such."[64] "Choosing" the lesser evil is not, therefore, properly a choice at all, but rather mere conformity with official, institutionalized norms and values. From Arendt's perspective, it amounts to promoting domination in the name of "doing the right thing."

Foucault characterizes modern societies' promotion of conformity (and obedience) in terms of "normalization." Unlike prevailing philosophies that conceive of norms as legitimating epistemological and moral claims, Foucault argues that norms are implicated in the "exercise" and legitimation of power.[65] In supporting this claim, Foucault distinguishes between "the idea of the norm" and particular norms. "The norm," Foucault argues, "circulates" between two different types of modern power relations: disciplinary power, which functions to mold and shape efficient but limited bodies, and regulatory power, which functions to control populations.[66] Given this circulatory function, the norm "can be applied to both a body one wants to discipline and populations one wishes to regularize," thus providing a link between individual bodies and populations along which power can travel and giving rise to what Foucault refers to as bio-power, "a power that has taken control of both the body and life or that has . . . taken control of life in general—with the body as one pole and the population as the other."[67]

If the norm gives rise to bio-power, then particular social norms can be considered to function as "nodal points" within the overall social power matrix that either facilitate or obstruct the flow of power. Since, as noted earlier, Foucault considers subjects to be free when they are able to modify, negotiate, reverse these relations—when in other words, the circulation of power within society is at least relatively unimpeded—norms that facilitate this circulation don't possess oppressive potential. Norms that promote the sedimentation of power, on the other hand, are implicated in what Foucault refers to as "normalization," a set of effects or techniques that result from the new form of power that takes the norm as its point of departure. Normalizing norms function "not to exclude and reject" but rather to "intervene and transform," and, as Foucault sees it, this intervention in and transformation of bodies and populations in accordance with some norm *is* potentially oppressive.[68] That is, while individual norms may or may not be oppressive, normalization always is; if norms become entrenched to the point that they are uncritically accepted as natural, necessary, and beyond deliberation, they can function in a normalizing and therefore oppressive manner insofar as alternatives come to be seen as deviant—as "abnormal." Bringing abnormal individuals into conformity with prevailing norms—even by force—is generally considered to be not only justifiable but also beneficial to society.

Foucault's brilliant and sobering analysis of early Christian practices of the self supports his contention that modern subjects constitute themselves as such in and through relations of power.[69] Specifically, by arguing that early Christian practices mark the beginning of the modern hermeneutics of the self, Foucault illustrates that modern subjectivity is in fact grounded in obedience to authority. Whereas initially this authority is external—as in the case of the relationship between young monks and their masters—later it will become internalized in the form of, for example, Kantian autonomy.[70] From early Christianity onwards, Foucault argues, subjects cannot reveal the truth about themselves without simultaneously sacrificing themselves: "No truth about the self," Foucault writes, "is without the sacrifice of the self."[71]

Western society has sought to rectify this situation by trying to figure out how to "[save] the hermeneutics of the self and [get] rid of the necessity of sacrifice of self which was linked to this hermeneutics since the beginning of Christianity."[72] Yet Foucault's point in showing the degree to which our subjectivity is bound up with our own subjugation is different. Insofar as we have done this to ourselves, he says, we can undo it.

> Maybe the problem is not to find a positive foundation for those interpretative technologies [the modern hermeneutics of the self]. Maybe the problem now is to change those technologies, or maybe to get rid of those technologies, and then, to get rid of the sacrifice which is linked to those technologies. In this case, one of the main problems would be, in the strictest sense of the word, politics—the politics of ourselves.[73]

A politics concerned with emancipation needs to take into account that pressure toward conformity and obedience is inherent within modern societies—it needs to be cognizant, in other words, to the degree to which such societies are normalizing. Within such a context, as David Hoy puts it, "Resistance to . . . domination may . . . be more complex than it appears on the surface" insofar as "the social features that are being resisted may produce the shape that resistance takes."[74] While such pressure has intensified within the post-September 11, 2001 United States, I think feminists have experienced such intensification in the form of pressure toward conforming with and being obedient to gender norms for a long time. The work of Arendt and Foucault can both facilitate insight into normalization and enhance existing analysis and negotiation of normalizing societies in ways that resist domination and promote freedom.

As I see it, then, the work of Hannah Arendt and Michel Foucault is valuable for feminist politics in at least two ways. First, it is valuable insofar as Arendt and Foucault are "pragmatic" thinkers who are concerned with negotiating problems pertaining to thinking and acting in the world; moreover, both thinkers are concerned with doing so in ways that promote freedom and resist domination. Such concerns, contrary to traditional interpretations of what it means to be pragmatic, do not require an articulation of what Foucault refers to as "blueprints for change." As I have shown in my analysis of their work, for both Arendt and Foucault, insofar as blueprints provide ready-made plans for action, they promote the kind of disengagement from the world that facilitates the maintenance of the status quo. For Arendt, both dictating and accepting in advance how to think and act conjures up the threat of totalitarianism, for Foucault that of domination. Critical engagement with predetermined and prevailing modes of thought and action, in contrast, is an expression of concern for the world. Thus, while Arendt's and Foucault's resistance to defining the terms of such engagement in advance has led to attempts to systematize their work, as well as to criticisms that they are unable to offer the positive framework that politics require, this "inability" is more accurately construed in terms of both a rejection and a refusal: a rejection of the idea that pregiven frameworks are either positive or necessary and, therefore, the refusal to provide them.

The second way in which Arendt's and Foucault's work is valuable to feminist politics, then, is precisely through asserting the idea of politics without blueprints. This is the kind of politics that I see being facilitated by these thinkers' conceptualizations of agonism, creativity, nonidentitarianism, thinking differently, and antinormalization. Such a politics provides no guarantees that domination will be resisted, that practices of freedom will be expanded, yet what should we make of desires for certainty, for clear direction about how to think and act in the face of the uncertainties and conflicts that have only increased within the United States since I wrote the original version of this chapter? Arendt's and Foucault's work points to the harmful potential of such desires, at the same time that it affirms political engagement with the world in its complexity. I have suggested that feminist political endeavors reflect both of these commitments; I believe that especially in the face of increased pressures toward conformity and obedience they need to continue to do so.

Notes

1. "Introduction to First Principles Series," *The Nation*, April 14, 1997, 11; original emphasis.

2. Ibid.

3. Susan Bickford, *The Dissonance of Democracy: Listening, Conflict, Citizenship* (Ithaca, NY: Cornell University Press, 1996), 15.

4. Bickford, *The Dissonance of Democracy*, 16.

5. Bickford critiques Jürgen Habermas' distinction between communicative and strategic action. Communicative action is "interaction in which all participants are motivated solely by the desire to reach understanding" and consensus (p. 17). Participants in communicative action seek to "rationally motivate" others, and the

"more rational argument" prevails (p. 17). In strategic action, a speaker seeks to "influence" others by "causing" them to come around to her or his way of thinking (p. 17). Bickford argues that such a distinction is not sustainable, and that Habermas himself frequently blurs the boundary between communicative and strategic action. Moreover, insofar as Habermas attempts to rid the argumentative process of strategic action, Bickford thinks that he "obscures the difficult complexity of actual political interaction, in which strategic and communicative action are intertwined." (p. 18) Within certain formulations of unification discourse, consensus-oriented delibera-tion encounters the same problems: It facilitates the assertion of a single, dominant viewpoint by seeking to reduce or eliminate conflict. Like Bickford, I am similarly unconvinced that the "intertwining" of communicative and strategic action "should be regarded with regret." See Bickford, *The Dissonance of Democracy*, and Jürgen Habermas, *The Theory of Communicative Action*, vol. 1, trans. Thomas McCarthy (Boston: Beacon Press, 1984).

    6. See Judith Butler, "Merely Cultural," *New Left Review* (January/February 1998): 33–44.

    7. Ira Katznelson, "The Fight for Liberalism," *The Nation*, July 14, 1997, 23.

    8. Ibid.

    9. Ibid.

    10. Habermas critiques such a liberal solution in "Struggles for Recognition in the Democratic Constitutional State," in Charles Taylor et al., eds., *Multiculturalism: Ex-amining the Politics of Recognition* (Princeton, NJ: Princeton University Press, 1994), 107–148. Habermas' own proposed solution, however, is also problematic. He argues that an "individualistically constructed" theory of rights, if properly understood as "[protecting] the integrity of the individual" insofar as she or he is a member of a community," is adequate to the task of adjudicating between conflicting claims for justice (pp. 107, 113). While Habermas is correct that individuals are not distinct from social contexts, his acknowledgment of the "substantive" aspect of ethics is merely formal, and so he ultimately appeals to a notion of "the ethical as such" which is ultimately not sustainable.

    11. Jeff Faux, "A Progressive Compact," *The Nation*, April 14, 1997, 12–15.

    12. Iris Marion Young critiques the prevailing liberal construction of benefits and burdens. Young agrees that insofar as citizens "have rights to basic liberty, respect, and tolerance from their fellow citizens and from the state," it is perfectly acceptable to expect these citizens "to contribute meaningfully to the social fabric." (p. 127) She argues, however, that defining "meaningful contribution" merely as "economic con-tribution" is problematic. See Iris Marion Young, "Mothers, Citizenship, and Inde-pendence: A Critique of Pure Family Values," in *Intersecting Voices: Dilemmas of Gen-der, Political Philosophy, and Policy* (Princeton, NJ: Princeton University Press, 1997), 114–133.

    13. Faux, "A Progressive Compact," 12.

    14. Judith Butler discusses the relationship between the orthodox left and the new social movements in "Merely Cultural."

15. Faux, "A Progressive Compact," 12.

16. Paul Wellstone, "If Poverty is the Question . . .," *The Nation*, April 14, 1997, 15–18; Richard Rorty, "First Projects, Then Principles," *The Nation*, December 22, 1997, 18–21.

17. Barbara Ehrenreich, "When Government Gets Mean: Confessions of a Recovering Statist," *The Nation*, November 17, 1997, 11–16.

18. Ellen Willis, "We Need A *Radical* Left," *The Nation*, June 29, 1998, 18–21.

19. It is important to note that indicating ways in which economics and culture intersect or, to make an even stronger statement, are interconnected, is not to argue that they are "the same." Willis', Butler's, and my own intention is not to collapse the distinction between economics and culture, but rather to challenge their supposed mutual exclusivity.

20. Willis, "We Need a *Radical* Left," 19.

21. Ibid.

22. Ibid.

23. Todd Gitlin, *The Twilight of Common Dreams: Why America Is Wracked by Culture Wars* (New York: Henry Holt and Co., 1995), 176.

24. Bickford, *The Dissonance of Democracy*, 112.

25. Butler, "Merely Cultural," 37.

26. Ibid.

27. Ibid.

28. For social histories of the women's liberation movement and its relationship to the New Left, see Alice Echols, *Daring to be BAD: Radical Feminism in America 1967–1975* (Minneapolis: University of Minnesota Press, 1989) and Sara Evans, *Personal Politics: The Roots of the Women's Liberation Movement in the Civil Rights Movement and the New Left* (New York: Vintage, 1980).

29. My substantive analyses of this issue are forthcoming, but for an overview see Dianna Taylor, "Foucault's Ethos: Guide(post) for Change," in *Feminism and the Final Foucault*, eds. Dianna Taylor and Karen Vintges (Urbana: University of Illinois Press, 2004), 258–274. Giovanna Borradori's interviews with Jacques Derrida and Jürgen Habermas, as well as her own commentary on and analysis of these interviews, offer important philosophical analysis of the September 11, 2001 attacks. See Giovanna Borradori, *Philosophy in a Time of Terror* (Chicago: University of Chicago Press, 2003). For provocative philosophical analyses of the post-September 11, 2001 United States, see *Constellations* 9, no. 4 (2002).

30. Bickford, *The Dissonance of Democracy*, 2.

31. Young, *Intersecting Voices*, 17.

32. Ibid.

33. Judith Butler makes this point in "Contingent Foundations: Feminism and the Question of 'Postmodernism,'" in *Feminists Theorize the Political*, eds. Judith Butler and Joan Scott (New York: Routledge, 1992), 3–21.

34. On this point see Judith Butler, *Gender Trouble: Feminism and the Subversion of Identity* (New York: Routledge, 1989) and "Contingent Foundations."

35. Bonnie Honig, "Toward an Agonistic Feminism," in *Feminist Interpretations of Hannah Arendt*, ed. Bonnie Honig (University Park: Pennsylvania State University Press, 1995), 157.

36. Hannah Arendt, *The Human Condition* (Chicago: University of Chicago Press, 1958), 175.

37. Ibid.

38. Honig, "Toward an Agonistic Feminism," 157.

39. Arendt, *The Human Condition*, 176.

40. Michel Foucault, "Power, Moral Values, and the Intellectual," November 3, 1980. IMEC Archives, folder FCL2. A02-06.

41. Ibid.

42. Ibid.

43. Ibid.

44. Moya Lloyd, "A Feminist Mapping of Foucauldian Politics," in *Feminist Interpretations of Michel Foucault*, ed. Susan Hekman (University Park: Pennsylvania State University Press, 1996), 257–258.

45. Michel Foucault, "Sex, Power, and the Politics of Identity," in *Ethics: Subjectivity and Truth*, ed. Paul Rabinow, trans. Robert Hurley et al. (New York: The New Press, 1997), 163–173 and "The Ethics of Care for the Self as the Practice of Freedom," in the same volume, 281–301.

46. Michel Foucault, "The Subject and Power," in *Michel Foucault: Beyond Structuralism and Hermeneutics*, Hubert Dreyfus and Paul Rabinow (Chicago: University of Chicago Press, 1982), 221.

47. Foucault, "The Ethics of Care for the Self as the Practice of Freedom," 283.

48. Arendt, *The Human Condition*, 176.

49. Hannah Arendt, *Between Past and Future* (New York: Penguin, 1968), 27.

50. Arendt, *Between Past and Future*, 26.

51. Hannah Arendt, "On Hannah Arendt," in *Hannah Arendt: The Recovery of the Public World*, ed. Melvyn Hill (New York: St. Martin's Press, 1979), 301–339. Arendt states that "thinking without a banister" is her "metaphor" for the phenomenon of "groundless thinking": "As you go up and down stairs you can always hold onto a banister so that you don't fall down. But we have lost this banister." (pp. 336–337)

52. Arendt, *Between Past and Future*, 14.

53. Hannah Arendt, "Personal Responsibility under Dictatorship," in *Responsibility and Judgment*, ed. Jerome Kohn (New York: Schocken, 2003), 37.

54. Michel Foucault, *The Use of Pleasure*, trans. Robert Hurley (New York: Vintage, 1990), 9.

55. Michel Foucault, "What is Critique?" in The Politics of Truth, eds. Sylvere Lotringer and Lysa Hochroth (New York: Semiotexte, 1997), 32.

56. Ladelle McWhorter, "Practicing Practicing," in *Feminism and the Final Foucault*, eds. Dianna Taylor and Karen Vintges (Urbana: University of Illinois Press, 2004), 141–162.

57. Foucault, *The Use of Pleasure*, 9.

58. Arendt, "Personal Responsibility under Dictatorship."

59. Arendt, "Personal Responsibility under Dictatorship," 25.

60. Hannah Arendt, "Thinking and Moral Consideration," in *Judgment and Responsibility*, ed. Jerome Kohn (New York: Schocken, 2003), 178.

61. Ibid.

62. Arendt, "Personal Responsibility under Dictatorship," 26.

63. Under totalitarianism, Arendt argues, "There is no office and indeed no job of any public significance, from advertising agencies to the judiciary, from play-acting to sports journalism, from primary and secondary schooling to the universities and learned societies, in which an unequivocal acceptance of the ruling principles is not demanded." See Arendt, "Personal Responsibility under Dictatorship," 33.

64. Arendt, "Personal Responsibility under Dictatorship," 26.

65. Michel Foucault, *Lectures at the College de France, 1974–1975: Abnormal*, eds. Valerio Marchetti and Antonella Salomoni, trans. Graham Burchell (New York: Picador, 1999), 50.

66. Michel Foucault, *Lectures at the College de France, 1975–1976: Society Must Be Defended*, eds. Mauro Bertani and Alessandro Fontana, trans. David Macey (New York: Picador, 1997), 252–253.

67. Foucault, *Society Must Be Defended*, 253.

68. Foucault, *Abnormal*, 50.

69. Michel Foucault, "Christianity and Confession," October 21, 1980, IMEC Archives, folders FCL 3.4 and FCL2. A03-04.

70. Foucault, "What Is Critique?"

71. Foucault, "Christianity and Confession."

72. Ibid.

73. Ibid.

74. David Couzens Hoy, *Critical Resistance: From Poststructuralism to Post-Critique* (Cambridge: MA: MIT Press, 2005), 3.

Index

~

About the Contributors

Amy R. Baehr is assistant professor of philosophy at Hofstra University. Her work explores the relationship between feminism and liberalism. She is editor of *Varieties of Feminist Liberalism* (Rowman and Littlefield, 2004). Her papers have appeared in the *Journal of Social Philosophy*, the *Journal of Political Philosophy*, and *Hypatia*. Her most recent paper, a critique of feminist perfectionism, will appear in *Law and Philosophy*.

Alison Bailey (Ph.D., University of Cincinnati) is the director of women's studies and an associate professor in Philosophy at Illinois State University. Her philosophical work is largely motivated by issues of social justice. She is the author of *Posterity and Strategic Policy: A Moral Assessment of U.S. Strategic Weapons Options* (1989) Her research on gender and race privilege has appeared in *Hypatia: A Journal of Feminist Philosophy*, *The Journal of Social Philosophy*, *Whiteness: Feminist Philosophical Narratives* (2000), and *Feminist Ethics Revisited* (2001). She is currently coediting a special issue of *Hypatia* on the reproduction of whiteness with Jacqueline Zita. She is also coediting *Feminism and Philosophy: An Introductory Reader* (McGraw Hill) with Chris Cuomo. Her current research project explores epistemologies of ignorance. She is an enthusiastic Iyengar yoga practitioner.

Cathryn Bailey is professor of philosophy at Minnesota State University. The focus of her work is on feminist thought, especially ethics and epistemology.

Marie-Claire Belleau is a full professor at the Faculty of Law of Université Laval. She also teaches Feminist Legal Theories and Identity Politics in graduate programs at the European Academy of Legal Theory in Belgium and at the Oñati International Institute for the Sociology of Law in Spain. Professor Belleau has an S.J.D. and an LL.M. from Harvard Law School and a D.E.A. from Université Paris II. Her research focuses on feminist legal theories, identity politics, legal theory, judicial dissent and power, family mediation, comparative law, and the history of legal thought.

Sigal Ben-Porath received her Ph.D. in philosophy from Tel-Aviv University. She was a postdoctoral fellow at Princeton University's Center for Human Values, and currently teaches at the University of Pennsylvania's Graduate School of Education. Her research focuses on the intersection between political philosophy and education. She has published articles on the regulation of intimacy, civic education in wartime, and just relations between adults and children. Her book, *Citizenship under Fire: Democratic Education in Times of Conflict*, was published in 2006 by Princeton University Press.

Marlene Benjamin's interdisciplinary interests date from her undergraduate work in the "Great Books Program" at St. John's College. Her Ph.D. is from Brandeis University. She has taught at Clark, UMASS/Boston, Harvard University's Extension School, and at Richmond College in London. Benjamin is the recipient of numerous awards and honors, including a dissertation grant to work on the theoretical foundations of human rights claims, the highest category award in the Massachusetts Artists Foundation Fellowship Awards for her essay on philosophy, cancer, and the idea of the self, and an NEH Summer Institute Fellowship to study the writings of R. W. Emerson and his role as the first American philosopher. Her current project, *The Catastrophic Self: Philosophy, Memoir, and Medical Trauma*, examines three routes by which the self reconceptualizes itself and operates in response to the embodied experience of catastrophic illness.

Marla Brettschneider is professor of political philosophy and feminist theory at the University of New Hampshire with a joint appointment in political science and in women's studies where she is also coordinator of queer studies. She is author of *Cornerstones of Peace: Jewish Identity Politics and Democratic Theory*; *Democratic Theorizing from the Margins*, and *The Family Flamboyant: Race Politics, Queer Families, Jewish Life*. Marla has edited numerous works on Jewish diversity politics including *The Narrow Bridge: Jewish Perspectives on Multiculturalism*, with a forward by Cornel West. She has also published in special issues of such academic journals as *The Journal of Femi-*

nist Studies in Religion; Nashim; and *Race, Gender, and Class.* She is the winner of the Gustavus Meyers Human Rights Award.

Morwenna Griffiths is professor of classroom learning at Edinburgh University. Her research interests are in social justice, philosophy, and the interaction of educational theory and practice. She has previously taught in primary schools in Bristol, and at the University of Isfahan, Iran, at Christ Church College HE in Canterbury, and at Oxford Brookes, Nottingham, and Nottingham Trent Universities. Her books include *Action for Social Justice in Education: Fairly Different* (Open University 2003); *Educational Research for Social Justice: Getting off the Fence* (Open University, 1998); *Feminisms and the Self: The Web of Identity* (Routledge, 1995); and (with Carol Davies) *In Fairness to Children* (David Fulton, 1995).

Birge Krondorfer, Ph.D., studied theology, philosophy, group dynamics, and political science in Frankfurt, Vienna, and Klagenfurt. In her teaching and research, Krondorfer is combining these fields with her expertise in feminist studies and gender relation. She has taught courses in Austria, Germany, Switzerland, Hungary, and the United States. She also received degrees in coaching, conflict mediation, and adult education, and is the cofounder of *Frauenhetz*, an autonomous feminist center in Vienna (www.frauenhetz.at). Her publications include articles, edited volumes, and books on feminist and gender concerns. She currently is part of a European Union project on the integration of migrants in the labor market. Contact: birge.krondorfer@chello.at.

Marjorie C. Miller is professor of philosophy, women's studies, and Asian studies at Purchase College, SUNY. Her interests in American pragmatism, Chinese philosophy, and feminist philosophy have developed over the course of a teaching career spanning over a quarter century. Publications include many articles in all three fields, as well as coediting a special issue of the journal *Metaphilosophy* on philosophy and feminism.

Deborah Orr wrote her doctoral thesis on concepts of understanding in the mature philosophy of Wittgenstein. She is an associate professor who teaches in the areas of gender, ethics, and embodiment in the Division of Humanities at York University in Toronto, Canada. She has published in various journals in the areas of Wittgenstein, pedagogy, moral logic, and moral development. Recent work includes "The Crone as Lover and Teacher: A Philosophical Reading of Zora Neale Hurston's *Their Eyes Were Watching God,*" *Journal of Feminist Studies in Religion* 18, no. 1:25–50; "Developing Wittgenstein's Picture of the Soul: Toward a Feminist Spiritual Erotics," in *Feminist Interpretations of Wittgenstein,* eds. Naomi Scheman and Peg O'Connor (University Park, Pennsylvania:

The Pennsylvania State Press, 2002); *Holistic Learning and Spirituality in Education: Breaking New Ground*, coedited with Jack Miller, Diana Denton, Salia Karsten, and Isabella Kates (New York: SUNY, 2005) which includes her "Minding the Soul in Education: Conceptualizing and Teaching to the Whole Person:" and "The Uses of Mindfulness in Feminist Anti-Oppressive Pedagogies: Philosophy and Praxis," *Canadian Journal of Education* 27, no. 2. She coedited *Beliefs, Bodies and Being: Feminist Reflections on Embodiment*, with Linda López McAlister, Eileen Kahl, and Kathleen Earl (Lanham: MD: Rowman & Littlefield Publishers, 2006), also from the IAPh Conference in Boston. She is also working on a book about embodied spirituality with the working title *The Art of Love: The Logic of a Feminist Spiritual Erotics* and a book about the use of yoga and meditation in antioppressive pedagogy with the working title *Mindful Pedagogy*. She teaches Iyengar yoga and meditation in Toronto.

Dianna Taylor is assistant professor of philosophy at John Carroll University in Cleveland, Ohio. Her research focuses on twentieth-century French and German philosophy, especially the work of Michel Foucault and Hannah Arendt. She is the author of articles on Foucault and Arendt and is coeditor, along with Karen Vintges, of *Feminism and the Final Foucault* (University of Illinois Press, 2004).

Jutta Weber is guest professor for interdisciplinary studies at the University of Duisburg-Essen (Germany). She is a trained philosopher as well as a science studies scholar. In her Ph.D. thesis she did a comparative study of concepts of nature in postmodern epistemology, science studies, and artificial life. Her main interests are cultural studies of science and technology, epistemology, philosophy of science, social theory, gender studies, and inter-/transdisciplinarity. As a senior researcher she conducted theoretical and empirical research in the field of robotics, computer science and artificial intelligence at the Department of Philosophy of Science at the University of Vienna. She is coediting an issue on "Ethics in Robotics" as a guest editor of the journal *International Review of Information Ethics* 2 (2006) (together with Karsten Weber and Daniela Cerqui). Other publications include "From Science and Technology to Feminist Technoscience Studies," in *Handbook of Gender and Women's Studies*, eds. Kathy Davis, Mary Evans, and Judith Lorber (London: Sage 2006); "Helpless Machines and True Loving Caregivers. A Feminist Critique of Recent Trends in Human-Robot Interaction," *Journal of Information, Communication and Ethics in Society* 3, issue 4, paper 6 (2005); Umkämpfte Bedeutungen: Naturkonzepte im Zeitalter der Technoscience. Campus 2003 ["Contested Meanings: Nature in the Age of Technoscience"].